The Character of Criticism

The Character of Criticism

Geoffrey Galt Harpham

R Routledge
Taylor & Francis Group
New York   London

Routledge is an imprint of the
Taylor & Francis Group, an informa business

Earlier versions of chapters 2, 3, and 4 were published in *Salmagundi*, *Representations*, and *Critical Inquiry*, respectively.

Routledge
Taylor & Francis Group
270 Madison Avenue
New York, NY 10016

Routledge
Taylor & Francis Group
2 Park Square
Milton Park, Abingdon
Oxon OX14 4RN

© 2006 by Taylor and Francis Group, LLC
Routledge is an imprint of Taylor & Francis Group, an Informa business

Printed in the United States of America on acid-free paper
10 9 8 7 6 5 4 3 2 1

International Standard Book Number-10: 0-415-97133-0 (Softcover) 0-415-97132-2 (Hardcover)
International Standard Book Number-13: 978-0-415-97133-1 (Softcover) 978-0-415-97132-4 (Hardcover)
Library of Congress Card Number 2005036248

Library of Congress Cataloging-in-Publication Data

Harpham, Geoffrey Galt, 1946-
The character of criticism / Geoffrey Galt Harpham.
p. cm.
Includes index.
ISBN 0-415-97132-2 (acid-free paper) -- ISBN 0-415-97133-0 (pbk. : acid-free paper)
1. Criticism--History--20th century. I. Title.

PN94.H39 2006
801'.950904--dc22   2005036248

Visit the Taylor & Francis Web site at
http://www.taylorandfrancis.com

and the Routledge Web site at
http://www.routledge-ny.com

For Joan Barasovska,
who has taught me most of what I know about character.

Contents

CHAPTER 1

The Character of Criticism

1. What Matter Who's Speaking

Many years ago, I acquired a marvelous book called *Memoirs of Extraordinary Popular Delusions and the Madness of Crowds*. Written by Charles Mackay in 1841, it had been reissued in paperback in 1970, one year before I found it in the legendary Papa Bach Bookstore on Santa Monica Boulevard in West Los Angeles.[1] The book detailed instances of popular enthusiasm, in which large groups of hitherto sane people became convinced that black was white, up was down, one could safely leap before looking, tulips were more valuable than any other commodity including money itself, witches were plotting among them, or that the Crusades were an excellent idea easily realized. Throughout history, Mackay wrote in his preface, "we find that whole communities suddenly fix their minds upon one object, and go mad in its pursuit; that millions of people become simultaneously impressed with one delusion, and run after it, till their attention is caught by some new folly more captivating than the first" (xix). I found the book endlessly entertaining, partly because I was untroubled by any suspicion that I was at that very moment at the margins of an event that might have qualified for inclusion in an updated edition.

Just two years before Mackay's book was reissued, Roland Barthes wrote a brief essay that immediately became a classic. It was called "The Death of the Author," and in it he argued that "the author," a personage whose existence had long been taken for granted, was in fact "a modern figure," conjured into being by a combination of "English empiricism, French rationalism and the personal faith of the Reformation."[2] The author was unknown, Barthes contended, until the modern era of "capitalist ideology," when "the prestige of the individual" was first conceptualized, along with a host of other ideas that have become so deeply ingrained that it is difficult to think without them. Indeed, the "image of literature" to be found in "ordinary culture" is "tyrannically centred on the author," in whose person, life, tastes, passions, and ideas are sought the work's meaning or *"explanation"* (143). The author blocks our access to a deeper, richer truth, for, buried beneath the ideological deposits of recent centuries lay an unconstrained semiotic infinitude that Barthes presented as if it were both an ancient verity and a modern discovery. "We know now," he reported, in a tone that sounds today like the anthem of 1968, "that a text is not a line of words releasing a single 'theological' meaning (the 'message' of the Author-God) but a multi-dimensional space in which a variety of writings, none of them original, blend and clash" (146).

The implication was inescapable: we must now replace the ideologically useless figure of the Author with that of the "scriptor," who is to be conceived as simply a kind of writing machine possessed of a dictionary from which words are drawn; and we must replace our veneration for the point of origin with an equally intense but disintoxicated interest in the "destination" of language in the act of reading, which is itself "without history, biography, psychology" (148). The tone of austere derision that Barthes commanded so expertly during his brief period of infatuation with linguistic "science" was, especially to those for whom anything produced in that great year enjoyed a presumption of authenticity, extraordinarily effective in demolishing the prestige of the individual, and indeed prestige in general. The death of the author stood for other deaths—of humanism, subjectivity, literature, interpretation, authority, agency, originality, intentionality. All this—the entire melodrama of creation and its consequences—was now to be discarded, its place taken by the concept of writing, "that neutral, composite, oblique space where our subject slips away, the negative where all identity is lost" (142).

Like other popular delusions, this one had a bit of truth that had been inflated beyond its natural dimensions. It is reasonable to consider rare and beautiful things such as exotic tulips valuable, but they cannot bear the weight of an entire economy. Similarly, it was interesting and productive to historicize the figure of the author and to consider that this figure supported a wide range of unreflected ideological and historical forces; but when this argument was puffed up into a general statement about the nature of language and deployed in the service of a general repudiation of "humanism," gross distortions crept in. One of the most aggressively antihumanist thinkers was Michel Foucault, who, one year after Barthes published "The Death of the Author," issued a kind of companion essay called "What Is an Author?" in which he repeated Barthes's attack on the phantasmatic figure of the author.[3] Attempting to detach language from any point of origin in the conscious or intending individual, Foucault insisted that the only object of a properly critical attention was "the functional conditions of specific discursive practices," for which the "paradoxical singularity of the name of an author" is merely a convenient, if reductive, name. The "essential basis" for writing, Foucault said, "is not the exalted emotions related to the act of composition or the insertion of a subject into language. Rather, it is primarily concerned with creating an opening where the writing subject endlessly disappears" (116). In perhaps the best-known comment he made in his entire, highly prolific career, Foucault noted that the very concept of man, of which the author is a special instance, is "an invention of recent date," brought into being by Enlightenment philosophy, copyright laws, and disciplinary and knowledge regimes, soon to be washed away like a figure drawn in the sand.[4]

Under this doomsday paradigm, which Foucault elaborated in *The Order of Things*, *The Archeology of Knowledge*, and with an even greater dramatic force in the subsequent "genealogical" phase of his work, the author is to be considered a function of discourse rather than its originator. This emphasis on the ways in which the self is shaped, formed, corrected, normalized, and documented by agencies and structures beyond its knowledge or control made it difficult to imagine how such a thing as a self-aware or self-determining individual might arise within the "regime" of modernity, with its proliferating sites of control. So powerful was the rhetorical force of this work that the "ethical turn" to a concern for the "care of the self" taken in Foucault's last works seemed to some of his readers almost a self-betrayal rather than a self-realization, thin and unpersuasive by comparison with his earlier and more magisterial antihumanism.

What the very late work lacked was precisely what made the earlier work so very compelling: an almost visible relish in the contemplation of forms of discipline, observation, and punishment; a certain eagerness to conjure up the thought of large inhuman structures that determined in their deepest interiority the small human subjects that had been under the impression that they had created those structures; a thoroughly awakened if icily uncompassionate interest in what he seems to be condemning. The late work lacks, in other words, the psychological complexity of what preceded it, and communicates instead a spirit of accommodation and resolution. In early and middle Foucault—the period in which Foucault was considered an exciting, corrosive, and dangerous figure—a line of inquiry and critique is pursued with such fascinated antipathy for the humanistic figure of the enlightened, autonomous, and self-determining subject that the work manages to communicate, beneath its formidable scholarly reserve, something else: a certain pleasure, which nearly deserves to be called perverse, taken in the experience of humiliation.[5]

Most of the schools of thought that were beginning to assert themselves in the 1960s and 1970s contributed something to this perversity. Foucault's teacher Louis Althusser rejected humanism in all its forms and argued for a more scientific approach that, for example, described ideology not as a coercive system of oppression or even as an ambient atmosphere of convention, but as a "process without a subject."[6] Lacanian psychoanalysis updated Freudian thinking by assimilating it to Saussurean linguistics, which had achieved "scientific" status by eliminating from language any consideration of the processes of communication in a social or historical milieu. Under the leadership of Fredric Jameson, Marxist criticism attacked the longstanding critical emphasis on "ethics," which focused on the choices and fortunes of the individual as a late-capitalist mystification. Jameson proposed instead that "history," inflected by structuralism and Lacanian psychoanalysis, should serve as the ultimate if unrepresentable horizon of critical reflection. Jean-François Lyotard contributed to this movement a meditation with the title of *The Inhuman: Reflections on Time*.[7] Jacques Derrida began his career with work of extraordinary power, range, and complexity built on a thematics of loss, absence, and fatality, in which language, exemplified by the letter or grapheme, was depicted as the ultimate rebuke to humanist fantasies, beginning with the fantasy of life. "Writing in the common sense," he wrote in 1967, "is the dead letter, it is the carrier of death. It exhausts life."[8] For these and many others, the figure of the reflective, expressive, communicating subject was an historical relic disproven by modern knowledge, like phlogiston or a benevolent God. For the jubilation of infinite semiosis to be released, it was necessary to embrace inhumanity, process, mechanism, and death.

Perhaps the most manifestly perverse form of the death-of-the-author argument was Paul de Man's account of language as "inhuman" and "mechanical." "There is, in a very radical sense," de Man wrote, "no such thing as the human"; in fact, "actual language . . . has invented the conceptual term 'man.'"[9] Once again, the theoretical advance came at the expense of "ethics," which, in de Man's view, had

> nothing to do with the will (thwarted or free) of a subject.... The ethical category is imperative (i.e., a category rather than a value) to the extent that it is linguistic and not subjective.... The passage to an ethical tonality does not result from a transcendental imperative but is the referential (and therefore unreliable) version of a linguistic confusion. Ethics (or, one should say, ethnicity) is a discursive mode among others.[10]

In the wake of the great scandal that arose in the late 1980s surrounding de Man's wartime journalism, when it was discovered that de Man had indeed been the victim of profound ethical confusion, all of his work was reread from a different perspective. Such passages were taken to signify de Man's wish to do away with the entire issue of ethical responsibility, to draw attention to the helplessness of the individual caught in the snares of history, or to argue for a scholarly obligation to set aside vulgar notions of propriety or good behavior in favor of rigorous analysis. A subdiscipline rapidly emerged that was devoted to the task of disclosing in de Man's work a series of deeply coded confessions, explanations, rationalizations, recantations, and apologies.

All these theoretical discourses understood themselves as committed to a principle of analytical rigor that was set against "naive" humanist illusions and mystifications, and all gathered to expression in the sentence from Samuel Beckett, quoted with great effect by Foucault in "What Is an Author?": "What matter who's speaking?" (115).

What matter who's speaking? A truly extraordinary popular delusion.

Whatever salutary effects this movement had—and the theory movement was in many respects extraordinarily vivifying, despite its sometimes macabre or mechanistic thematics—the defiant hostility to the question of who was speaking constituted an own-goal of massive proportions. For the single most compelling feature of the theoretical discourse of this era was not the new knowledge introduced into scholarly discourse, but the way in which it focused and channeled the energies of a truly remarkable set of *maîtres de penser*—powerfully individualized, charismatic, often deeply conflicted or troubled figures whose lives were dramatically visible not only in the world of events but in the mediated form of their work. Whether they understood it in this way or not, those who were drawn to the project of theory were attracted in part by the spectacle offered by theoretical discourse of complex and passionate minds engaged in vivid encounters with each other, with great figures from the artistic and philosophical past, and with the broader forces of culture, politics, and history. The identity of the speaker was one of the best things theory had going for it.

The de Man scandal—an astonishing case in which the most revered theorist was ensnarled in the ultimate evil—might actually have awakened a new kind of interest in theory or criticism, centered on the expressive subject. Disclosures of a past tainted by lurid and bloody forms of unreason in one who had posed as the apostle of cold-blooded lucidity had, after all, made possible a new reading of theoretical discourse in general. Instead, the de Man affair only resulted in general demoralization on one side and a sterile triumphalism on the other. With the deaths of Barthes (1980), Lacan (1981), de Man (1983), and Foucault (1984) (not to mention the incarceration of Althusser in 1980 for strangling his wife), the theory movement was already in difficulties. But by the time the revelations came in 1987, theory had become too broadly diffused and integrated into ordinary critical practice for academe simply to shrug off the episode and move on. What survived in departments of literary study was a general climate of professional occultation in which literature lost its aesthetic specificity and became enfolded within a generalized textuality, the study of which was said to be highly technical. Buoyed by the continuing interest of amateurs, literature survived; but literary criticism suffered by being subordinated to theory, with a circle drawn around the initiates.

Through the self-replicating process of education, the circle grew somewhat wider but no less exclusionary, until what began as professional autonomy began to seem, to those on the outside, like a phenomenon, an extraordinary popular delusion. The reasons an educated nonacademic reader might have for taking an interest in criticism dwindled, and, in a well-documented and widely lamented turn, critics themselves stopped buying each others' books. Eventually, the discipline of criticism found itself in the anomalous position of having failed to persuade the general public of anything except its own indifference to public concerns, and therefore its own irrelevance to the culture at large, on which point it had carried the day, sweeping all opposition aside. Having defined textuality as an oblique space where the subject slips away, academic critics now found themselves slipping, or rather being filed away, their disappearance unmarked, their absence from the cultural conversation unmourned and even celebrated.

Intellectual movements have a determined lifespan, and a movement as sharply articulated, difficult, and in some ways counterintuitive as the theory movement could not have expected to survive forever. What concerns me here, however, is not the process of inevitable decline, but the striking fact that, for a long season, it became not just possible but almost necessary to think that it did not matter "who's speaking" because language had its own structures and functions that could be studied independently of any particular human circumstance. For an argument that focused on the "destination" of all writing in the act of reading, this argument is determinedly ignorant of the fact that criticism is read not just for information, but for the sense of communication with another mind. If "we know now," as Barthes put it, that we do not need to concern ourselves with the other mind, but only with the linguistic structures on the page, then that reason vanishes, leaving in its place a merely academic interest in the behavior of semiotic units.

Some critics, to be sure, protested against theoretical antihumanism by insisting on the distinctive features of the feminine, subaltern, American, black, postcolonial, or queer identities; but their arguments were largely confined to literary texts.[11] And when critics or scholars did advance their own identities, they often did so in ways that were either immediately obvious, through memoirs or testaments; or reductive, through announcements of their "subject position" as members of a certain sexual, political, economic, national, or ethnic group. Sacrificing the author to language, theoretical criticism eliminated a primary source of interest in itself, and went a long way toward arguing itself out of an audience.

This book is an attempt to recover the real interest of criticism by demonstrating that it is, or can be at its highest levels, a richly expressive discourse. Criticism has been said to have any number of "characters," and it seems that almost any adjective can modify this term, depending on the argument being made. Foucault spoke of the "local character of criticism"; others have argued for the "historicizing," "scientific," "secular," "rational," "oppositional," and "equivocal" characters of criticism.[12] My argument here is that none of these terms designates the essence of criticism, but that all capture some dimension of it. The argument that supports this position is that criticism absorbs all these terms so easily because it is a discourse of character in general.

Criticism is a scholarly discipline that includes textual commentary, historical research, and theoretical reflection; it is also a human practice of reflection and meditation that enlists every intellectual, affective, and experiential resource that a person has. I will try to make this case by examining in detail the critical practice of four thinkers who make a particularly powerful claim on our attention. What Elaine Scarry, Martha Nussbaum, Slavoj Žižek, and Edward Said have in common and in abundance is the capacity to communicate in their scholarly work something more than just the scholarly virtues of intelligence, training, integrity, discipline, and imagination; what their work gives voice to is a distinctive way of being in the world that I will call character.

I distinguish character from mere personality, a collection of attributes expressed in the course of one's social existence. Criticism is not a medium for the expression of personality. One may be loyal, gluttonous, obtuse, inconstant, weak-willed, flirtatious, nonresponsive, or greedy in life, and never reveal these attributes in one's work; or, correlatively, the perspicacity, dullness, incisiveness, patience, conventionality, or rigor evident in one's work may not find expression in one's personal life. The character of the critic is implicit, not explicit, in the criticism, and may not be continuous in any obvious way with the critic's personality. Character in criticism is above all mediated through the conventions of scholarship and through the resources provided by the text being discussed. This mediation may take any number of forms. Criticism may be a refuge for alienated attributes that one cannot, or chooses not to, express directly; it may be a stage for attributes one chooses to display; it may be a safe place where one hides aspects of oneself that one wants to shelter from the warlike conditions of existence; it may be a confessional where one blurts out, in distanced or displaced forms, one's secrets. It may be all or any combination of these things, but what it is always is a particular form of expression different from the forms in which one engages with one's body, in real time. If we understand criticism as, at least in potential, a discourse of character—if we grasp, that is, the character of criticism in both senses—then we will not necessarily write differently, but we might become newly sensitive to what makes criticism a permanently valuable practice, and the value of that practice might rise in the general estimation.

The fundamental condition for the emergence of character in criticism is interpretive or speculative freedom. Criticism is a discourse of knowledge in which information is gathered, organized, described, analyzed, and reflected on. But the interest or value we attribute to criticism cannot be reduced to the information contained in it, for this information is not just accompanied or adorned by interpretation or speculation, but structured by them. And however disciplined or channeled by scholarly protocols they may be, interpretation represents a moment at which cognition is not absolutely bound by necessity to produce a particular result. All criticism, no matter how dryly technical, formalist, bibliographical, or philological, includes within its procedures this moment of cognitive freedom, and this moment serves as a portal through which character, an individual way of being in the world, enters the work.

How can we account for this speculative freedom, this x-factor, or factor of excess, in a discourse of knowledge? Perhaps the best way of accounting for it is to begin with the fact that criticism is a mimetic practice whose primary purpose is to produce an accurate representation of its object. In the case of criticism, this object is, paradigmatically, an "aesthetic" text presumed to be the product of a creative act undertaken by an individual author.[13] One aspect of that mimetic fidelity, therefore, must be a probing reentry into the process by which the text came to be produced. This entails not only a kind of sympathetic identification with the mind of the author, about which I'll have more to say later in this chapter, but also an effort that is both scholarly and imaginative to grasp the process by which this particular text came to be. The poet-scholar Susan Stewart describes this effort in terms of "obligation":

> I believe critics and artists have different obligations. Artists move forward in unanticipated ways and in the end must surprise themselves and their audiences. But the critic has an obligation to the intentions of the maker and to the work's formal integrity—the work is complete and must be addressed on its own terms. I often write about perceptual issues and not literary criticism per se, but when I am writing about someone else's work, whether living or dead, I try to keep pushing myself to go beyond my expectations and to come closer to the maker's intentions. And I try to infer what decisions were made that make the artwork what it is, so there's a mode of temporality that's retrospective. But there's a proleptic aspect, too, that in truth is closer to art-making itself, for I ask, "What am I not considering?" "What have I left out?" "Where else could I go?"[14]

This is, to be sure, the voice of a creator-critic, who might feel herself to be under a weightier obligation to reexperience the act of making than others who lack her direct experience of such acts. But no critic, regardless of orientation or commitment to any particular school of thought, could feel herself to be under no such obligation whatsoever, for the mimetic obligation of criticism to its object means that every critical act includes an experience of creative freedom, the experience of "moving forward in unanticipated ways." It is the distinctive combination of its obligations—to accuracy, fidelity, and verifiable truth on the one hand, and speculation, imagination, interpretive freedom, and creation on the other—that produces the character of criticism. And it is in the process of negotiating these various obligations that the character of the critic is disclosed.

2. Criticism As Confession

Let us imagine the primal scene of criticism. Let us say that, one day, a person—call him A—retires from the dust and disorder of the world to a quiet room. All his life he has been studying a text whose meaning has been disputed. Much depends on the meaning being made clear. If people really understood the text properly, he feels, their lives would be improved immeasurably, and the consequences of misunderstanding are far more serious than people realize. The premise of the text, which he thinks of as The Word, is that its call must be heeded—"Follow me," it says. But how? Controversies abound, and the meaning even of simple phrases is lost in the clamor. Something must be done. He decides to write another text.

He understands that, in an ideal world, a commentator would possess a complete understanding of the matter he presumes to explicate. He is far from certain that he has such an understanding; in fact, he is certain that he does not, for all his patient study and meditation have only brought him to an anxious appreciation of The Word's many difficulties and obscurities, which seem to him to indicate a deeper but more elusive truth than the certainties loudly proclaimed by others. He feels that some people have done themselves a profound disservice by grasping the meaning prematurely, without having suffered through a period of trial, of doubt and struggle, and that the meaning they have grasped provides false comfort by reinforcing mere custom and prejudice. His uncertainties notwithstanding, he feels that he has sensed the real and essential truth of The Word, its inner meaning. He feels that although The Word speaks to all the world, it has spoken to him with singular force, almost as if it somehow understood him, rather than he it. The Word has reached deep into his soul; it has illuminated, challenged, and fortified him. Reading it, he feels both addressed and expressed, apprehending it and his own identity at once, in dialogue.

He does not feel that The Word speaks only to him or even to him in his entirety. There is too much ordinariness, weakness, mediocrity, and habit in his life for him to feel that his entire being is comprehended by The Word, whose lofty and unchanging nature exposes his lack of constancy or focus, his vulnerability to distraction in all directions. He must somehow purge or clarify himself, setting aside those parts of his being that engage in family life, private meanderings, or public affairs, those animal parts that eat and sleep and desire. He must purify himself of arbitrary fancies, bodily promptings, and rigid habits so he can vibrate in perfect sympathy with the text, to see it as in itself it really is, with every faculty eager, open, and alive.

Everything begins with sympathy, which unlocks the flood of energy, releases one from the degrading limitations of custom and the body, and leads to transformation. On the other hand, however, sympathy is the source of a deep corruption that takes The Word for one's own utterance, a confusion that eliminates the very possibility of "following." There is nothing more exciting, and more misleading, than finding the promptings of one's own heart voiced in the text: one experiences that kind of extension and multiplication of self that we know as happiness. But, he reflects, his personal happiness is not the goal, and so he must somehow manage his sympathy so that he is summoned in the right way, and follows in the true path. He must block every fugitive wish to recognize, in the form of the text, himself again; he must destroy every trace of nonresponsive inertia, every stubborn desire to remain as he was. He must not insist on himself, but must, in a sense, forget who he is and even where he lives. He must become a kind of nomad, with no established identity, living a condition of transcendental homelessness. Only then can he make of himself a medium through which the text speaks; and only by this means can he realize his own true and essential nature. He will transcend himself by submitting to the text; his abjection will be his triumph.

Retreating to his quiet room, he focuses his thoughts, emptying his mind of everything but The Word. Reading is a discipline, a chastening, a self-transformation, a conversion of life. But The Word, too, must be converted. It must be transformed by the agency of his text from suggestive form into transparent meaning. Mere repetition will not accomplish this transformation. He must produce new and different words that, although faithful to The Word, speak the truth it does not speak itself. He will bring into the world the truth of the text as he understands it—the truth of the Truth. If he succeeds, other readers will be able to grasp this truth for the first time; inspired by his example, they will come to an understanding that is their own, and yet proper, legitimate, and warranted. His own text will dissolve in their minds and become indistinguishable from The Word, even as The Word becomes more fully itself, its vast potential liberated. If he succeeds, readers of The Word will feel as though a film or screen had been removed, or an accent mark placed over a letter—a sense of brightening, heightening, enlivening.

He is keenly aware that although he may hope to clarify The Word, he must never aspire to subdue or compete with it. Rather, he must bring out its power, which inspires respect, and its beauty, which draws us to it and makes us want to dwell in its presence. But beauty, he reflects, may be a problem. Excellence in beauty, after all, is not excellence in morals. Moreover, the relation of beauty to meaning is not clear, and may be a negative one. He does not understand to his satisfaction why he considers The Word, whose material form is just scratches on a surface, beautiful. It is not even clear to him whether beauty is a property or a feeling. If it can simply be described, then why do people disagree about it? And if it is a feeling—perhaps "judgment" would be a more precise term—then why does it seem so important that everyone should share this feeling? And why should we be concerned with beauty at all? When we are under its atavistic spell we begin to think of The Word as a thing apart, something to be admired, but what is really needed is a sharpened sense of the way it impinges on the world. He ponders these questions.

The one thing he must clarify above all, he determines, is the boundless fertility of The Word, whose power and value are measured by its capacity to respond to all questions put to it, and to exceed all accounts of it. The simplest points are also the deepest and most mysterious. What, for example, is meant by the words, "In the beginning God created heaven and earth"? The beginning of what? What kind of dimensionless vacuity preceded this primal act of creation? Is "the beginning" merely the first moment that words can describe? And why did God decide to do this? How, dwelling in the void, did he come to have a new thought? What provoked him to this deed? And once provoked, how did he create "heaven"—out of what? And—moving along, as though these questions had been answered—what is "the spirit of God"? Is God himself not spirit? On another level, how do we know that Moses was telling the truth about all these things? Or that the transcription that lies open on our table is an accurate representation of God's speech, acts, or mind? (Does God have a "mind"?) Is The Word the voice of God or the writing of Moses? Is it alive, or the record of life? Does it have its own form, as do things of nature, or was it given form like clay worked by a potter? And why is it not transparent? Why, if one can understand the words, are the sentences still puzzling? And how can one tell a true interpretation from a false one? What is the problem with The Word as it is? Does it have too much meaning to be contained in clear, rational sentences, so that the work of criticism consists of stripping, paring, reducing—or is something missing, which the critic must provide?

Our critic must enter into the spirit of The Word. But what, and where, is this spirit? As deep and fecund as it is, The Word is still mute, imprisoned within the letters on a page, these markings that anyone could make. Why does meaning take this degraded form—or any form? Why should The Word bear any resemblance to the meaningless chatter that one hears everywhere? Why should it be embodied in markings, which are powerless as a king without a kingdom until they are taken up and read? And what happens when they are read? This is a mystery even deeper than The Word itself. Somehow, when someone who, through the fortunes of the world has come to possess The Word, takes it up and reads it in the proper way, The Word itself is transformed, or converted, from matter into spirit, from marks into meaning, from potential into actuality. Taken up in the right way, The Word, like the reader, is miraculously transfigured. This is the destiny of The Word—and yet, it is not destiny, for everything depends on chance and circumstance.

Fixed and immutable, The Word is still part of the world, and worldliness is a condition of its being. Time, chance, and corporeality must be honored without being mistaken for the meaning, which is essential, living, and abstract. The entire mystery is contained, it seems, in the characters of The Word themselves, in the marks that are both word and Word. *Character*— our critic thinks to himself—is an interesting word. It refers, in the case of a person, to identity as revealed by the events of a lifetime. Character distinguishes one person from another, and seems entirely internal to the person, but it can only be revealed, discovered, or tested in the world at large. One has gifts, limitations, dispositions, to be sure; but without the opportunities and challenges provided by one's friends, enemies, parents, townsfolk, children, wife, mistress (our critic reflects)—the world at large—one is not truly oneself, but only a self-in-waiting or in suspension. It is very difficult to distinguish what is truly one's own from the accidents of life in which it emerges. In fact, it seems that one's character is precisely the self that is forged in the course of confronting those accidents. Characters on the page have the same character, both individual and collective. They are called characters because they give a particular and bodily form to meaning. They incarnate the spirit intended by the author, enabling that spirit to enter the world. They betray, in both senses, the thought of the author in that they exhibit it and falsify it; and the constant task of the reader is to distinguish these two senses. Like human character, textual characters are individual only in a narrow and misleading sense. The same scratches that have, in The Word, a singular and precious existence also swirl around the world like so much dust. And the very existence of those marks testifies to a mighty collective process of meaning-making. The Word could not have come into the world without paper, ink, and binding, and without people to make, sell, transport, and exchange. The arrival of The Word in one's quiet room testifies to many characters in addition to that of the author. Really, it testifies to the comprehensive character of the world itself.

One must read back through this deep mesh of character or characters to recover the spirit animating The Word. One must enter into the spirit of this spirit as it is revealed behind and within and by the characters. All these words are beginning to sound alike. But in the moment of illumination, if it arrives, one grasps it all together, the intention and the medium, the timeless message and the changing world it addresses and in which it exists. One grasps the character of The Word alive in the world.

Naturally, one's own character is also at issue. The act of writing a critical text reaches deep into oneself, testing one's acuity, responsiveness, erudition, and staying power. But critical writing also tests attributes normally considered as moral qualities, including the capacity to suspend one's own interests and desires and to make of oneself a perfect instrument for registering the truth of The Word. Above all, one wants the truth of The Word to be communicated without distortion, and this requires discipline, a principled indifference to himself, ascesis. There is no place in this task for self. One must stand not between the reader and The Word, like a child clamoring for attention, but modestly off to the side. Still, he reflects, one must admit that the act of critical writing responds to desire, even to many desires—to create, to contribute to the goods of the world, to know, to express, to be understood, to be legible to oneself and others, to be acknowledged as an authority, and to be clear and resolved in the eyes of the world. By losing oneself, one can become allied with The Word: praising it, one can claim a share in it. It is all very good. And yet—and here is where character is tested—these various pleasures cannot be indulged or even fully acknowledged. They must be satisfied without satisfaction, for the only permissible motive for writing is to speak the truth of The Word.

The pleasures of critical writing cannot be acknowledged, and yet they are not altogether dishonorable and must not be altogether disowned. Indifference to them would represent indifference to The Word, because the labor they spur on is entirely in its service. To represent The Word, one must be understood in a certain way, as a person who can be trusted. And so, naturally, one must desire that others see in their humble guide a host of virtues, all deployed in service to The Word and to themselves. One must, for example, wish to be regarded as a person who can overcome insubordinate impulses, remove clutter and distractions from the field of vision, isolate the main issues, set aside conventional views, persevere through difficulties, set high standards, see beneath appearances, form general propositions from particulars, see particulars within the context of general propositions, make rigorous and valid inferences from concrete evidence, be responsive without being obsessive, take delight without becoming besotted, concentrate without obsession, be suspicious without being withholding, be fair without being equivocal, be responsive to the moment without being indiscriminate in one's enthusiasms, and so forth. To serve one's readers as a model of the aroused intelligence, with desire mediated by judgment, passion guided by reason, deep experience gathered in profound reflection, one must wish to be so regarded. How can it harm me, then, our critic thinks, if I wish to be admired? Or loved? The great secret of morals is, after all, love, and one will only follow that which he loves. Wanting to be loved by the reader is almost the same—is it not?—as wanting the reader to follow The Word. He struggles with these issues.

So, eager for admiration, our critic still sets himself apart from his readers as a performer sets himself apart from his audience, to create the space across which he will be seen, understood, and appreciated. But the regard is mutual. How can he fail to think about the other who will retire from the dust and disorder of the world to his own quiet room with a book—his book? Simply to communicate The Word, the critic must imagine the person who might read his book; he must think about what sort of person his reader is, wants to be, thinks he is, ought to be, and can be encouraged or made to be by the reading of a book. To imagine a reader is to imagine a relationship and a strategy, the means by which the reader can be led along from a beginning position of more or less responsive but unproductive questing to the desired destination. What do readers—all those who might, in the vastness of space and time, take up a book and read—want? In the long term, they want the truth. But they also want to be regarded with respect for who they are, as they are. And, it must be admitted, they want pleasure as well, little garden patches of enjoyment along the stony path to truth. Once again, the desire for pleasure is a problem, because it is not properly a part of the search for truth. But ultimately, it is the solution, for The Word is full of virtue-breeding delightfulness; it instructs by enticing, and then by pleasing, giving the reader a cluster of grapes, that, full of that taste, he may long to pass further. Anyone who craves pleasure can be manipulated. In need of severer instruction, such a reader can be led to it by degrees by a skillful writer who can deploy the reader's appetites in the service of a loftier goal. After all, genius does not merely persuade an audience, but lifts it to ecstasy. Phrases and arguments can be devised to persuade the reader to suspend his resistances and permit his passive or unformed understanding to be shaped. A productive uncertainty, full of potential for transformation, can be created where none had been before. Objections and cavils can be anticipated and met. Assent to authority can be engineered so the illusion of free choice is preserved. All this is possible.

It is not, however, simple. Readers will only assent to the authority of one who seems to have no interest in exercising it. A reader's trust is extended only to one whose only interest is in helping them to see the truth as he, the critic, has seen it. Interested in themselves, readers distrust those whose interests lie elsewhere. What readers want in a writer is a person whose entire existence, as encountered in the text, is oriented toward them—a person who has experienced a profound conversion of life.

With supreme craft, our ur-critic appends his critical text to an account of the wandering and deeply imperfect life he led before committing himself, following a traumatic event in a certain garden, to service on behalf of The Word. One must, this technique suggests, spend a lifetime preparing for the task of criticism, the performance of which is an unforgiving measure of the character of his devotion. If one were still stealing pears (for example), if one's personal attachments remained excessive or incoherent, if one was veering from appetite to appetite, if one was still taking inordinate delight in the visible world, if one had become addicted to praise and approval, or if one were constantly distracted by meaningless details, then one would be incapable of criticism. But if one has learned—with the help of The Word—to resist these temptations at last, then one has earned the right to speak. Indeed, the very act of criticism testifies to and completes one's self-transformation. This is the story, and the strategy.

It is a delicate business, however, because although one's readers expect critical competence, they do not want to be lectured by a saint. They require assurances that the person who presumes to instruct them was once as fallible as they, and that he remains mindful of life's difficulties. If that assurance takes the form of confession, fine. In fact, all the better: signs in the critical text of unresolved struggle, especially if that text were to be appended to an account of prior transgressions, would be very helpful in encouraging identification and interest.

Detecting signs of untransmuted desire within the critical text becomes a kind of game with them. Readers—our critic reflects in an unguarded and admittedly unworthy moment—take up a book in part because they want, in addition to instruction, to see a performance by one who is willing to take the risk of authority. They enjoy watching him labor to construct an account of The Word that owes nothing to conventional wisdom on the one side or—he assures them—to any merely personal interests on the other. (Why, they ask themselves, would one wish to forego these?) They look not only for signs of rigor or method, but for indications of character as well. Measuring his words against The Word, which they can read for themselves, they can see what engages his attention and what does not; they can speculate about the reasons for both. They can assess his performance, with its strengths and weaknesses, its errors, omissions, distortions, and his insights and moments of brilliance, and can infer the mental habits, the philias and phobias, the tics and reflexes, the drives and compulsions and enthusiasms, the dead spots of indifference, the blockages of resistance that make up the mechanism of his mind as it negotiates the world. They can read his secrets, even, sometimes, his life story. They flatter themselves that they can discern in his text the lineaments of a confession even more candid and revealing than the story he tells when he is confessing.

Like him, they understand that every act of criticism is an act of confession. But they take particular satisfaction in the sense that they are receiving different confessions than the one he thinks he is giving. They read, in the very gestures of his scholarly humility, signs of other energies—the desire to impress, to display himself, even to eclipse The Word by substituting for it his own words. They grasp his need for applause, and are prepared to grant him their approval on the condition that it is understood that they have the power to judge him as he has judged The Word. They are not necessarily eager to interrupt their own rhythms or replace their comfortable beliefs with labor, doubt, uncertainty, and discontent. They read, in general, for confirmation that they are all right as they are, more or less. And they make sure that they receive this message by treating his text as the utterance of a man who is not converted beyond recognition, but who, despite having made some progress along these lines, has remained like themselves, more or less—someone who has borne their burdens, faltered as they have faltered, transgressed as they have transgressed.

When they open his book, they are pleased. They see not only ample evidence of conversion in the form of critical insight, but also intriguing indications that he has slipped back into the patterns he claims to have transcended or overcome, signs that he has managed to remain his inconstant, vainglorious, insecure, preening, distracted, lusting self. They read not only stunning confessions of weakness, error, and desire, but also something else whose appeal is subtler and more compelling: confessions that masquerade as explication. In those passages in which he probes The Word for its secrets, they see not the elusive truth alone but also the desperate man. They are fascinated by the drama of consciousness that unfolds as he weighs alternatives, poses questions, complains, appeals, and contradicts himself. They note signs of an illicit author-love: "I write this book for love of your love"; they mark his uncertainty: "Can it be that I am confusing the corporeal works which [you have] accomplished . . . with the clear understanding of these mysteries?"; and they note his rationalizing indecision: "How can it harm me if I understand the writer's meaning in a different sense from that in which he understands it?"[15] They note all these with an illicit but unembarrassed pleasure. "Wasn't this the fellow who told us that the sole meaning of the Bible was the 'pulling down of the dominion of lust'?" they ask each other.[16] "Didn't he congratulate himself for leaving his mistress? And now he says that St. Paul 'begot children in the Gospel,' and that the entire world bears witness to the commandment to be fruitful and multiply! He is definitely confusing corporal things with understanding. He has found another mistress in The Word! I've heard stories about him from my friends in Carthage—what a fellow!"[17]

Even as he attempts to demonstrate his profound understanding of and total adherence to The Word, our critic provides his readers with the gripping spectacle of a man falling, falling, all over again—with the added amusement that he manifestly believes himself to be rising. With a sickening certitude, he recognizes that such judgments by his readers do not strike him as perverse because—perversely—he is actually soliciting them out of a desire, perhaps driven more by pride than humility, to be chastened even further. Doubtful of the completeness of his conversion, he seeks further correction in the judgment of his readers. They—usually so easily bored, distracted, or indifferent to his needs—are in this respect eager to help.

3. Griffes of the Great

Introducing his brilliant book *The Art of Living: Socratic Reflections from Plato to Foucault*, Alexander Nehamas notes that philosophy is widely considered to be "a theoretical discipline" with few implications for everyday life.[18] This view, he points out, is actually a quite recent invention—even more recent than "the author." Philosophy is not by nature theoretical; it has become so. If we return to the classical roots of philosophy with fresh eyes, we would see a persistent emphasis not on theory in itself but on a *life* of theoretical activity. "One could not lead such a life," he says, explaining the premise of classical philosophy, "unless one acquired not only a number of philosophical views but also, over time and through serious effort, the very particular sort of character whose elements and presuppositions Aristotle described" (2). In this older but, Nehamas insists, still-viable account of philosophy, the views one holds and the ways one articulates and defends them indicate a certain way of being in the world, a conception of life. Philosophy as theory versus philosophy as the art of living: one conception "avoids personal style and idiosyncrasy as much as possible. Its aim is to deface the particular personality that offers answers to philosophical questions . . . . The other requires style and idiosyncrasy because its readers must never forget that the views that confront them are the views of a particular type of person and of no one else" (3). In the case of this second type, the defense of which is the point of Nehamas's book, "the construction of character" is a central preoccupation; and indeed, at the very end of his book, Nehamas reflects that, in his readings of Plato, Montaigne, Nietzsche, Foucault, and others, "I, too, have tried to construct a particular character" (3, 188).

One may wonder why, given his central argument, Nehamas waited until the final paragraph to acknowledge that character construction was part of his own project. The answer, I believe, is that he could not make such an acknowledgment without undermining the integrity of his work. Criticism, which is what he is doing, is neither the first type of philosophy, in which character counts for nothing, nor the second, in which it counts for everything. It is a discourse of knowledge whose expressive dimension cannot be admitted, much less consciously manipulated or "constructed" by the author, without compromising the entire project. Character in criticism cannot be consciously performed; it can only be inferred. The instant the critic confesses his desire to construct a character for himself in his work, a crucial innocence is lost and criticism comes to an end. When the reader suspects that the critic is at all concerned with self-presentation, the game is up.

The reason for this has as much to do with the character of criticism as with the character of character. And here we must be very precise. The term *character* is misapplied to a discourse in which "style and idiosyncrasy" are front and center; a more appropriate term for such a discourse would perhaps be *personality* or *persona*. It is in criticism that character is revealed with great clarity and force not by the performance of attributes or qualities but by the particular way in which one notices and describes things, formulates arguments, negotiates difficulties, sets and solves problems, makes assessments, weighs evidence, draws inferences, and arrives at judgments or conclusions. Criticism betrays the mind's tensile strength, responsiveness, and especially its adaptability, the ways in which it conforms itself to its subject and its subject to itself.

Character is revealed, in the first instance, by the choice of subject, which provides the field of evidence. Because this choice is as free as choices ever are, it provides the first indication of a critic's sensibility by disclosing what sort of thing the critic wishes to spend his time thinking about. Critics choose their projects for a variety of reasons, but the most powerful criticism is often produced by those who make their choice on the basis of elective affinity, another term for which might be sympathy as Adam Smith and David Hume defined it: a capacity both moral and aesthetic to extend one's concern beyond the self, to feel the anger, fear, enthusiasm, sorrow that another feels.[19] Sympathy in this broad sense includes the ability to experience a work of art as if it were somehow an expression of oneself; and such an experience can, under the right circumstances, eventuate in criticism. If it does, the criticism that results might well be character-revealing, disclosing to the reader not just factual knowledge or an illuminating perspective, but a nearly legible or perceptible ethical dimension, a system of values, concerns, and desires informing the production of knowledge. In the very broadest sense, sympathy describes any response to another in which character is probed, tested, or defined, whether by affinity or by antagonism, a sense of sameness or a sense of difference, a relation of harmony or of counterpoint.

The indication of character provided by subject choice is still, however, preliminary; the truest index is not the subject alone but the angle of vision or "take" on the subject, which is less purely volitional and therefore less within a critic's conscious control. The Shakespeare depicted in the criticism of Samuel Johnson, S. T. Coleridge, William Hazlitt, G. Wilson Knight, Phyllis Rackin, and Stephen Greenblatt is a different Shakespeare because, inmixed with Shakespeare in each case is the critic's own sensibility: all of these critics, recognizing a part of themselves in their subject, cast the Bard in the image not of their personality, a more or less conscious social construction, but of their aptitudes, capacities, orientations, interests, concerns, and deep values—their character. For each one, "Shakespeare" represents, in addition to a monumental oeuvre and an historical figure, a form of self-knowledge.

A discourse informed by sympathy will be irreducible to system. But here, once again, precision is required. It is tempting, following Nehamas's lead, to conceive of an opposition between sympathy and system; but what criticism really demonstrates is their ultimate compatibility. Indeed, what I am calling character is precisely the combination of the two, the subjection of sympathy to system and the destabilization of system by sympathy. Thus Camus's famous formulation in *The Fall*—"when one has no character one *has* to apply a method"—is inexact. Character is demonstrated by the way one deploys method. Method—conventions, rules, regularities, the general spirit of argumentative and scholarly rigor—does not represent the dead force of law, to be opposed to sympathy; it is, rather, a condition of sympathy's accession to the status of character, the resistance it must overcome in order to achieve itself.[20] Character cannot be reduced to method, but neither can it be altogether differentiated from it. The canonical formulation of this position is in Max Weber's "Science as a Vocation": "Ladies and gentlemen," he begins sternly, "in the field of science only he who is devoted *solely* to the work at hand has 'character' (*persönlichkeit*). And this holds not only for science; we know of no great artist who has ever done anything but serve his work and only his work."[2] Method functions for the critic as a principle of "unconsciousness," a set of rules and precedents that engages the attention and permits the self-forgetfulness that is the condition of self-disclosure.

And so, paradoxically, the various factors of objectivity and impersonality in criticism—the text, method, the institution of criticism, academe, the conventions of communication, professional expertise—actually secure criticism's expressive dimension. They are part of the reason that criticism, to a far greater extent than any other academic discipline, can be considered a personal undertaking. To a greater degree than any other scholarly discipline, criticism is not merely something that one does, but an index of who one is. Readers of criticism encounter the character of the critic in mediated form, expressed indirectly through the protocols of a particular scholarly discourse that provides an accepted traditional form for individual response, ensuring both transparency and a certain kind of authority or power.

Criticism is the record of an encounter between a living mind and a text. This encounter is not directly reflected in the text, which typically proceeds as though the drama of understanding—of initial interest and curiosity, of gathering and arranging evidence, of probing and exploration, of quickening excitement, of speculation and growing conviction—had been completed before the writing had begun. But it is, in some criticism, discernible, or perhaps recoverable, and in these instances the reader can sense the form and force of the process that eventuated in the critical text. Because this drama is unrepresented and in fact unrepresentable, it is rarely discussed; indeed, most accounts of criticism simply ignore it. But it is there, and constitutes one possible feature of our experience of reading criticism.

It is a possible rather than an essential feature because not all critical texts are rewarding to read in this way. But the critical works that strike us as powerful, illuminating, and likely to endure do so because, in addition to the information they convey about their subjects, they give us the record of a character-in-action or a character-in-formation. On rare occasion, this is conceded. In 2002, a memorial service for the critic Thomas Greene was held at Yale University, where he taught for many years. One of his former graduate students, Leonard Barkan, began his tribute by saying that "It is the mark of great scholars that their work demonstrates a personal signature, a griffe, that weaves its way through a great diversity of subjects and concerns."[22] Such an account of criticism is more appropriate at a memorial service, where the focus is on appreciative reminiscence, than in professional discourse about criticism. A character-centered account is actually seen as a threat to the basic premise of criticism, that it is a discourse of knowledge informed by a certain aversion to display, a humility before the text under discussion that was exemplified by the old custom of the *Times Literary Supplement* to publish only unsigned articles. It is not a truth generally acknowledged that a measure of "greatness" in scholarship is a "griffe" or characteristic set of markers that identify one's work as one's own. The conditions of critical greatness are rarely, in fact, discussed at all. The very notion that criticism has a "personal signature" that is inscribed regardless of the subject matter would strike many as a degradation, as if the venerable institution of criticism were being seen through the lens of *People* magazine.

But Barkan persists, and the truly significant point is the next one. If a personal inscription in a critical work is a sign of greatness, he says, it is only in the even rarer case of the "very great scholar that this set of ongoing individual markers is also the bearer of moral, ethical, spiritual conviction, quite apart from, but woven together with, the matters of learning, of history, of critique, of interpretation." Only those whose characters display patterns of responsiveness and evaluation in which extrapersonal commitments are registered can convert their "personal signatures" into bearers of meaning and value. In the case of the very great scholar, the personal is not just the political, but also the moral. Or, to put it another way, the personal signature of the very great scholar is no longer a matter of style and idiosyncrasy, but carries a public meaning, signifying beyond itself. Nehamas makes a similar distinction between the ordinary and the extraordinary cases. "In the cases of great individuals," he says, "like Socrates, Montaigne, Nietzsche, and Foucault, the private and the public, the aesthetic and the political, are as entangled with one another as the 'life' and the 'work'" (180). The work of some critics reaches deeper and lasts longer than the work of others because, in the case of the great and very great, there is no clear distinction between public and private, but rather a fertile confusion. When readers discern in the critical text not simply insights into Shakespeare or Goethe or Sophocles but a pattern of responsiveness, attention, and discrimination from which can be inferred a distinctive way of being in the world, then criticism expands its reach and becomes both political and ethical. In these cases, public or historical issues and energies become legible as personal concerns or attributes, and the critical work itself is invested with a more general force.

It was the versatile Barthes who provided the first "theoretical" formulation of this account of critical greatness. Fifteen years before he wrote "The Death of the Author," Barthes wrote *Writing Degree Zero*, a youthful effort intended as a reply to the passivity of Sartrean existentialism, in which the function of literature seemed restricted to the bearing of witness, the providing of lucid insights into hopeless situations.[23] Barthes began by describing two aspects or dimensions of writing that were given rather than chosen. The first was language, the untranscendable horizon of history within which the writer works; and the second was style, a kind of idiolect that is closer to the biological processes of the body than to social convention. In neither domain could the writer claim to exercise freedom. Even style, Barthes argued, was like a compulsion; it always had "something crude about it: it is a form with no clear destination, the product of a thrust, not an intention . . . a vertical and lonely dimension of thought."[24] Both language and style should, he proposed, be considered "objects" and distinguished from a third "function" (as opposed to object) in which the operations of freedom could be detected. Barthes's compelling articulation of this function, which he called writing, or *écriture*, effectively ended the reign of Sartrean existentialism and announced the arrival of the era of theory in France.

By the time a translated version of this concept reached the monolingual shores of the United States in 1968, Barthes himself had long since left behind heroic notions of freedom in favor of semiology and the scientistic elimination of the personal. The 1953 version of Barthes was actually more congenial to 1968 America than the 1968 death-of-the-author Barthes; and in her preface to the English translation of *Writing Degree Zero*, Susan Sontag offered as a more precise translation of *écriture* the phrase "personal utterance," a term better able to indicate a commitment consistent with political urgency of the quasi-libidinous kind then current (xiii). "Personal utterance" occupied a middle ground between the historical and the merely personal, a space of freedom in which form unfolded as the product of a human intention. Barthes's example of greatness in the domain of personal utterance was "Hébert, the revolutionary," who

> never began a number of his news-sheet *Le Père Duchêne* without introducing a sprinkling of obscenities. These improprieties had no real meaning, but they had significance. In what way? In that they expressed a whole revolutionary situation. Now here is an example of a mode of writing whose function is no longer only communication or expression, but the imposition of something beyond language, which is both History and the stand we take in it. (1)

Hébert was not a revolutionary because he used language; nor was the burden of revolution carried by his "style." The specifically revolutionary force of his work lay in the domain of *écriture*, where his freely undertaken and constantly reaffirmed decision to introduce pointless obscenities marked the morality of form, placing him emphatically in History.

The two most telling characteristics of Hébert's utterance, for Barthes, are gratuitousness and consistency. The former implies a personal decision unmotivated by any necessity, and the latter suggests that this decision reflects an attribute of character rather than a mere gesture. Consider, in this context, Dr. Johnson's account of character:

> The most authentic witnesses of any man's character are those who know him in his own family, and see him without any restraint or rule of conduct, but such as he voluntarily prescribes to himself. If a man carries virtue with him into his private apartments, and takes no advantage of unlimited power or probable secrecy; if we trace him through the round of time, and find that his character, with those allowances which mortal frailty must always want, is uniform and regular, we have all the evidence of his sincerity that one man can have with regard to another; and, indeed, as hypocrisy cannot be its own reward, we may, without hesitation, determine that his heart is pure.[25]

For Johnson, character is not a matter of conscious self-invention or dutiful obedience to law; but neither is it a matter of strictly reflexive unconsciousness. It is, rather, a function of that particular kind of freedom we experience when we feel secure in our privacy; it is displayed in the routines we follow when we are unwatched, the rules we give ourselves when we can gain no advantage by, and suffer no consequences for, our behavior. Character, Johnson suggests, is most revealingly disclosed in those moments when one is following a routine one has determined for oneself without the experience of conscious choice, when one is behaving in a characteristic fashion without feeling that one is "behaving" in any particular way at all. As Barthes's *écriture* stands between the personal and the historical, Johnson's character stands between the unconsciously random and the fully self-aware experience of following the rules. As is often the case with Johnson, there is classical precedent, this time in Plutarch, who introduces his life of Alexander with the comment that "the most glorious exploits do not always furnish us with the clearest discoveries of virtue or vice in men; sometimes a matter of less moment, an expression or a jest, informs us better of their characters and inclinations, than the most famous sieges, the greatest armaments, or the bloodiest battles whatsoever."[26]

Criticism lies somewhere between expressions or jests on the one side and armed combat on the other. For this reason, criticism is actually superior to either of these as a medium in which character is revealed, and is one of the very best ways of revealing character in all its depth and complexity. Criticism is especially good at revealing the particular features of that disciplined kind of character that respects and values truth and is willing to submit to the constraints imposed by a conventional and scholarly discourse. This characteristic is not uniformly distributed across the human species, but critics have it in abundance. They find in criticism an opportunity to discover and record the truth, and a way of doing so that registers as well, albeit in ways they cannot fully explain or even acknowledge, their distinctive singularity.

In the chapters that follow, I have tried to describe these ways in the work of critics who seem to me full of interest in this respect. In an earlier book, I had attempted a few career studies in which I tried to delineate the evolving and essential arguments of certain critics I admired greatly. I found the task challenging and rewarding in equal measure. Reading criticism in this way enabled me not just to acquire a richer understanding of certain critics, but to appreciate a new dimension of the genre, to see it not just as an analytical or descriptive discourse, but as a richly human testament in which a distinctive sensibility tests and defines itself in—and is in turn challenged and exposed by—the encounter with a text. After several such studies, I was able to formulate to myself a larger and deeper project, which was to develop not just a different way of reading but a new concept for criticism itself. The essays in this book differ from their predecessors in that they were written in full awareness of this concept and are as a consequence much fuller and more detailed.

Each of the critics discussed in this book answers in his or her own way to Barkan's recipe for the "very great critic" in that not only do they have their distinctive griffes, but their griffes bear "moral, ethical, spiritual conviction"—to which I would add that they also register historical and political energies. The work of each is exceptionally good at illuminating the subject under consideration, of course, but it also suggests a distinctive way of being in and acting on the world. I find all four problematic in some ways; in fact, I find them on occasion conflicted, wrongheaded, misguided, and even foolish. This does not diminish my admiration for their accomplishments; in fact, in some instances, it intensifies that admiration. What manifests itself as a compelling singularity, even peculiarity or oddness, testifies to a certain integrity, a difficult identity sustained over time despite the manifest sacrifices exacted in terms of plausibility, descriptive adequacy, and readerly confidence.

One measure of their peculiarity is the atmosphere of controversy that surrounds their work. I am particularly intrigued by debates not about the meaning of their work but about its value. Serious differences among intelligent readers on the fundamental question of whether critical work is good or bad signal the presence of a protracted singularity that cannot be reduced or accounted for by anything other than the force of character. Although each of my four main subjects here is a sharply etched individual, the trait they have most conspicuously in common is force, or brute critical strength.

To read criticism as a document of character requires a certain kind of analysis that may appear to be radically, even inappropriately, personal. But according to the rules I have set myself, I will, in the discussions that follow, use only materials that are publicly available. I have some personal acquaintance with two of the critics treated here, and none with the other two. But in all four cases, I have restricted the field of evidence to the published work or to those facts that are widely known and uncontested. This seems to be the only way in which an argument about the character of criticism can proceed. And if I am right about the singular power of criticism to convey character, then it might be that this is the very best way to develop a truly intimate understanding. I am not attempting to describe four human beings, with their private qualities, concerns, circumstances, or aptitudes, but rather four critics. In the end, I am describing certain expressive capacities of criticism as exemplified by these four instances, and suggesting that there could be, and are, many more.

CHAPTER 2

Criticism as Reverie: Elaine Scarry and the Dream of Pain

Introducing Elaine Scarry to an immense audience at the 1999 Modern Language Association convention, Edward Said asserted that, "There is no one even remotely like Elaine Scarry for the depth and originality of her thinking in the humanities today." A stunning assertion, especially given that the presidential panel he was chairing included Pierre Bourdieu, Michael Fried, and Noam Chomsky, not to mention himself.[1] Of these, Scarry was much the youngest and least prolific, despite having published, just a few months before, two books. Clearly, her claim to such stature, which Said is not alone in according her, is based not on the quantity of her work, but on its singular and striking quality, its character. Praise of Scarry's work typically takes the form of praise of Scarry herself, her ethical seriousness, her "bravery," her brilliance, her iconoclasm, and her profundity. And so it is particularly noteworthy that the quality of Scarry's work is its most controversial aspect. Attacks on Scarry generally take the form of an exasperated incredulity that such thoughts as hers even qualify as thoughts, or that anybody could seriously think them. Her account of the imagination, James Wood writes, "has a zany academicism more outré than the most frigid theorist's"; her theory "is sometimes stimulating, but

ultimately it is very strange, very speculative, and very obviously erroneous."[2] All her contentions about torture are vitiated, Peter Singer writes,
by "a blithe disregard for the ordinary canons of argument."[3] The critiques
most unresponsive to Scarry's work dismiss it as insubstantial froth,
marred—indeed, constituted—by errors of fact and reasoning so numerous and glaring as to make sustained refutation manifestly not worth the
effort, because the source of error lies too deep to be correctable. Concentrated at the extremes with astonishment the only constant, Scarry's
reputation is not the kind that normally attaches to a scholar; there is,
in the reception of her work, none of the commonplace respect typically
accorded to a life of quiet industry and perseverance, the life of the mind.
Hers is rather the kind of reputation more typically associated with a charismatic political leader revered by ordinary people but loathed by the elite,
with the difference that Scarry's reputation, as Said's introduction and her
position at Harvard attest, is strongest among the elite.[4]

Reputation is often an unreliable guide to the value of a scholar's work.
A more conventional approach is to compare what a writer says about a
given subject with the facts of the matter. But in the case of Scarry, the
incoherence of her reputation actually indicates, far better than an independent assessment of her subjects would do, the true character of her
contribution. To understand exactly what Scarry has been doing for the
past twenty years, we must suspend for a moment the impulse to decide
between worshippers and denigrators, and try to comprehend them both
in a synthetic understanding that attends to the genuine strength, the hyp-
notic appeal, the incredible gaps and flaws, and the almost overpowering
peculiarity of her writing. So, rather than assessing Scarry's statements on
pain, torture, war, creation, beauty, and imagination by measuring these
statements against the things themselves, we will begin by taking Scarry's
work as that sort of thing that excites radically divergent and convinced
assessments. Trying to understand why this is so, we will try to infer the
features of the mind and sensibility that produced the work, with insight
into the subjects she takes up being reserved as a possible byproduct of
this approach. We will begin, in other words, by assuming that the determinants of Scarry's texts are internal as well as external, and that these
texts constitute a whole—a "body of work"—rather than a scattered set of
discussions of various subjects.

The reputation in question rests on a very few items, including her first
and most famous book *The Body in Pain* (1985); an extraordinary feat of
autodidactic, interdisciplinary mastery, "The Fall of TWA 800" (1998)
and subsequent articles on other airplane crashes (2000); the defiantly
"naive" treatise *On Beauty and Being Just* (1999); and the compellingly

strange exploration of the mechanisms of the imagination, *Dreaming by the Book* (1999). She is also the author of five heterodox essays included in *Resisting Representation* (1994); the introduction to, and one essay in, a collection of English Institute essays titled *Literature and the Body* (1988); and diverse texts concerning issues related to war and social contract, presumably fragments of a major work yet to appear. More recently, she has written on the Patriot Act and on the impact of 9-11 on traditional rights and freedoms in this country. This list is not exhaustive, but it can be stated unequivocally that her stature rests chiefly on the very first of these, *The Body in Pain*. Without that book on her résumé, Scarry's other works would lack the presumption of substantiality and seriousness that makes them something to reckon with; but with it, even the most diaphanous of her productions commands attention. (Indeed, one of the primary sources of interest in reading Scarry lies in the effort to grasp the fact that the same mind produced these lesser things and that very major one.) In fact, in some respects, nearly all of her more recent work is explicitly anticipated in *The Body in Pain*.[5] One four-page passage (147–150) contains preliminary articulations of the "thinness" of images (a principal tenet of *Dreaming by the Book*); the relation between nuclear and conventional war with respect to the social-contract issue of "consent"; and the relation, to which she has often referred, between "making-up" and "making-real."[6] Elsewhere in that book, she refers to "thinking in an emergency," the title of an article she has read on a number of occasions; the concept of "work," subsequently elaborated in an essay on Hardy in *Resisting Representation*, dominates Chapter 3, as does "imagination"; and the emphasis throughout *The Body in Pain*, but especially in Chapter 4, on bodiliness and materiality reappears in her work in *Literature and the Body*.[7] An essay from the early 1990s on "The Difficulty of Imagining Other People" takes as evidence for this difficulty the human willingness to inflict pain.[8] If, a generation later, Scarry remains the author of *The Body in Pain*, it is because this great and strange book constitutes the first, and often the most productive account of subjects that have occupied her ever since.

The appearance in 1985 of *The Body in Pain* constituted one of the most stunning academic debuts in memory; the book remains today one of the most formidable, ambitious, and original works to have been produced by a scholar trained in the humanities. Then not yet forty years old and completely unknown, Scarry had written a book that both brilliantly synthesized the diverse energies then current in academic discourse, and triumphantly announced and initiated a new orientation. Its methods and effects were, however, scarcely academic at all. Sweeping with great assurance over a huge range of materials and generating a maze of secondary arguments, the text enacted a Dantean ascent from an initial meditation on the grisly intimacy of torture, out to warfare, and from there on to the relations between pain and creation; finally, with a great swelling movement, the text fanned out to a spacious and large-souled consideration of the nature of human imagination and human making. Despite the stupendous scale of its project, the extremity and abstractness of its subjects, and the often wildly counterintuitive positions Scarry took, the book was characterized by a pacific spirit, an undisturbed methodological regularity and orderliness, and a writerly facility that produced countless pauses or openings in the argument in which unexpected metaphors and ruminations were permitted to exfoliate at length and at leisure.

The book undoubtedly won part of its initial audience by appearing to respond so fully and forcefully to its moment. It addressed the then-obligatory issue of language, insisted on the pertinence of Marx and material culture, and introduced that emergent force, "the body." But Scarry's perspective on all these issues was radically out of step. Although most theorists then saw the body as the site of social or cultural "construction" and language as the privileged site of "deconstruction," Scarry saw the opposite. She argued that bodily pain "deconstructed" the sufferer's "world," whereas language could be applied to a compensatory and restorative labor of construction. She discussed Marx respectfully and at length—and paired him with the Bible. At a time when "the metaphysics of presence" served as one of the most comfortable targets of academic contempt available, Scarry declared that the human imagination realized itself directly in material objects, investing them with sentience. And whereas the concept of language had become firmly identified with uncertainty, with a vague sense of liberation resulting from demonstrations of the subversion of the tyranny of reference by figurality, Scarry contended that a figural or fictional use of language could be associated with torture, sadism, injury, and war, and that referential solidity alone would save us. Without so much as noting that fashionable criticism was wedded to such terms as license, excess, freeplay, and aberrance, she declared that language was bound by moral obligations. In fact, all the book's central concerns—bodily pain, belief in God, imagination, and the metaphysics of creation—were, in 1985, under a general proscription in academic discourse.

In an era dominated by such figures as Paul de Man, Julia Kristeva, and Michel Foucault, when the concept of "the inhuman" had acquired great theoretical prestige, most respectable academic writing cultivated a sere and rationalistic tone; by sharp contrast, *The Body in Pain* was notable for its thickly affective atmosphere of intelligent compassion, of tender regard for the vulnerable human being, and also for a committed moral optimism that was jarringly discordant with the witty and sophisticated disenchantment prevalent then and now. At one point in the mid-1980s, it was rumored that Scarry was being considered for a position at a leading university in the field of "literary theory," but everything about her orientation could, in the context of that field, have been considered a mark of "resistance to theory." A glance at the index to *The Body in Pain* reveals no references to de Man, Foucault, Derrida, Barthes, Jameson, Benjamin, or Kristeva; their places are taken by von Clausewitz, Amnesty International, the Greek Colonel's Regime, and the Nuclear Test Ban Treaty.

To say that Scarry's career begins with *The Body in Pain* is to say that it begins in the spectacle of torture. For Scarry, torture represents the unredeemable nadir of the human experience. Aspiring to "the totality of pain," torture substitutes for the world at large a world of hurt; as the torturer exercises absolute power, his victim is deprived of any anchor in the world and reduced to the smallest possible compass, his own subjectivity. Perhaps the most frequently cited sentence in the book claims that "intense pain is world-destroying" (BP 29). Torture is so savage, so maximally aversive, that no worth or rationale can be attached to it. "There has," Scarry writes, "never been an intelligent argument of behalf of torture (and such an argument is a conceptual impossibility)" (139). Even in these opening gestures, it is clear that Scarry is uninterested in the facts about torture. The Spanish Inquisition, to mention only the most conspicuous example, has furnished historians with a wealth of "intelligent" arguments on behalf of torture, and those who, such as Joseph de Maistre, defended the Inquisition on religious grounds implicitly defended the practices in which it engaged.[9] Torture also has its contemporary defenders, even in the enlightened American academy.[10] It is easy to imagine circumstances in which torture is the only honorable course, as in the "ticking bomb" scenario often invoked in debates on torture, in which the man who has planted a bomb timed to go off somewhere in the school in an hour is apprehended, refuses to divulge the location even when asked politely, and scoffs at mere threats. Scarry's relegation of such considerations to a labored footnote suggests a positive distaste for complicating counter-instances (BP 352 n. 160). Insisting on the negative moral purity of torture, Scarry ignores practical distinctions that might make all the difference in assessing the meaning and value of the experience, such as whether the victim possesses the information being sought, the kind of cause for which the victim suffers, the degree of commitment to that cause, the training of the torturer, and the personal character and cultural conditioning that victim and victimizer bring to the experience. For Scarry, torture is not really a practice at all, but a concept or even a kind of position, the possibility of absolute pain, absolute deprivation, absolute moral zero.

War is subjected to a similarly generic reduction. Scarry does not discuss any particular war, but rather war's "interior structure," as if the Punic Wars, the Hundred Years' War, World War I, the insurrection in East Timor, and the Gulf War were elaborations on a single theme of violent contest, with a single aim of producing injured bodies. All wars have, to her way of thinking, the same structure, whether they are just or unjust; whether they are fought by citizen-soldiers, conscripts, proxies, or mercenaries; whether they are undertaken for conquest, liberty, or self-defense; or whether the issue is real estate, wounded pride, ideology, or wealth.

Nor, to continue this list of things in which Scarry shows little interest, does pain receive an adequate or even a minimally acceptable treatment. She argues that intense pain is destructive and aversive, but the world is filled with examples of nonstandard pain thresholds. The Party of Pain includes those recovering from surgery or healing from spinal paralysis, for whom pain indicates a restoration of responsiveness; athletes and ascetics who operate on the no-pain, no-gain principle; those eager to prove, test, or martyr themselves; those for whom the material world and the pain experienced in it are mere illusions; and those for whom pain is erotically exciting. What Scarry calls pain and regards as aversive, these call by different names and regard as desirable. To this number must be added the vast legions for which pain is such an inescapable dimension of daily life that it excites no particular response and indeed scarcely has a name. Not feeling their pain at all, Scarry treats as an immediate and monochrome physical experience, a baseline of reality, what is in fact a combination of sensations, dispositions, cultural circumstances, and explanations, a phenomenon involving body, mind, and culture. She has, in other words, misconceived the character of pain precisely by giving it a character, by treating it as a fact—a brute fact, the first and final fact—rather than as an interpretation. So rhetorically or internally filigreed, Scarry's thoughts on pain, as on torture and war, are, when matched against the things themselves, strikingly undeveloped.[11]

To understand the "internal" significance, the placement, of pain in Scarry's thinking, we must compare it with the concept of beauty as articulated in *On Beauty and Being Just* (BBJ).[12] This astonishing text, eschewing scholarly protocols of argumentation and evidence in favor of a whispering first-person testimony, argues—if that is the word for it—that beauty has been the object of a misguided academic taboo and should be cherished not only because it is charming and delightful, but also because it is allied with truth and fosters justice. Perceptible through tears in the surface of the world that suggest some vaster space, beauty inculcates in attractive forms the principles of symmetry and selflessness, and creates a certain incentive to replicate in the world the kind of "fairness" on which justice must, she says, be based. Beauty can do all this because it contains within itself, perhaps within its interior structure, an "impulse toward begetting" that operates according to "a deeply beneficent momentum" (BBJ 9, 6). Also a system of tears in the surface of the world, pain, especially in its purest form of torture, is based on inequality; it deconstructs rather than liberates the self, creating a psychic state at once cramped and empty; it produces not selflessness but self-hatred. Pain is as sterile, repellent, and constrictive as beauty is fertile, attractive, and expansive.

And yet, as each other's mirror, pain and beauty are, in Scarry's thinking, much alike. They both have a definite relation to morality, they can both be considered as concrete abstractions detachable from particular instances, and both compel a focused but distant regard that entails no sense of coimplication between observer and observed. The torture chamber is a spectacle so gruesome as nearly to overwhelm the capacity for humane response. We can, however, bear a certain kind of witness, to which *On Beauty* gives the proper name: the "simplest" response to beauty, Scarry says, in terms that could also describe her general response to torture, is "the everyday act of staring" (5).[13]

So perfectly do these concepts invert each other that one suspects that the prior concept of pain has determined the concept of beauty, which is formed implicitly as a negative of pain, or rather a positive of pain's negative. It may be for this reason that Scarry's beauty deviates so sharply both from the beauty of Nietzsche, who cites Plato in support of his contention that "all beauty incites to procreation" and is more intimate with arousal than with justice; and from the beauty of Burke, Kant, and others who position it in some relation to the sublime, which Scarry sees as the hypermasculinized concept favored by those who would demote or banish beauty from the world (*see* BBJ 82–86).[14] Scarry's beauty tends to the condition of sky on a nice day, partly cloudy. The notions of a beautiful uppercut, a beautiful mushroom cloud, a beautiful suicide, or a Yeatsian "terrible beauty" are, for Scarry, oxymorons, because "beauty is pacific" and "is associated with a life compact or contract" (107, 128 n. 5). Even though her account of beauty is feminized to the point of desiccation as a consequence, Scarry is constrained to reject any relation between the beautiful and the sublime because for her, the first requirement of beauty is that it provide a counterweight to pain, and, according to Kant at least, the feeling associated with the sublime includes an irreducible quantum of pain.

Because pain has been determined to be concentrated in the victim and unable to take objective form, beauty must therefore lie entirely on the surface, available to public view. Scarry seems disconcertingly unaware of the fact that her notion of beauty as a visible property of material objects contradicts a long and largely unchallenged tradition of thought. She has produced perhaps the only treatise on beauty in recent centuries that does not stress the constitutive function of the eye of the beholder. Indeed, the beholder, reduced to a mindless gaping that "copies" the beautiful object, is curiously passive, especially when compared with the Kantian observer. The real locus of beauty for Kant lies not in the object at all, but in the object's power to suggest a common human faculty of understanding. The standard of beauty is within the subject: perceiving beauty's "purposiveness without purpose," we come to a disinterested appreciation of formal qualities and relationships, and formulate a judgment that all people could be expected to share if they could set aside their prejudices, interests, and desires. The aesthetic enjoys, in Kant, a qualified autonomy from ethics, which it can only represent by analogy. This distance from any particular ends, even moral ends, implies, for Kant, the possibility of a just civil society based on the common possession of reason, and above all a common investment in freedom.

Scarry's much more direct moralization of beauty proceeds along entirely different lines. It is based not on a community of free minds, but on the desire of individuals to see more of what they like. When something beautiful—palm fronds, cloudy skies, butterfly wings—strikes our eye, Scarry says, we are stopped in our tracks, incapable of thought, "decentered," stunned out of ourselves. No longer the heroes of our own stories, we are equalized with all others and stand in a position of "opiated adjacency" (BBJ 114). But, she continues, we then find ourselves hungry to realize in the world the kind of symmetry and repose we have just seen. Beauty compels us to copy it, first in our staring perception, then by replicating the object, then by sharing it with others. This compulsion to copy constitutes a form of "begetting," a term on which Scarry insists as a way of claiming that beauty suggests a world of abundance (in opposition to pain's emptiness). The emphasis thus falls not on understanding and taste, but on sensation and desire; not on a civil society of free and rational beings but on a disaggregated crowd of hungering monads, alike in their apolitical vacuity. Where Kant speaks of rational freedom, Scarry speaks of drugged compulsion.

Kant's account of the aesthetic is famously vulnerable to critiques of the "aesthetic ideology," exposés of the real conditions that underlie and structure the ideal *sensus communis*. Convinced that beauty is an objective property of visible things, something we perceive rightly or wrongly, Scarry has persuaded herself that critiques of the aesthetic are profoundly misguided attacks on beauty itself. But if she thought of beauty as an experience rather than a property—a happy convergence of a culturally conditioned receptivity, a good mood, and a congenial object—she might be more alert to the senses in which beauty could be a snare, a sublimation, a mystification, a distraction, a principle of superficiality, an ideologically generated illusion, a mask, a category mistake, a momentary lapse of critical analysis. Such thoughts, which are virtually automatic for many academics, never occur to Scarry because the determining context of her thinking on beauty is not the subject of the aesthetic and its long philosophical tradition, but her own thoughts on pain.

If the inversion of a monochrome account of pain does not produce a satisfactory version of beauty, it results in an even more defective version of justice. Based on a theoretical condition of symmetry and equality, Scarry's justice does not describe a conflict-ridden world in which people have different interests, needs, abilities, characters, positions, values, and resources. As Scarry's one-time student Joseph Valente has argued, justice in a democracy is not achieved by the mechanical application of a single concept, such as "fairness." People come before the law, Valente points out, in different positions, and these differences must be respected if justice is to be rendered.[15] Justice is always "rough" because it involves not calculation but a more complex and risky act of negotiation between conflicting but equally worthy principles. Scarry would surely endorse this argument had she thought of it. Her failure to think of it suggests, once again, the priority of the internal determinants of her thinking, the relation of concept to concept in her system, over the referential matching of descriptions to material facts.

This is curious because linguistic reference, although never the subject of explicit theorization, is the single most important principle in Scarry's thinking. So rooted in the "incontestable reality of the body" and its afflictions, *The Body in Pain* (BP) is actually more vitally concerned with language (BP 62). The worst part of torture's pain, in her account, is inflicted by language. Although most accounts of torture explain it as part of a process of interrogation, Scarry argues that interrogation is a part of a process of torture, with the interrogation itself representing one form of torture. The first sentence of her book declares that, "Nowhere is the sadistic potential of a language built on agency so visible as in torture." Torture not only conscripts language (or "is a language") but exploits a capacity for cruelty always present in language. This capacity is centered in fiction: the torturer tries, by inflicting pain, to make his or her victim believe in the absoluteness of the power of the regime, a power that is in fact "highly contestable" and so, fictional (27). But pain is also the consequence of the substitution of fiction for reality. We experience pain when confronted, in language, with the torturer's version of the world.

And yet, in a characteristically sinuous movement, Scarry suggests that an opening created by language permits a slender shaft of light to penetrate the profound abyss of torture. The way it does so constitutes a fascinating instance of the power of a conceptual system to generate possibilities not immediately apparent in practice. The "closest analogue" of torture, Scarry asserts, is war. Both produce pain by injuring bodies, and both exploit a certain aggressiveness in language. Wars are provoked when each party attacks the "interior national self-description" of the other, and waged over the right to the control of language (BP 129). Then war itself destabilizes language by undermining, or "deconstructing" reference: in the chaos of conflict, injured bodies produce a "fluidity of referential direction" as part of war's general "verbal unanchoredness" (115). But on the conclusion of the conflict, the work of reconstruction begins, and words reestablish intimate relations with reality.[16] War, like torture, exploits the power of language to shear off from reality—"War is in the massive fact of itself a huge structure for the derealization of cultural constructs"—but because war ultimately produces a rejuvenated practice of reference, war has a "moral ambiguity" that torture does not (137).

As this ambiguity gradually resolves itself in the course of the extraordinarily complex, hundred-page fourth chapter of *The Body in Pain*, on the Bible and Marx, reference emerges into even greater prominence as the agent of transformation. Scarry holds a belief that might be hers alone in the field of literary studies, that language honors the world when it refers to it and dishonors or threatens it when it does not, that fiction and other failures or refusals of reference are derelictions of linguistic duty. This argument is never made explicitly in *The Body in Pain*, but it is perceptible just below the surface of, for example, the assertions that the torturer engages in "the fiction of absolute power," that warring parties seek to fictionalize the enemy, or that wars begin when nations have become fictions to themselves (BP 27; *see* 128–33). And it determines, too, Scarry's reading of Marx, in which *Capital* constitutes "an exhausting analysis of the steps and stages by which the obligatory referentiality of fictions ceases to be obligatory: it is an elaborate retracing of the path along which the reciprocity of artifice has lost its way back to its human source" and has become "internally referential" (258, 260). The Marxian commodity is a material fiction that has somehow lost its "original referent," the human being who made it; the point of Marx's analysis of such objects, Scarry says, is the restoration of this referent so we can understand the object's "original function" (272). In these instances, fiction is set against the truth of reference as a malicious kind of idling in which language refuses the tasks appropriate to it.

To understand fully the role Scarry envisions for reference, we must first grasp the original function of material making, which she calls "rescue." According to Nietzsche's Zarathustra, the morally good person "cannot create" and creation is, at its root, a form of morally equivocal violence; Scarry takes a different approach, contending that all created things are good because the interior structure of making as such is benign.[17] All created objects, she insists, are brought into being by an underlying spirit of compassion for the body, whose pain they are dedicated to relieving. How they do so is pure magic. Created objects relieve the pain of sentience by "redesigning" body parts in such a way as to extend their functioning while removing some of their hurtability. In effect, they absorb pain into themselves, which they can do, already having absorbed the maker's pain in the process of being created. Thus all artifacts are fashioned in the form of an implied wish: "perceived-pain-wished-gone" (BP 290). A handkerchief, blanket, and bucket of white paint, for example, contain a "wish for well-being: 'Don't cry; be warm; watch now, in a few minutes even these constricting walls will look more spacious'" (292). All created things share a single origin, and it is good: "It is the benign, almost certainly heroic, and in any case absolute intention of all human making to distribute the facts of sentience outward onto the created realm of artifice" (288). The world's objects are designed, in their deep interiors, with a single purpose in mind, "to remake human beings to be warm, healthy, rested, acutely conscious, large-minded" (311).

Not fully theorized in *The Body in Pain*, the relation of reference to rescue becomes much clearer in a text written soon after, the introduction to *Literature and the Body* (I).[18] Here, Scarry takes the occasion of introducing a number of essays from a recent English Institute to argue more fully the imperative that governs language's "referential obligations to the material world" (xiv). Considered on its own, she writes, language has only a weak or diminished bodiliness; but it can, like the shroud of Turin, absorb bodiliness into itself, "registering in its own contours the contours and weight of the material world." According to what we might call the Brawny theory of reference, language that has absorbed some worldliness into itself becomes "endowed with the referential substance of the world," and acquires thereby the power to act on the world (xxv). By "inlaying" narratives and descriptions into things, language produces "language-soaked" artifacts (xiii, xiv). In this way, language can be said to have an "interventionist" capacity.

This is not a serious discussion of linguistic reference. The issue of context, within which reference might at least be theoretically measurable, is never raised, much less addressed. The issue of intention is raised, but addressed incoherently. Scarry notes that language "does not, independently of us agents, just happen to absorb us or empty us from its content. The users of language regulate the degree to which language describes or instead discards the material world" (I xv). But many other passages imply the reverse, as when she says that "language constantly aspires to bring about a mimesis of materiality," or that words "only acquire the material attributes of the world—mass, weight, substance—through their referential transparency," and not, apparently, through any intention on the part of a speaker/writer/interpreter (xv). Insofar as reference is a quality that some bits of language have and others don't, her account is functional; but insofar as reference is an aspiration, her account is moral. (The issue is sometimes presented as one of life or death: if language doesn't refer properly, things or even persons may be "subjected to a linguistic fatality") (x). Scarry never defines reference, or provides a criterion for deciding whether language is or is not referential; nor does she sort out the referential gearing of even simple figures of speech such as *grease monkey* or *hot shot*; nor does she mention any of the other factors that dominate the academic discussion of reference, including citation, intertextuality, representation, rhetoric, or metaphor.

Nor does she credit an argument favored by poets and philosophers, that the real power of language is centered in its ability to describe either counterfactual states of affairs or abstractions that can acquire the force of theory in relation to worldly practice. In both cases, language interferes with the reproduction of the status quo. For Scarry, by contrast, the reproduction of material reality is the condition of intervention, and language that does not reproduce can only be justified when it "supplement[s]" rather than subtracts or distracts from, "'the sensuously obvious'" (I xx). Committed to ever-increasing abundance as a good, Scarry seems unable to conceive of a positive value for negation, and anything other than the capillary form of linguistic materialism seems to her a form of negation.

If this is not a serious account of reference, then what is it? It is an invocation of a principle of homeopathy that is, Scarry says, inherent in the universal phenomenon of language, a principle by which one thing transfers its attributes to another, with a slight alteration. Scarry is committed to such a principle because it is the one on which *The Body in Pain* and indeed all her thinking is based. In her emergent system, pain is alleviated by flowing from one site to another, in the same way that heat is dissipated from the warmer to the cooler surface. Without such a principle in place,

Scarry would lack grounds for her signature moral optimism. But with such a principle, she can posit a series of finely graded healing touches or "modulations" beginning with the analysis of the ethical nullity of torture, proceeding to the discovery of an analogue for torture in war, moving from there to the conception of war as "the most unceasingly radical and rigorous form" of work, and then to the observation that war's work ends in construction, and concluding with an analysis of the anaesthetic and restorative properties of material making. At each step, her writing draws off a bit more pain, so although the world is left untouched, the reading experience is one of gradual relief.

Eventually, Scarry arrives at the work of imaginative creation, which is plainly constructed as the perfect inversion of the absolute pain of torture—as pure a good as torture is an evil, as compassionate in its fecundity as pain is aversive in its deprivation. Most important, imaginative creation is as real, as genuinely powerful, as the torturer merely pretends to be—it is capable, Scarry says, of "a revolution of the entire order of things, the eclipse of the given by a *total reinvention of the world*" (BP 171). And so, from humble beginnings in the torture chamber, *The Body in Pain* concludes with the pronouncement that

> the realm of her [the imagination's] labor is centrally bound up with the elementary moral distinction between hurting and not hurting; she is simply, centrally, and indefatigably at work on behalf of sentience, eliminating its aversiveness and extending its acuity in forms as abundant, extravagantly variable, and startlingly unexpected as her ethical strictness is monotonous and narrowly consistent (306).[19]

How is the imagination, which is both nonmaterial and notoriously illicit in its operations, conscripted for this vision of what Scarry candidly calls "ethical monotony" (BP 323)? To answer this question, we must turn to the recent *Dreaming by the Book*, where the concept of the imagination is fleshed out.[20] Here Scarry describes an interior structure of imagining that is at once unexpected and, in the context of her thinking, inevitable. She describes the imagination as having, like language, a quasi-material form. Mental images themselves strike us as light, transparent, gauzy sorts of things; even images of charging rhinos, rock masses, or exploding land mines are still tissues of the mind. Scarry says that we can work these flimsies as if they were real, and lists several "genres of acting on the image," including "folding the image, shaking it, tearing it, pulling it out all around its circumference, pulling a small piece at the center—as if pulling the membrane of a tambourine toward you while keeping the frame steady" (DBB 121). The entire account of the mind seems to be modeled on *Doonesbury's* Duke, whose head sometimes pops open, revealing a smaller version of himself who takes care of business when Duke "himself" is too stoned to function. But this miniature figure can at least stand in Duke's skull. In the Scarryan imagination, there is no such foundation, and so one has to be laboriously created. This is why writers describe ground—earth, pavement, floors—as a way of providing "a fiction's *vertical floor* that, by promising to stop our inward fall, permits us to enter into the projective space without fear" (14).

Like language, the imagination has its obligations and responsibilities toward the material world. We imagine improperly, Scarry argues, when we daydream, a state she describes with distaste as a kind of mental limbo, idling in a dead zone where images drift like jellyfish this way and that, without vivacity or point (*see Inferno* IV. 25–30). Imagination functions properly when it restricts itself to the materials provided by perception. The emphasis on perception at the expense of an already creative memory has the effect of limiting, in a sense both ethical and functional, the range of the imagination. The most striking feature of the entire account is its restrictiveness, the way in which the imagination is carefully distinguished from any faculty of invention, combinatorial freedom, or even general intelligence.

Imagining is a specific kind of work; doing it, we become specific kinds of workers. Because mental images, lacking a will of their own, naturally stay put, we need to move them around to create an impression of life. But the imagination does nothing without a work order. Hence literature, in which authors replicate in their texts the deep structure of sensation that occurs in perception, giving us "an intricate array of small instructions" on how to conceive and manipulate images (DBB 37). Note that there is, in this account, no necessary or natural connection, maintained in the memory, between the perceived world and the imagined one; we must always dream by the book. Scarry adduces five ways in which books guide our imagining, making it possible for us to construct an image, make it visible, and then to make it fly, stretch it out, or position it near other images—thus miming, in the imagination, our perception of real life. If, in the world, we require light to see, then, in books, we require "radiant ignition." One way to achieve this is "to place the moving persons inside a large radiant envelope," an example of which would be Apollo's placement of the body of the dead Hector in Homer's *Iliad* inside a golden cloud (84). Another way is to place flashes of light "not in the persons who move but in the things the moving persons are asserted to be passing": thus, Homer will speak of the "glistening" robes of the women past whom men run. Walled off from invention or intelligence, the imagination seems to be more than a little autistic, finding the ordinary conventions of perception to be deep mysteries requiring patient explanation.[21]

It is difficult not to be grateful to a book that gives you ideas you never had before, but *Dreaming by the Book* beggars all gratitude, informing its readers that it is easy to imagine flowers because they are about the same size as your head (merely to name a flower is to offer it "as something which, after a brief stop in front of the face, can immediately pass through the resisting bone and lodge itself and light up the inside of the brain" [47]); that it is easier to imagine small light things as being in motion than big heavy things; that there are nine kinds of "stretching" to which mental images are subject; that it is easier and more humane to stretch an image in the mind than it is to stretch "embodied persons" and so authors often "embed the image in cloth [i.e., represent it as being clothed] which we already know to be flexible" when they are going to represent someone as moving or stretching (128); that it is easy to imagine a stationary figure moving "when a scroll of ice is pulled along behind it" (195); that "spherical shapes roll and wheel through the mind with great ease" (196); and that while, to make a bird's tail bob up and down in the imagination, we might need to "mentally attach a thread or filament" to its tail and then jerk on the filament, an "amazing thing follows" when we discover that the second time the filament is no longer required (125).

In many ways a thoroughly mystifying production, *Dreaming by the Book* enables us to comprehend in its full dimensions the rhetorically magnificent salute to the powers of the imagination at the conclusion of *The Body in Pain*. The internal determinants, the implicit beliefs that drive this salute, include the convictions that the imagination, like language, is properly referential and obedient to material reality; that it, like language, is in danger of thinning out into self-referentiality, or daydreaming; and that it, like language, must therefore be subjected to a certain discipline that is both moral and mechanical. The imagination derives its ethical stature not from its powers of penetration or invention, but from the opposite, its subjection to an elaborate set of conditions that constrain its potential lawlessness or waywardness. And with the vision of a tireless, omnipresent work of the imagination doggedly devoted to the relief of pain, *The Body in Pain* concludes.

What can, or must, we say about the sensibility behind this high and extraordinary argument? We can make a beginning by treating Scarry's work as if it answered to her own concept of work, a process in which we take on a manageable amount of pain in order to create something that helps us make a "movement out into the world that is the opposite of pain's contractive potential" (BP 169). Examining Scarry's work in this light, we will, then, be looking for the mark of pain and the means by which pain is transmuted into its opposite.

Where, in Scarry's work, is the pain buried; where is its sign, its X? We can at first only guess, but it may be possible to detect the pulsing of pain deep below the surface of Scarry's remarkable sense of structure. Scarry has a facility that might be called uncanny for detecting order in domains that appear to be disorderly, spontaneous, ungovernable, or mindless. *The Body in Pain* begins with the assertion that an analysis of torture is made possible by the fact that even "moral stupidity . . . has an unconscious structure" (28). Scarry clearly feels that her analysis of this structure both faithfully replicates torture (on the principle of "referential obligation") and goes some way towards binding up torture's wounds by moving them out into the world of rational public discourse. The functional rules she posits for the imagination may have the same neutralizing function. *Dreaming by the Book* constitutes an elaborate compendium of ways that the imagination ignites, stretches, folds, and tilts images in response to instructions provided by literary texts. The continual surprise of this book is the kind and number of rules said to be followed by creators, who mime the deep structure of perception; by literature, which exists to give readers orders; and by the imagination, which, when working properly, works to rule. So intricate are these rules, so extensive is their reach, so severe are the strictures against slacking, that one must infer that the prospect of an ungoverned imagination is, for Scarry, the site of an anxiety so sharp that she is willing to risk the most wildly counterintuitive and implausible statements for the sake of fencing it in.

The most structural of thinkers, Scarry also uses lists as fences. Perhaps the most densely list-infested site in the *oeuvre* is a fourteen-page section of an essay on Thackeray's *Henry Esmond* that has no fewer than four lists, just one of which has fifteen questions, just one of which has three kinds of answers, just one of which has three specific answers.[22] But the most exorbitant instance of interlocking structures must be the entire edifice of *The Body in Pain*, which, from this point of view, constitutes a vast, obsessive-compulsive nesting of stipulations concerning the interior structures of things: torture, war, injury, imagination, creation, and artifacts. To read this book is to feel as if one is negotiating the proliferating planes of an M. C. Escher composition. Torture, for example, is organized around four sets of oppositions, while the "structure" of torture displays three "simultaneous phenomena" (BP 51). In the second of these phenomena, pain displays eight aspects; the third phenomenon, denial of pain, enables a Moebius shift back to the first, infliction of pain. Injuries are also more complicated than one may have thought. They have four vocabularies, which are assessable by three ways. They also have many functions, the second of which depends on two attributes of injury, "and it is these two attributes that are the third and fourth of the central conclusions here . . ." (12). Analyzing pain, Scarry says at one point, we may take "a third backward step . . . into the realm of human hurt alone. Even here two separable categories exist, with only one allowing the forward movement up through the successively more benign displacements from human hurt to animal hurt to, finally, no hurt" (148). Nothing in Scarry is out of place, or without a place; indeed, analysis consists largely of discovering something's place, or places.

If an obsession with placement is the X, a deep concern with the general possibility of disappearance must lie buried beneath. One cannot read Scarry for long without encountering some scenario in which something apparently solid and present simply vanishes. The experience of pain makes "the world" disappear. In the misleading discourse of war, injuries can disappear by "any one of six paths," beginning with "omission" (BP 80). Material objects make pain disappear. Novels bring "into being a small population of characters, and then [cause] them to disappear" (I ix). In a passage in Hardy, even the "heavy sensuous surfaces of the cows suddenly evaporate like quicksilver into momentary cartoon or undergo mystical self-dissolution into the mist."[23] The body itself can disappear from language unless protective measures are taken. If certain academics had their way, Scarry suggests, beauty would disappear from the world. In Scarry's work, our grip on things is weak, our hold on place tenuous, the need for the reassurance of structure great.

From an insistence on structure we can infer an acute sense of exposure; from exposure we can infer some trauma, by which I mean a form of violence inflicted by an external agent acting on a mechanical or "inhuman" principle.[24] Among Scarry's singular strengths as an intellectual is her unwavering moral and theoretical poise even when contemplating extreme experiences. But her very assurance in this respect testifies to an understanding of trauma of a kind that is not given to all, and suggests that her interest is not strictly driven by a scholarly desire to clarify.

The most indicative text in this regard is the one of the boldest interventions into worldly affairs undertaken by a scholar in the humanities, the monumental essay, printed as a "Special Supplement" in *The New York Review of Books*, on "The Fall of TWA 800: The Possibility of Electromagnetic Interference."[25] Reportedly written on spec and submitted cold to the presumably astonished editors of *The New York Review of Books*, this amazing production seems at first to be written by some person altogether unrelated to the author of *Dreaming by the Book* and *On Beauty*; in fact, her authorship of these two deeply personal, even dreamy books compromises for some the case she argues at immense length in "TWA 800." But many readers, caught in the grip of this massively detailed text and unaware of what the author was shortly to publish, must have felt that Scarry had spent years in the continuous study of electrical engineering, the construction of aircraft, civilian transportation systems, avionics, the labyrinths of the military, and airplane disasters, and had devoted the previous twenty months to gathering all available facts about this incident. Although the argument and its factual basis have been subjected to skeptical critique, "TWA 800" is by any measure an unusual production, especially for one untrained in technical disciplines.[26]

The thesis is that a freak conjunction of lines of electromagnetic radiation issuing from other craft in the vicinity of TWA 800 might have been responsible for the plane's sudden plunge into the sea. To make this case plausible, Scarry marshals a mass of information concerning the planes, ships, and helicopters in the area at the fatal moment, including their exact positions, missions and equipment, and their patterns of interaction, both probable and possible. "TWA 800" would be a remarkable text by any author, but it gains a certain kind of significance when considered as a work by Elaine Scarry. Why, one wonders, would an English teacher with a full life and no apparent personal investment devote so much time and energy to the task of producing it?

The event must have summoned Scarry in an especially intimate and commanding way. To see why, we must consider her analysis, which is shared by very few. The official National Transportation Safety Board inquiry rapidly determined that an explosion occurred in the fuel tank. Some asserted that the explosion was caused by a bomb; others, that a chemical reaction in the fuel tank caused ignition; still others argued, on the basis of eyewitness accounts of streaks in the sky, that the plane was hit by a missile.[27] Scarry, and Scarry alone, proposed that the explosion was neither innocent nor sinister, its cause neither random nor planned. In her analysis, TWA 800 was a trauma involving the disappearance of 235 people, the official explanations of which had failed to retrace the path from event to origin. It was, in other words, the event for which she had been preparing herself for many years. Her response was to commit herself utterly to an inquiry into the event on the premise that even mysterious and apparently causeless occurrences have an unconscious interior structure. Her analysis "stares" at the catastrophe, restoring, at least in speculation, the original referent that had threatened to disappear along with the plane itself.

Readers who made it through the 19,000 words of "TWA 800" may have been struck by a feature common to a number of Scarry's texts, the argument's radical reducibility, the striking ease with which the complex entirety can be telescoped to a few relatively banal statements. If *The Body in Pain* can be summed up in the statements that pain is bad but can be relieved, or that we ought to find a better way to settle disputes than war, "TWA 800" concludes its mighty course with the suggestion that electromagnetic interference may have been responsible for the crash, that the inquiry ought to be reopened to consider that possibility, and that the military ought to share more information with civilian airlines.[28] *The New York Review of Books* refused to print any reader's responses to the text to which they had devoted so many pages, and so effectively suppressed a relevant fact: that, because the precise conditions in the air and in the plane at the moment of the explosion could never be perfectly reproduced, her hypothesis could never be definitively proven or disproven; an inquiry opened to consider the possibility of electromagnetic interference would never be closed, with the only consequence being that the fear associated with air travel would be increased. "TWA 800" not only registers and anatomizes trauma; it adds to it.[29]

At the Modern Language Association panel at which she was introduced by Edward Said, Scarry argued that "radical" argumentation and documentary thoroughness were strictly compatible. In her own recent work, however, she has succeeded in separating them almost completely. If "TWA 800" represents documentation without argumentation, *On Beauty and Being Just* succeeds in being the opposite, all argumentation without documentation. Interestingly—endlessly interestingly—Scarry was frantically researching and writing the former at the same time she was delivering the latter as the Tanner Lectures in Human Values at Yale. The contrast between these two texts, one so armor-plated and the other so terribly exposed, could hardly be greater, and yet they are identifiable as products of the same hand. "TWA 800" has its own cold beauty as a text; and the very thought of the airspace over Long Island on that fateful night in 1996, humming with crisscrossing lines of radiation, invisible filaments extending from craft to craft, has aesthetic qualities as well. What requires more demonstration, however, is the notion that *On Beauty* contains traces of trauma.

If, in other texts, structure itself serves as the "representative" in the work of the trauma that structure seeks to neutralize, the strategies of *On Beauty* for incorporating trauma are even subtler—so subtle, in fact, that they eschew disguise altogether. Meditating on certain paintings by Matisse, Scarry for some reason chooses to include in the text her own pen-and-ink renderings of these compositions. She is not a talented draftswoman, and the drawings are undistinguished, even inept. Included in all of them is a palm tree, which, in Scarry's account, comes to stand as a token of beauty itself. Scarry's version of the palm, however, assumes several forms, none of them beautiful, some of which resemble a tarantula on a stick, and others a beetling blotch that suggests to the unmystified eye not the heart of beauty, or even the heart of palm, but a kind of stain, a principle of aversion at the center of beauty, and the thought of beauty.

Aversion to what? This is the question that will take us to the deep interior of Scarry's thought structure. Scarry, the reader notices, mentions human beauty only occasionally, and then typically in a series that includes other forms of beauty. Her example-rich text includes "a beautiful boy or flower or bird" (BBJ 3), different kinds of butterflies, the arrival of "a new student" (16), various trees, "a blossom, a friend, a poem, a sky" (28), and "blue sky, musical sounds, cakes, roses, and the body's soft, smooth surface" (100). Most frequently, it is the cloudy sky on a pleasant day, a little bird, or, most insistently, a flower in full bloom that stands for beauty itself. The unremarked inclusion of human beings in such lists suggests that beauty inheres equally in sentient and nonsentient forms, and that the presence of a mind behind some beautiful surfaces counts for nothing in the experience of beauty.[30] This implication actually supports an argument Scarry tries to refute about beauty's indifference to the human condition, and undercuts her central assertion, that when we behave justly—or rather, in her own strikingly passive construction, when we are "being just"—we do not realize specifically human ends, but simply follow instructions provided by beauty itself, so that justice consists of a miming, in the human world, of the appearance of flowers.

A floral and entirely visual beauty is an inhuman beauty, one that neutralizes the faculty of judgment. For Scarry, but not for Kant, our apprehension of beauty is not an act of free intelligence, but is in the first instance a simple recognition, a perception, a kind of certainty that Kant associated with mathematical or theoretical, rather than moral or aesthetic, reasoning (see BBJ 11–33). An insistence on visible surfaces, on the various "promptings" and "requirements" imposed on the observer by beauty, and on the suddenly dispossessed and staring response appropriate to beauty, coordinates with the emphasis on rules and instructions in Scarry's treatment of the imagination, with her insistence on "the referential obligation" in discussing language, and even with her advocacy on behalf of "consent" in the conduct of war.[31] All these converge on a single point: the association of the free and uncertain mind with pain, and of the bound mind with relief. Scarry always speaks warmly of those occasions on which volition is suppressed and guided, or in which choice is exercised in the decision to follow instructions or higher imperatives (*see* DBB 104, 244). And she seems to experience a sense of threat in the presence of indeterminacy. To associate injury with "referential fluidity" during time of war is brilliant, original, and even profound; but to conceive of referential fluidity as a kind of injury suggests, in its gratuitousness, an acute vulnerability to the ordinary fluidities of interpretive and interpersonal life.

In fact, Scarry seems not fully at home, and certainly not at ease, in the everyday world of misunderstanding, duplicity, half-realized intentions, and conflict. The title of Stuart Hampshire's recent book, *Justice is Conflict*, has no echo in Scarry's thinking.[32] If Scarry does not live in the clouds, she stares at them, dreams of them, and would refashion the world on their pacific model if she could. What redeems her work is not its vaguely religious emphasis on redemption, however, but rather the far more fascinating way in which she builds into even her most anodyne ruminations—on her garden, the bird in her garden, her friends' gardens, the markings on hummingbirds, the prospect of justice based on perfect equality—the dark spot, the trauma these ruminations are intended to heal.

On rare but revealing occasion, Scarry actually evokes entirely gratuitous images of horror, as when, in the course of elaborating the idea of consent in *The Body in Pain*, she notes that, in peacetime, one demonstrates consent to the state when one "alters" one's body by, for example, lifting one's eyebrows to view the flag; similarly, she says, in war, a soldier might give his consent, by "entering a certain terrain and participating in certain acts," to another kind of alteration: "to the tearing out of his forehead, eyebrows, and eyes" (BP 112). Scarry is also no stranger to the numbing effects of beauty on sympathy. In the "Introduction" to *Literature and the Body*, she cites a passage from one of the essays, which concludes with the statement that "the victim of chapter 19 [of a Biblical text], who is dragged from house to house and gang-raped and killed when expelled from the house, will be called *Beth*, house." "I cite this passage at length," Scarry writes with an impressive *sangfroid*, "because of its beauty" (I x).

Such moments deepen and enrich our understanding of Scarry's moral vision, which is considerably darker and more troubled than most of her admiring readers would admit. But evidence of a sort of complicity with the forces against which she argues is scattered throughout her work, and helps explain a number of its curious features, including her tendency to cite in support of her thesis precisely the evidence that undercuts it. In the book on beauty, for example, she quotes a passage from Iris Murdoch's *The Sovereignty of Good*, in which Murdoch notes that beauty has the power of "unselfing" the observer, a concept Scarry conscripts for her argument about beauty's capacity to "decenter" us (BBJ 113). "It is clear," Scarry concludes, "that an *ethical fairness* which requires 'a symmetry of everyone's relation' will be greatly assisted by an *aesthetic fairness* that creates in all participants a state of delight in their own lateralness" (114). But Murdoch's analysis takes a different direction. In her more compact work *The Fire and the Sun*, Murdoch speaks with a dark knowingness of how "the bad side of human nature is secretly, precariously, at work in art. There is," she says, "a lot of secret cruelty there . . . How this becomes beautiful is a mystery" (82). For Murdoch, art's interest in beauty is decidedly equivocal. For Scarry, such a thought seems to be unthinkable—except that she has, by citing Murdoch, already thought it, by proxy.[33] In another passage, in which she describes beauty's power to disarm us and reduce us to staring, she cites Pater's description of Leonardo, who used to "follow people around the streets of Florence once he got 'glimpses of it [beauty] in the strange eyes or hair of chance people'" (BBJ 6). Scarry's helpful insertion of beauty constitutes a highly aggressive reading. In Pater's source, Vasari notes that Leonardo was fascinated not by beauty but by "striking" appearances, especially "a strange head of hair or beard"; the results of his researches are a series of sketches known as "Grotesque Heads" or "Caricatures."[34] Leonardo tailed not the Beatrices of Florence, but the monstrosities.

We recover the power and drama from the languorous preciosity of *On Beauty* when we consider it not as an analysis of beauty and its entailments, but as the record of a powerful recoil from disorder, deformation, evil. Still, the most compelling drama to emerge in Scarry's work concerns the masked violence of her own thought and expression.

So delicate, so evocative of lacework in its spirit and intricacy, Scarry's thought is not without its own kind of force, beginning with the strict and prejudicial delimitation of evidence. Scarry almost never, in her texts, appears to subject herself to the kind of reciprocal interrogation that characterizes real critical reading. Although her theory of imagination is devoted to mimesis, her analytical practice involves the imposition of a crushing mastery. On those few occasions when she engages in literary criticism, her approach is so narrowly focused that her reader loses sight of the text in its totality, or even of such large-scale patternings as character, theme, or plot, which are bracketed to concentrate on a sentence, a phrase, a detail. And even these are often expressed in terms the author would never have conceived, as when, in *Dreaming by the Book*, certain sentences or lines from Hardy, Homer, or Flaubert are studied as instances of the construction and character of images. As James Wood complained in his *New Republic* review, this approach ignores the careful work of the author in constructing character and scene and atmosphere; it "orphans detail, and puts it in the workhouse," so that the authors she discusses emerge as collaborators on Scarry's project, "consciously devoted to Scarry's theory of picturability" (30). Texts emerge from their encounter with Scarry decidedly "altered," that is, dismembered and reassembled.

Nor does Scarry bother with the ordinary erudition associated with mere scholarly competence. Unusually learned in some areas, Scarry is almost defiantly indifferent to scholarly conventions on precedent. One could construct an impressive negative bibliography composed of thinkers on beauty who are not given serious consideration in Scarry's book on the subject, including all classical, medieval, and Renaissance thinkers, Burke, Kant, Shaftesbury, Schiller, Hegel, Schopenhauer, Ruskin, Nietzsche, Wilde, G. E. Moore, Freud, Brecht, Adorno, and Lacan. And on the one occasion when she is forced to take issue with other critics, the results are almost amazingly bad. Nearly thirty pages in *On Beauty* are devoted to refuting the arguments of those responsible for "banishing beauty from the humanities in the last two decades"; none of these villains is mentioned by name, much less quoted, and the arguments are constructed in the weakest possible way in order to ensure their easy demolition (57).

What we are considering here is not really a matter of scholarly incompetence, but rather a pronounced tendency to co-opt or overwhelm her objects. The single most graphic demonstration of this tendency is perhaps her pen-and-ink renderings of Matisse in *On Beauty*. Scarry "translates" not only Matisse's paintings, but also his titles, one of which is given as "My Room at the Beau Rivage" (BBJ 37). Thus Matisse is not only dispossessed of his work, but evicted from his room. Considering that Scarry's career begins in the torture chamber, or *chambre*, in which one person has all the power and the other is wholly bereft, this small accommodation of the monolingual English reader might also be seen as a quiet reinscription, within the heart of beauty, of the initial circumstance: the threat of domination or even obliteration by the other mind.

Scarry is also capable of occupying other rooms by assuming positions and arguments that it seems she ought to oppose. At the end of a book that centrally concerns the horrors of torture and war, she argues at length that, regardless of the intentions of makers and consumers, material artifacts—including, presumably, all the instruments at the torturer's disposal and all the machines of war—have but one "absolute intention," to relieve sentient being of its pain. She claims, in other words, that guns don't kill, people do. The same deep intention ennobles the material objects that clog first-world consumer culture, even though many of these were produced in sweatshops, many appeal to unenlightened appetites, and many are in fact illegal drugs, which relieve pain but can scarcely be called benign. Defending the right to bear arms—a right that cannot extend to nuclear arms and so can be used to bring the legitimacy of nuclear war into question—she lends aid and comfort once again (and disclaimers notwithstanding) to the National Rifle Association. Insisting that beauty provides the measure for a just social order, she provides unexpected support for formalist claims made by the southern agrarians, Roger Scruton, and others on the aesthetic right wing.[35] By moralizing beauty, she aligns herself with ideologues on both the right and on the left. And by defining justice as all-around symmetry and equality without difference, she seems to be reverting to the position of old-line communist ideologues. If one is known by one's enemies, Scarry presents something of a puzzle in that her only enemies seem to be—her friends.

Reviewers of Scarry's work often find themselves at a loss to say what she is, a literary critic, a philosopher, a "thinker," a "theorist," or a mere "English professor." She does not meet the conventional criteria of any of these. Nor can she be considered a moralist, despite the ethical aspirations of all her work, for much of the burden of ethics falls on things, or on "the imagination," rather than on specific people. She does not urge a more rational or equitable distribution of goods; for her, it is enough that goods are all around. Nor does she, in the manner of, say, Ruskin, praise beauty to condemn the unlovely world of materialism; in fact, she has given materialism an endorsement it could scarcely have anticipated. She is rather a dreamer, and, secondarily, a writer. Her subjects have a certain worldly urgency, but what makes them her subjects is the cluster of private meanings they acquire in the course of her meditation. Her work (like the work of others and scholarly work generally) consists of the mapping of a certain set of internally determined meanings and energies onto a series of external subjects. What distinguishes it is not its descriptive accuracy or logical irrefutability, but the intricacy, rhetorical power, and suggestiveness of that mapping. Reading Scarry as she negotiates a difficult passage, as between beauty and justice, or wounding and creation, one often feels as if one is watching a sleepwalker. Her admirers are those who do not want her to wake up.

She has been criticized by brainy graduate students, theoretical diehards, and traditional scholars for what they consider her underresearched and underconceptualized aestheticism, her lack of ideological self-awareness, her "very obviously erroneous" theories, her "blithe disregard" of the protocols of scholarly rigor. Many find her unpersuasive. But Scarry's work does not really solicit agreement. It is best considered not as a succession of arguments but as an ongoing creation, an artifact to gaze at, to admire even to the point of stupefaction, without regard for its utility. It is the product of what was once called a beautiful soul. To the unenchanted, Scarry seems an ultra-academic figure, sheltered at Harvard, where students apparently arrive one at a time (rather than in ragged gangs of 186, many wearing baseball caps turned backwards) and at various centers and institutes from California to Europe, spinning theories with no purchase on the world, oblivious to everything except her own thought processes. To others, however, she is a kind of contemporary Emily Dickinson (*see* "The Soul has Bandaged Moments," "These are the Days when Birds Come Back," or "This World is not Conclusion") fortunately settled in the academy, which both nurtures and brings out, by contrast, her autodidact's independence, her complete lack of cynicism, the earnest peaceability of her singular intelligence. Stressing her goals over her achievements, her fans actually join up with those of her detractors who emphasize her failure—which is to say, her noble, if unrealized, aspirations.

But Scarry is most interesting, even fascinating, when her work is understood as a success, even if we have to locate this success in some other project than the one she says she is engaged in. She bears witness to traumas that are recognizable as common to the era, and struggles with kinds of pain that she is not alone in suffering. Her responses, moreover, include the deployment of tools central to the life of the mind: wide reading and a scholarly, even scholastic, sense of order; and an urgent sense of worldly responsibility motivated by passion, with its roots deep in the dark soil of human hopes and fears. If these last are still legible in her work, if the task of sublimation has not been fully accomplished, this may be grounds not only for dismissal on grounds of descriptive or theoretical inadequacy, but for identification. So exotic a plant, Scarry may yet be understood as a representative figure for the life of the mind in a time of trauma. We could do worse.

CHAPTER 3

Criticism as Therapy: The Hunger of Martha Nussbaum

Academics are impressed and depressed in equal measure by the spectacle of extraordinary productivity in others, and Martha Nussbaum has occasioned far more than her share of such ambivalent discomfort. The gross flood of words appearing under her name is stunning. A bibliography on the Web tells the tale.[1] Between 1985, when she really hit her stride, and 2001, Nussbaum published, according to this *partial* count, more than 180 articles (some nearly book length), chapters, and reviews, one coauthored book, and eight books of her own—seven appearing between 1994 and 2001, all on different subjects, even in different fields. Setting aside the nine books and two special issues of journals she edited or coedited during that time, it appears that Nussbaum has gotten into a rhythm of publishing around seven or eight hundred words a day, 365 days a year; in a good year, of which she has had many, she can double that. One of her books, *Women and Human Development* (WHD), is a wide-ranging and ambitious 300-page tome that draws on a remarkable variety of materials and reflects extensive experience in various milieux, especially India.[2] In the preface, Nussbaum describes it as a mere 10K race in comparison to the "marathon" book that will ultimately complete her work in this area. Moreover, in addition to her publications, she has worked full time in other areas, teaching, giving numerous interviews, engaging in many high-visibility public debates, traveling constantly, interacting with hundreds of scholars in various fields, giving lectures beyond number, doing extensive work for a United Nations agency in Helsinki and India, examining issues of curricular reform at fifteen universities in the United States—and, incidentally, honing herself into marathon shape.[3]

Apart from the issues raised in this thronging body of work, the very size of the body raises its own set of questions. Academics, for whom each hyperscrupulous sentence is a separate feat of restrained daring, have two ways of accounting for exceptional productivity. The first is that the writer is a closed-minded narcissist who has established an intellectual framework that generates questions and answers almost automatically, so the time-consuming labor of open-ended research, the sifting of information, the gradual detection of emergent patterns, the generation of conviction and with it a point of view, the articulation of an argument—all this happens with a wondrous but suspect efficiency. The second explanation for unseemly productivity is that the author is a deeply troubled person driven by some unresolved internal conflict that seeks expression in argumentation about some comfortingly, if misleadingly, external object. For authors of this itchy and overstimulated kind, life presents an endless series of irritations or affronts, little burrs that provoke, knots that cry out to be undone, injustices that call for remediation, contradictions that demand to be sorted out because they are distanced forms of an obdurately internal difficulty.

Nussbaum may be a rare instance in which both accounts are combined. In one sense, she is always herself, always at rest, always saying the same things. Her entire career has been spun like a spider's web from a single passage in the Aristotelian text about which she wrote her dissertation and around which she constructed her first book, *De Motu Animalium*:

> Now we see that the movers of the animal are reasoning and *phantasia* and choice and wish and desire. For both *phantasia* and sense-perception hold the same place as thought . . . . Wish and spiritedness and appetite are all desire, and choice shares both in reasoning and in desire. So that the first mover is the object of desire and also of thought; not, however, every object of thought, but the end in the sphere of things that can be done.[4]

Here, deep in one of the lesser known, indeed disputed texts in the classical canon, immured in a work of scholarship that serves as the occasion for a stunning display of several kinds of scholarly mastery, one finds the emphases on the animality of the human, the mutuality of thought and desire, perception, and practical action—and of course "Aristotelianism" itself, with its focus on concrete particulars, virtue, and human flourishing—from which Nussbaum has never deviated. But Nussbaum's mind, as we will see, is also in a state of constant, self-transforming turbulence, ceaselessly discovering not just new fields to master but occasions within these fields for intervention, provocation, response—so many occasions, in fact, that one suspects a certain need for controversy that seeks out opportunities.

The very existence of boundaries seems to provide Nussbaum with an incitement to discourse. Oversized in every respect, her work is positioned at the seams of philosophy and numerous other disciplines, including literary study, legal theory, economics, classics, and education, and claims to have implications as well for cultural change, educational reform, quality-of-life assessment, and public policy. Her work is driven by a kind of yearning to forge a new and larger whole from what had been perceived as discontinuous elements. In her work, the cohabitation of different academic disciplines generates, or is intended to generate, a super-discourse oriented not toward the cultivation of increasingly refined vocabularies and distinctions but toward action in "the sphere of things that can be done." The great spew of words that is Nussbaum's oeuvre is animated both by a vast, almost unfathomable hunger and by a principle of immense fecundity. Nowhere in contemporary academic discourse is the desire to speak the transdisciplinary truth so clearly marked as in Nussbaum; from no other writer do we hear calls to "live as human," to embrace erotic passion as our highest good, or to refashion our lives on the model of the great philosophers, artists, and fictional characters.[5] Nowhere else in academic writing do we find such an undisguised desire to further the cause of justice, remedy social ills, or promote moral health. No other philosopher treats the classical canon as a repository of sound advice for ordinary people today. Nowhere else do we find technical tools of scholarship applied directly to the purpose of articulating a "radical proposal for the transformation of our lives" (LK 112). Nussbaum works at the margins of discourses as a way of exploring, exposing, exploiting, and ultimately escaping the constraints of academic discourse itself.

This, at least, might be the most generous way of accounting for one feature of her work that has troubled many of her readers, who, however, often have no explanation for it at all. Despite the ubiquitous evidence in Nussbaum's work of a superb education, rigorous training, scholarly accomplishment, a bold imagination, moral seriousness, and uncommon rhetorical skill, she routinely makes arguments that appear wildly implausible; her work is full of what seem to many to be unjustified claims or inferences, plain misreadings, or simple failures to think through her own arguments. Bristling with footnotes, heavily armored in every professional respect, backed by a confidence that can only be called massive, Nussbaum's arguments still seem to many readers self-evidently false, and the disconnect between the quality of mind manifest in the arguments and the arguments themselves creates real bewilderment. Judgments are sometimes harsh. Reviewing *Sex and Social Justice* (1999), a book that contains the texts of a number of high-profile lectures given at renowned universities all over the world, and drawing on concepts that Nussbaum has worked on for over a decade, Mary Beard describes "an undergraduate-style political optimism" marred by "repeated oversimplifications" and a "narrowly overconfident, simplistic and ahistorical reading of world culture." The overarching argument, she concludes, is "a frightful muddle which verges on the ludicrous."[6]

Some slips are perhaps inevitable, given Nussbaum's rate of production. But this is not the most interesting way of understanding what I would contend are integral features, rather than flaws or accidents in her thinking. Nussbaum's work is not essentially sound but occasionally misguided; it is what it is through and through, and discovering what it is will be the burden of this essay. To begin with, Nussbaum should not be considered a scholar with social concerns, but a moral and social reformer who uses scholarly methods and materials. She is engaged in an enterprise, or as she prefers to call it, a "project" of a kind for which the contemporary academy has a profound distrust. Its ultimate aim is not enlightenment but betterment in a more comprehensive sense, and not for intellectuals but for the population at large. Heavily invested in academic thought, Nussbaum is not committed to its values, protocols, or hierarchies. The most heroic description of her work is that she attempts to unearth alien and buried energies within the massively sedimented heritage of the western philosophical tradition, and to set them free in the world where they can do their work of furthering justice, freedom, and human flourishing. She is, in other words, addressing herself not to academic specialists but to human beings. The end determines some of the means, including those means that seem, from a professional perspective, flawed. Granting Nussbaum her *donnée*, we must begin by trying to separate the muddles that are frightful from a specific and limited point of view from those that may remain no matter what the point of view.

The task is intriguingly similar to the one that confronted readers of Jacques Derrida a generation ago. Like Nussbaum, Derrida also attempted to unearth long-buried energies within the philosophical tradition, attempting to revolutionize philosophy even as he produced work that resisted traditional disciplinary classifications. He, too, insisted on the enduring relevance of classical philosophy, arguing that we must "become classical once more," and that we cannot escape philosophy: "one always has to philosophize."[7] Both warned about philosophy's excessive faith in rational orderings, and did so by advancing the cognitive claims of "literary" discourse—figuration for Derrida, narrative for Nussbaum. Derrida's reading of Plato's *Phaedrus* in *Of Grammatology* could be compared with Nussbaum's reading of the *Symposium* in her breakthrough book *The Fragility of Goodness* (1986). In both cases, a detail ignored by the mainstream reading of the work serves to unlock a new reading of the text and to launch a broad critique of the tradition that had ignored it. Derrida's fierce attention to Plato's comments on writing as an "exterior" and degraded form compared to speech provides him with an acute angle of vision on an entire tradition of prizing the "presence" and "immediacy" of speech, a tradition that is, he asserts, based more on moral preferences than on the facts of language.[8] The early Derrida especially is drawn to the "logic of the supplement" by which an element that a given system tries to exclude is admitted to the system, but only in negated or degraded form; "deconstruction" consists of demonstrating that the supplement—writing, in the case of Plato, de Saussure, and others—contains the secret principle that determines the entire system. Similarly, Nussbaum focuses on an event long thought to be incidental to the main argument of the *Symposium*, the sudden and disorderly appearance of Alcibiades, who charges that Socrates, in his theorizing about love, has ignored the fact that one must love someone in particular—as he, Alcibiades, loves Socrates. Nussbaum builds this incident into a general critique of Socrates and a revitalized understanding of the whole Greek tradition.[9] Insofar as Nussbaum's entire career has consisted of raising what Derrida might call "supplemental" details from classical texts—an emphasis on the "madness" of love, the superiority of "fragility" or exposed vulnerability to an overly controlled approach to life, the centrality of literature to a full appreciation of human life, the cognitive value of emotions—to the level of main arguments, one could say that the logic of Nussbaum's career has been "deconstructive" from the start.

Nussbaum herself would resist this suggestion with some force, for she has always been critical, even contemptuous, of Derrida, whose work she finds obscure, conceptually anarchic, ethically desiccated, and politically counterproductive. Reading Derrida, Nussbaum says, creates in her "a certain hunger for blood" (*Love's Knowledge* [LK] 171).[10] Flouting Derridean doctrine, Nussbaum proclaims herself a firm believer in a determinate conception of the human good and the projects of moral and social reform that can follow from such a conception. Whereas, in the climate of Derrida, a guarded hesitation and a proliferation of preliminary questions were the most authentic marks of sagacity, Nussbaum's work invariably betrays an impatience, even an impetuosity. The mighty forces of "*différence*" and "dissemination," sources of endless fascination for Derridean analysts as they traced the recession of meaning from sign to sign, context to context, are from Nussbaum's point of view indices of a virtually criminal timidity. On the other hand, her understanding of philosophy as edification, instruction, and therapy (as in *The Therapy of Desire*, 1994), a discourse of concentration rather than dissemination, in which concepts and distinctions are cashed out in the forms of policy recommendations and moral prescription, seems, from a Derridean perspective, naive, premature, even anti-intellectual.

The common interests of Nussbaum and Derrida only throw their differences into greater relief. The most intriguing such interest concerns their account of ethical responsibility. Initially, Derrida treated ethics as one dimension of the "metaphysics of presence" that had dominated Western thinking since the Greeks and sought to explore the root condition, "the nonethical opening of ethics"; but over the years he became more invested in the notion of a multidimensional "responsibility" extending, theoretically, to infinity. His thinking drew closer to such thinkers as Immanuel Kant and Emmanuel Levinas. The "ethics of discussion" that reached its most mature form in the late 1980s centers on the kinds of obligations— to the text, to context, to language, to history, to accepted procedures of research and analysis, accepted protocols of presentation—that regulate a conscientious act of interpretation.[11] Nussbaum, too, describes the act of reading as "a moral activity in its own right," but her premises and points of orientation are so different as to make one wonder how the concept of ethics can contain them both (LK 339). Derrida never mentions, and seems indifferent to, the feelings of the reader; nor does he hold reading to be instructive with respect to specific virtues, attitudes, or moral behavior. For Derrida, reading is many things, but it is not the source of a fundamental life transformation.

Arguments for transformation can be found not somewhere, but everywhere in Nussbaum, especially in what I will call "phase one" of her thinking, whose fullest expression is *Love's Knowledge* (1990). Her ideal reader is not a mind bound by obligations, but a whole being responsive to the excitations represented in and by the text. Whereas, for Derrida, "literary" figuration undercuts the truth-function of language and thus interferes with philosophy's ability to guide and instruct, Nussbaum sees the matter differently. For her, literature, centered in plot and character, both reveals the true nature of ethical decision-making as a constant testing of general principles against specific instances and, because of its superior vivacity, teaches virtue far more directly and effectively than philosophy ever could. Derrida avoids paraphrase on principle, focusing on textual details; Nussbaum is one of the boldest paraphrasers imaginable, fearlessly extracting lessons for living from texts written hundreds, even thousands of years ago. Derrida's approach to texts presumes their alien character, their refusal to lend themselves to their readers' purposes, their insistence on remaining "undecidable," and thereby requiring readers to remain in a state of unsettled inquiry. Nussbaum, by sharp contrast, insistently blurs the distinction between books and life, recognizing no such refusal, no such undecidability, no such submission. Texts may represent alien or distant worlds, but the texts themselves help readers overcome that distance. Readers who come to Nussbaum after being steeped in Derridean ascesis experience a giddy sense that, suddenly, everything is permissible; for the very things Derrida blocks—unmoderated humanism, a desire for direct moral instruction, and a preference for certainty over doubt—are, for Nussbaum, the essence of the enterprise. Derrida's imagined reader, although described as self-regulating and morally autonomous, is engaged in a test of disciplined intelligence; but Nussbaum's reader, as we will see, is not just instructed but constructed by novels themselves as sensitive, empathetic, imaginative, and concerned with others. For Nussbaum, if you're reading novels, you can't go wrong.

One final difference will take us to the heart of Nussbaum's thinking. No matter how classical Derrida gets, he always seems to approach his subjects from the perspective of the future. That is, he seems to have seen through to the end of certain traditional problems and assumes a position logically posterior to them; the critical practices that have been affected by his work typically designate themselves "post-," as in poststructuralist, post-Marxist, postmodernist, postfeminist, and even posttheoretical. With no interest, except a negative one, in post-anything, Nussbaum invariably attacks from the rear, challenging contemporaries from a point of view long forgotten, dormant, fossilized. Insofar as she seeks to renovate contemporary thinking by resuscitating its own tradition, her work typically reaches back to the future. Philosophers reading her work have been startled, sometimes pleasantly, to encounter powerful claims for the Greek tradition that they had long ago relegated to "classics" and treated as the prehistory of philosophy proper, which, they got in the habit of saying, began with such thinkers as Descartes, Hume, Rousseau, Spinoza, and Kant. Most of those who take issue with Enlightenment thinking today represent themselves as anti-, counter-, or post-Enlightenment thinkers. Nussbaum is defiantly Aristotelian and therefore pre-Enlightenment; her slogan might be "Antiquity—An Incomplete Project."

Not all of Nussbaum's regressions, however, can be traced back to Greece. Her reading habits seem to have been formed by an early reading of Adam Smith's "Theory of the Moral Sentiments," and especially of Lionel Trilling's *The Liberal Imagination* (1940), which emphasized, in an anti-Stalinist spirit, the importance of the novel as an agent of "the moral imagination, as the literary form which most directly reveals to us the complexity, the difficulty, and the interest of life in society."[12] Trilling's advice to liberals to turn away from "agencies, and bureaus, and technicians" and cultivate instead a "lively sense of contingency and possibility" seems to have made a deep impression on Nussbaum. And her references to Derrida have the same direction and tone as Trilling's dismissals of Cleanth Brooks and the New Criticism—a debate that, in Nussbaum's mind, is still worth replaying.[13] Soft words about Trilling are scattered throughout her literary critical work, sometimes accompanied by respectful comments on the moral seriousness of F. R. Leavis and, as a contemporary instance, Wayne Booth's *The Ethics of Fiction*.[14] In all three cases, Nussbaum responds to a set of linked convictions: that literature speaks to and of the human world, not some merely textual or fictional world; that literature's relation to life is essentially, if variously, a moral one; that "aesthetics" has no autonomy from the life world; that literature creates and reflects interpersonal "communities"; that literature synthesizes thought and feeling; and that the greatest literature is essentially liberal and democratic in spirit, even if it serves as a modern and secular version of religion.

What Nussbaum contributes to these interlinked convictions is a far greater degree of specificity concerning the moral character and impact of literature, and a far weaker sense of the distinction between literature and life. Neither Trilling, Leavis, nor Booth would feel at all comfortable with statements that are routine in Nussbaum about how novels construct moral readers by soliciting empathetic identification; or how they foster a supple and yielding way of being. They never venture arguments of the kind Nussbaum repeatedly advances, that "the novel is itself a moral achievement," that "the artist's task is a moral task," and that novels constitute a set of "universal prescriptions" (LK 148, 163, 166). Their writing gives no support to the notion that "the well-lived life is a work of literary art" and that "our whole moral task . . . is to make a fine artistic creation" (LK 148, 163). Their nonprescriptive understanding of the ethical arises from the sense of dignity and worth imparted to a particular way of life by a novelistic representation that both records details and provides a sense of overall patterning, not from models of moral behavior or virtues implicit in the form itself. Leavis's account of Dickens's *Hard Times* registers the feel of life in Coketown, oppressed by hard material conditions compounded by bad social and educational theory; it does not extract maxims that could guide contemporary policy makers, economists, or jurists, as Nussbaum does with hammering repetitiveness in *Poetic Justice*.[15] There is, to my knowledge, no place in the collected works of Trilling, Leavis, and Booth in which any of them confesses, as Nussbaum does in *Love's Knowledge*, to falling in love ("rushing into the eager volatility of desire") with a fictional character (James Steerforth of Dickens's *David Copperfield* [LK 335]).

In short, although Trilling, Leavis, and Booth may be old-fashioned in some respects, they are modern readers. Nussbaum seems something different. Her literary criticism seems, from a disciplinary point of view, not just iconoclastic but almost precritical, even archaic. In Nussbaum, the specificity of literature as a discourse, an object of professional study, is almost altogether erased, and replaced by a conception that treats it bluntly as moral philosophy.[16] The aesthetic is made to serve the aims of culture and morality in a dedifferentiated unity rarely seen in the modern world except in certain ("Wagnerian") fantasies, a unity repudiated by most modern theories of aesthetics, the repudiation constituting nothing less than modernity itself.

It seems implausible that someone as well educated as Nussbaum could sustain such out-of-phase attitudes. But it also seems that Nussbaum did not learn them in school, and nothing she did learn in school has succeeded in driving them out. Her relation to literature, and to the world of the mind in general, appears to have been based on the most "primitive" of all readerly responses, identification with fictional characters. By her own account a solitary, bookish young girl growing up in Bryn Mawr, Pennsylvania, Nussbaum (or Craven; she took her husband's name and converted to the Jewish religion after marriage in the late 1960s) spent much of her time alone, reading in the attic, dreaming her way into the worlds of thought, action, and love. She wrote an early paper on "recognition" in Aristophanes (*see* LK 11). But her most powerful experience of recognition came elsewhere. "I read Plato's *Phaedrus* when I was an adolescent," she has written, "and found that account of male-male love the most appealing paradigm of love I had seen." At once philosophical and literary, reasoned and passionate, logical and mythological, Plato's account of erotically charged pedagogy represented a compelling picture of the "shared concern" that constitutes love at its best. "It described what I myself wanted from love," she says, "(albeit with a man)" (*Cultivating Humanity* [CH] 241). Offered as a simple autobiographical vignette, this unembarrassed narrative opens a window on what amounts to a primal scene of reading, recollected and recounted as a formative experience in which emergent personal identity and dreams of love were crystallized in the particular hybrid form of the fantasy of philosophical mastery and the delirium of literary self-loss.

Later—after two years at Wellesley (a classmate of Hillary Rodham), some time in a professional theater group performing classical drama, an undergraduate degree at New York University and a Ph.D. in philosophy at Harvard, followed by an appointment in classics at Harvard, where she was denied tenure—she would continue to insist, with all the resources at the command of the mature philosopher and scholar, that the essence of philosophy was its capacity to transform lives, that the most life-altering texts in philosophy were those of the classical period, that Aristotle and especially Plato were the leading figures in the classical canon, and that the *Phaedrus* and the *Symposium* were Plato's most important works. In the *Phaedrus*, Nussbaum says, Plato suggests that intense erotic love "plays a central role in motivating us to grow ethically and to pursue our search for true beauty and goodness . . . . Indeed I believe he goes further still: he allows that this specialness of response to a beloved person is of *cognitive* value as well . . . . We need to follow his lead" (LK 122–23; *see also* LK 324–33, and *The Fragility of Goodness* [FG] 200–33). In her first major works, including *The Fragility of Goodness, Love's Knowledge*, and *The Therapy of Desire*, Nussbaum herself "followed his lead," producing a dense mesh of arguments that, taken as a whole, validated her initial identification with characters in Plato's text and affirmed, too, the value of identification as a way of knowing. One of the idiosyncratic features of Nussbaum's understanding of reading is her emphasis on the powerful bonds of identity formed between readers, authors, and characters, all of whom become, in the act of reading, a kind of composite macroperson, with the reader eagerly abandoning her (and with Nussbaum, it is always "her") critical exteriority. And, at a deeper level, one of the distinctive features of her identity as a scholar has been the especially close and admiring relation she has formed with figures of authority, including not only the giants of classical philosophy, but also such authors as Dickens and Henry James, such precursor figures as Trilling, and more recently such scholars as Amartya Sen and Kenneth Dover, with whom her attachments retain the aura of ardent apprenticeship that was, in her account, her first access to the world of the mind. At the very deepest level, her enduring and profound faith in classical philosophy as a master discourse has organized virtually all of her thinking.

So compelling, apparently, was this initial experience that many of Nussbaum's mature positions have continued to reflect the mindset of a teenager in love. In the most extreme arguments of *Love's Knowledge*, love truly conquers all, and is even said to surpass in human depth morality itself.[17] Especially in the late novels of Henry James such as *The Golden Bowl* (which Nussbaum read some years later in another lonely room [LK 18]), she discovers a warrant for urging her readers to dispense with rational self-control, to be vibrantly responsive and acutely perceptive, to fall in love, preferably in a "universe of moonlight and magic" (LK 352). Few philosophers have been willing to argue, as Nussbaum does, that "the tender susceptible heart is morally finer than a firm one" (LK 237).[18] Having read Plato during the Johnny Mathis years, Nussbaum may have taken to heart the great crooner's phrase about being helpless as a kitten up a tree; one can almost hear a thousand violins begin to play as Nussbaum recommends, in *Fragility of Goodness, Love's Knowledge,* and *The Therapy of Desire,* the virtue of "passivity . . . the strange sense (or lack of sense) of self" as the highest human attainment.[19] Aristotle advocated what has come to be called, by Bernard Williams and others, "moral luck," or the acceptance of contingency and of circumstances beyond one's control as an inevitable part of life and a measure of one's responsiveness and flexibility. Nussbaum's version of moral luck emphasizes "trust, the acceptance of incompleteness" (LK 282; *see* "Luck and Ethics"). "What I am after," she says in a misty moment in *Love's Knowledge,* "is a noncontrolling art of writing that will leave the writer [in this case, herself] more receptive to love than before" (LK 321). At the end of this admittedly "experimental" essay, "Love and the Individual," she promises herself, in a tone blending youthful anticipation and a will to self-deception that reflects a certain experience in this line, that "tomorrow I'll see my current lover. . . . I'll say how happy I am. It will be true" (333).

Nussbaum's moony account of love suggests another feature of her sensibility that remains, despite the indisputable professionalism of her presentation, "adolescent" in character, her tendency to think categorically, and to advocate one-dimensional formal solutions to complex problems. Her promotion of contingency, specificity, and exposure tends to obscure the extent to which her key terms are monochrome reductions of far more complex experiences. Her version of love, for example, tacitly excludes most of what goes by that name. Many people have been "in love" without ever experiencing, or wanting to experience, the one-way surrender she describes. And her use of such terms as "passion" or "emotions and emotional activity" is strikingly undifferentiated, as though these terms designated simple wholes with a positive moral value, and were incompatible by definition with hatred, contempt, envy, lust, and aggressivity (LK 291). "Perception," which she treats in *Love's Knowledge* as the foundation of the moral and of the aesthetic, the indispensable faculty by which norms are tested against concrete particulars, receives a similarly undifferentiated treatment, as though it was an unequivocal good—both a "created work of art" and a "moral achievement" (LK 155, 153).

Most disturbingly, literature itself, which Nussbaum represents as the very voice of particularity and contingency, is flattened out into a category with a single moral value: good. Her weakest—repetitive, reductive, and dull—book, *Poetic Justice* (PJ) (1995), argues this case at considerable length. Literature, she says, is a valuable supplement to formal reasoning in moral and legal theory; novels in particular are good at portraying the consequences of public policy on human beings, the pressures under which real people operate, and the true complexity of human life.[20] Reading novels, people are forced to imagine the lives of others, to feel their feelings and understand their problems in a way that unaided rationality will not enable them to do. Judges, economists, and policy makers should therefore become more literary as a way of doing their jobs better. This argument would surely have surprised Ian Watt, who contended, in *The Rise of the Novel*, that this genre developed in a climate of rationalism and emergent capitalism; and it must surprise any reader of Dostoevsky, Kafka, Anne Rice, Jerzy Kosinski, and other writers who seek to provoke very different responses, and often seem to want to expose tender susceptibility as a self-destructive romantic fraud. Nussbaum might have confined her argument to a few specific novels, for she is well aware of the threat to the reader represented by bad novels (PJ 76, 124 n. 2). But in the main, she insists that compassionate identification is "a feature of the genre, a feature of the way realist novels solicit and cultivate the imagination," and that "the very form constructs compassion in readers" (30, 66). When the Unabomber, alone in his mountain fastness, reads Joseph Conrad's acidic *The Secret Agent*, with its suggestive account of a retarded boy blown to bits, his heart flutters in sympathy, just like that of a Bryn Mawr teenager.

If a tendency to posit formal or categorical solutions to complex problems constitutes an "adolescent" frame of mind, then Nussbaum's understanding of literature, which informs so much of her work, continues to bear witness, like a scar, to that traumatic first encounter with Plato. The one-sided solitude of that encounter seems also to have remained as a model for the reading experience, and for interaction generally. She typically writes about people not as the bearers of traditions, customs, or cultures, or even as members of various kinds of groups, but as monadic individuals, autonomous choosers. Sensible as an account of reading, this approach through the "I" is notably undeveloped as a way of understanding the kinds of issues and choices that arise in social life. Still, what is really striking in Nussbaum is how plastic and heterogeneous that "I" can be. One of the primary features of the literary experience, in her account, is the way in which reading fictional stories exercises the mind and expands the imagination by soliciting identifications or experimental identities in a way unavailable in reality and thus enables one to get a new perspective on one's own life: even a teenaged girl in the late twentieth century may imagine herself as the heroine, and object of seduction, in a text that concerns only long-dead males. Part of the appeal for the young Nussbaum may have been that the love relationship described by Plato was an improved version of the modern heterosexual scenario, which, in fiction as in life, was commonly marred by inequalities or exploitation (*see* CH 241 ff.). It was, in other words, not only easy for Nussbaum to identify with the younger or "passive," that is feminized male, but imaginatively advantageous to do so, because this passivity did not, in the Greek context, seem to imply a lesser status; in fact, although the Aristotelian association of passivity with the female has been taken, by Luce Irigaray and others, as an early assertion of a masculine desire for "mastery" in reproduction, the kind of passivity that Socrates describes in the pedagogic relationship is reserved for males, and so represents a form of masculinity that one could "do" while remaining in the traditional feminine position.[21]

Further reading in the Greek corpus disclosed to Nussbaum, however, a more troubling point of affinity in the form of a pervasive indifference to the pleasure of the younger partner, which was contrasted to the pleasure felt by women. It appears, Nussbaum discovered, that the Greeks understood and valued female pleasure, whereas in more recent times women have been made to suffer the consequences of "the total denial, by whole societies and groups, of the reality of female pleasure" (*Therapy of Desire* [TD] 189; *see* 183–91). If the boy in ancient Greece was made to play the role of the woman with respect to passivity, then women since then have been cast in the role of boys with respect to pleasure. An identification that, in the first instance, gave Nussbaum access to an augmented experience of passion, power, and pleasure in the realm of the imagination seems to have given her new insight into the exclusion of women from those experiences in the historical world.

In Nussbaum's youthful identification with the younger or passive partner in a homosexual relationship, we can, then, posit a complex and highly charged scenario in which she not only came to understand herself in terms of the Platonic text, but also came to understand the social and moral shortcomings of contemporary society, especially with respect to women. Such an experience would be bound to change one's life, and in Nussbaum's case, this transformation happened in two stages. In the first, Nussbaum imagines herself as both transformed and transformable—that is, as the young boy taken under the wing, and into the bed, of the pedagogue ("Naturally," Socrates tells the dazzled Phaedrus, "it is not long before these desires are fulfilled in action.").[22] In the second, the mature Nussbaum, a student who has learned her lessons, assumes the position of the master, with its augmented and expanded range of powers and pleasures. Nussbaum's advancing mastery, to the point where she could represent and even criticize the ancients' conception of the male-male love relationship, and on the basis of that critique attack her own society as well—undiluted gratification!—constitutes in effect a claim to pleasure. It does not constitute a renunciation of her first identification with the unpleasured lad, but rather the complete success of that identification. As a scholar of classical philosophy, Nussbaum is a member of the otherwise misogynistic society of such scholars; but by insisting on passivity as a virtue learned from the Greeks, Nussbaum remains faithful to the boy that, in her imagination, she once was.[23] This combination of medium and message represents the fully developed, or passive-aggressive, form of Nussbaum's mature work, which is, in "phase one," predicated on the "female" virtues of sensitivity, passivity, perceptiveness, tenderness, caring, erotic passion, and, in a more fundamental sense, on the possibility and desirability of radical transformation.

And so we can see why, when Nussbaum paints the picture of her early reading, it is the *Phaedrus,* rather than a heterosexual romance, that is described as the catalyst for the formation of her intellectual persona. The dangerous and equivocal character of man-boy love constituted the *Phaedrus* as a kind of charmed circle that a brilliant, alienated adolescent might feel privileged to enter. The liberal spirit with which all parties in Plato's dialogue take for granted what modern bourgeois society regards as taboo may well have produced for such a reader the thrilling sense of being inducted into a deeply suppressed, because unusually broad-minded, society of initiates. For the young Nussbaum, homosexual pederasty was to philosophy as fertilizer is to fruit.

Readers of *The Fragility of Goodness* or *Love's Knowledge* who picked up a copy of the *New York Times Magazine* on November 21, 1999, may have been taken aback by the photograph accompanying Robert S. Boynton's article on Nussbaum, "Who Needs Philosophy?"[24] Expecting, perhaps, Sarah Bernhardt, they saw instead a chiseled athlete in a tight black tank top, glaring fiercely at the viewer with the lizard eyes of a killer. Can a heart that beats forty-two times a minute, they may have wondered, be tender and susceptible?

In fact, just as *Love's Knowledge* was published in 1986, Nussbaum was undergoing a conversion experience. From 1986 to 1993, she worked with the World Institute of Development Economics Research and as a consultant for the United Nations Development Programme, in projects relating to quality-of-life assessment, especially among women.[25] Spending a month each summer at the United Nations' office in Helsinki, and considerable time in India, China, and other countries, working with other scholars including the economist Amartya Sen as well as with numerous women and women's groups, Nussbaum encountered "traditional" life forms, including many that deprived women of what people living in advanced liberal democracies regard as basic human rights. Exposure to the legally sanctioned inequalities under which millions of women suffer, she says, "transformed my work, making me aware of urgent problems and convincing me that philosophy had a contribution to make toward their solution" (WHD xv).

It is difficult to avoid the impression that the United Nations experience awakened Nussbaum to limitations in her own work. By comparison with the sufferings of so many others, tender susceptibility to particulars may have come to seem a paltry thing. In the harsh light of the Indian experience, the argument that one should accept, under the name of "moral luck," one's fate by submitting to what lies beyond one's control, could well have appeared as self-destructive, even perverse. As a consequence, the status of passivity in her work drops precipitously. Emotions, once earnestly cultivated as ends in themselves, now begin to be seen as part of the problem, all too easily deformed by prevailing customs and norms, and must now be "properly limited and filtered" before they are put to use (PJ 4).[26] Earlier injunctions to heedlessness and headlong dashes into passion are now accompanied by the phrase "so long as you think first."[27] Other "phase-one" formulations such as those in *Therapy of Desire* in which love is figured as "a dangerous hole in the self," and the passionate life as "a life of continued gaping openness to violation" are less and less frequent, their literal meaning presenting difficulties for one who has met many women whose lives are dangerous and open to violation, but not as a consequence of romantic passion (TD 442).

Where others might have given up philosophy altogether under the pressure of this avalanche of new information, Nussbaum reworked her understanding of philosophy itself as a healing discourse that could help to reduce violence and promote justice. The scene of philosophy was radically expanded, its function redefined, its audience enlarged; the perception of concrete particulars gave way to "non-relative virtues."[28] The result was a shift of emphasis so decisive that it must be considered a kind of narrative turn, a "phase two" in which all her concepts are, if not actually rejected, turned inside out as she shifts from desire to therapy, ecstasy to equality, rapture to rights, love of man to love of Man.[29] Phase-two Nussbaum conceives herself not as a subversive feminine presence operating at the disciplinary margins of the academy, but rather as a theorist at large whose thinking has literally global consequences.

For this task, two concepts with which Nussbaum was already familiar lay ready to hand. The first was the concept of cultural difference, announced in a quiet way in the beginning of *Fragility*, when she urged her readers to try to see the Greeks as they really were as a method for estranging our own culture, freeing us to think differently. Whereas, in phase one, Nussbaum advocated a revision of our emotional orientations in light of information about other cultures, the emphasis in phase two fell on the revisability of laws.[30] Cultural difference merged into cultural construction as Nussbaum began to press for different principles and values, and for specific reforms. But cultural difference, according to which the practices and values of one culture cannot serve as norms for another, was altogether incapable of providing any leverage for judgment, much less reform: partisans of cockfighting, female genital mutilation, and dowry all take refuge in the principle of cultural difference. Nussbaum needed another principle to complete the work, and found it in a place most multiculturalists had failed to look: reason. In arguments that advance steadily in scope and confidence through the 1990s, she promoted human reason as the adjudicator of disputes generated by clashes of values.

The most brilliantly compressed application of both principles comes in what is perhaps Nussbaum's most famous dispute. In 1993, Nussbaum was called to testify briefly in a Colorado courtroom as an expert witness on ancient Greek attitudes toward homosexuality. The issue was the constitutionality of a statute that prevented homosexuals from claiming special protection against discrimination on the grounds of their sexual preference. Although the judge did not take Nussbaum's testimony into account in issuing his ruling, that testimony was followed by the appearance on the stand of John Finnis of Oxford and Robert George of Princeton, who argued that Nussbaum was wrong, and that the Greeks condemned homosexuality on moral grounds. Convinced that they were bad philosophers, incompetent scholars, and homophobic reactionaries, Nussbaum went to war with angry faxes, letters, maneuvering, interviews, and polemics. The most extraordinary document of all that followed was her prodigious 1994 *Virginia Law Review* article, "Platonic Love and Colorado Law: The Relevance of Ancient Greek Norms to Modern Controversies."[31] This tour de force, one of the great "I'll Take My Stand" position papers in recent years, weighed in at 136 pages, and included four appendices and 468 footnotes. The dispute even crested the surface of *Lingua Franca* and the *New York Times Magazine*.[32] With contemporary issues of justice and law, not to mention her scholarly and personal reputation, hanging on such minutiae as interpretations of brief passages and even single words in Socratic dialogues, the differences between editions of an ancient Greek lexicon, and—shades of Rosemary Woods! a whited-out ampersand—well, for a scholarly debate, it just doesn't get any better than this.

"Platonic Love and Colorado Law" argues that the Athenian culture we venerate today had very different attitudes towards male-male love than we do, and that we would profit from a careful reading of Greek philosophy. Such a reading, Nussbaum argues, would teach us that our own views are not natural or inevitable—in fact, she ventures, contemporary homophobia can trace its roots back only as far as Christianity. The Greek example, by contrast, suggests that homosexuality, regulated by "a complex system of caveats or reservations" that sought to protect the younger partner from exploitation and the dangers of developing a habit of "feminine" passivity, could be the object of respect and serve a valuable civic function ("Platonic Love" 1546, 1641). Plato is the primary example, and the *Phaedrus*, no longer understood as an account of the kind of love a Bryn Mawr teenager might aspire to but rather a culture-specific text that makes a "stirring defense of male-male desire and love and gives an extraordinary role to erotic love within the life of philosophical aspiration," is one of the key texts (1578). In this new context, love is no longer the end of life; now, Nussbaum says that "the moral end of love is to transcend itself in friendship" (1591).

As she discovered, Finnis, and especially George, were also warriors. Undaunted by a Nussbaum fax that seemed to threaten legal action, George wrote a long article defending his position and attacking Nussbaum's, "'Shameless Acts' Revisited: Some Questions for Martha Nussbaum."[33] An interesting figure, George is certainly one of very few Ivy League professors associated with the Catholic Natural Law movement, the Civil Rights Commission, and the Gary Bauer presidential campaign. "'Shameless Acts'" focuses largely on what George saw as Nussbaum's deliberate misrepresentations of the work of other scholars, especially Kenneth Dover. Both George and Nussbaum take Dover's *Greek Homosexuality* as the most authoritative text on the subject, and Nussbaum made a point of identifying herself with Dover, saying she was "in all major points in agreement" with him (PL 1538).[34] Suspecting that Nussbaum would attempt to enlist Dover's support and confident that she was misrepresenting Dover's views, Finnis wrote to Dover asking for clarification of certain key passages, and received the following response:

1. It is certainly my opinion that the Socrates of Plato and Xenophon condemned homosexual copulation as such, and did not confine the prohibition to any particular relationships. I certainly meant to say that on pp. 159 f. of my book. . . . At the same time he expected any normal male to experience homosexual desire, and he did not think that occasional copulation—in an unguarded moment—completely vitiated a non-physical relationship (p. 163). It is like a temptation to commit adultery or various forms of dishonesty or violence; natural and normal to experience the temptation, but wrong to yield to it.

2. Where one can distinguish Plato from his—Socrates' (i.e., in Laws), Plato condemns all homosexual copulation (pp. 165–68 in "Shameless Acts")

As it happened, Nussbaum was indeed enlisting Dover's support, and had persuaded him to coauthor an appendix to "Platonic Love" specifically to refute Finnis. In this appendix, Nussbaum—and Dover—argue that, appearances notwithstanding, Dover "never claimed that Socrates condemns this copulation as wicked, shameful and depraving. Thus Finnis's use of Dover's letter to support Finnis's own position is inappropriate" (PL 1645). It is enough to make the head spin, just thinking about the elderly Dover being pulled in two directions by people who know how to pull.[35] But the case lies, in the end, with George. Overinvested in the *Phaedrus* to begin with, Nussbaum proliferates side issues, superfine distinctions, and debater's points, aggressively distracting attention from Dover's plain statements and George's plain quotations of them.

But another reason for Nussbaum's bellicosity is that she believes that recognition of the rights and dignity of homosexuals is a simple matter of reason. "To defend the basic civil rights of the powerless," she writes, "we need reason, a force whose dignity is not proportional to its sheer strength. I am convinced that reason supports basic civil rights for homosexuals" (PL 1606).[36] Thus cultural differences explain the variance between the Greeks and us as two paths that might be taken, neither one of which is necessarily natural. But the signal distinction of Greek culture was its commitment to reason, a principle that transcends culture and provides a standard of judgment for all times and places. When we ask ourselves which view of a given matter is more reasonable, theirs or ours, the question is prejudged: the Greek view is better because the Greek view is the reasonable view. In the case of Greece, if in that case alone, the argument from cultural difference gives way immediately to an appeal to reason.

One of the moves that defines phase two involves, however, the ascendancy of reason over Greece. As Nussbaum realizes, Athenian reason had not supported basic civil or human rights for slaves, women, children, or non-Greeks, and so if reason were to function as a weapon against injustice, it had to be cut loose from its cultural and historical origin. Like others seeking to defend universal rights, Nussbaum turns to Kant; unlike others, she treats Kant as a late flower of the Stoic tradition. In *Fragility*, *Love's Knowledge*, and elsewhere, Kant's abstract universalism had fared badly, especially when compared with the "virtue ethics" of Aristotle. In fact, Kant is held responsible for the low esteem in which Greek thought has been held, a situation Nussbaum devotes herself to correcting (FG 4– 6). In phase two, however, Kant becomes indispensable for a series of post-Stoic arguments about human commonality—the insistence that morality means people as ends not means, that reason is a universal human possession, and that reason forms the basis of a universal human community of law.[37] In other texts written during the mid- and late-1990s, Nussbaum cites contemporary neo-Kantians John Rawls and Jürgen Habermas as persuasive spokesmen for a conception of reason without cultural origins or biases.[38] And so, while promoting the causes of cultural difference and cultural construction, Nussbaum also finds herself arguing against other constructionists who list a purified and impartial reason as one of western culture's more violent and prejudicial delusions.[39]

The emergent master concept in phase two is actually neither cultural difference nor reason, but a concept that embraces them, a redefined notion of "the human." Once, Nussbaum argued that human being was essentially fallible, contingent, concrete, passionate, as well as rational. To try to "transcend" the human was the very definition of a moral mistake (*see* LK 365–91). Now, however, humanity becomes a concept of universality in which local passions such as patriotism, patriarchalism, racism, and homophobia are transcended by identification with a global community. To support this revised and restricted account of the human, some adjustments are required. Aristotle, the phase-one philosopher of the concrete, becomes a phase-two philosopher of "human essentialism," the first thinker to try to pick out those features of human life most distinctive of humanity and therefore most worth cultivating; in this spirit, Nussbaum begins to speak with increasing frequency about "common humanity" and "common human functioning."[40] Missing from the inventory of acceptable human passions are aggression and anger. Behind Nussbaum's praise of the Stoics in *Therapy of Desire* is a disturbed if temporary obsession with the destructive force of negative emotions, especially anger in the erotic life (TD 439–83). "Human beings," she writes at about this time, "are born for mutual aid and mutual concord, and . . . the removal of anger will remove the vindictive and destructive elements in war, and cut down greatly on the world's total of conflict." Only those passions that are, in a sense, dispassionate and responsive to the patient work of philosophy are to be considered part of the human essence; the rest are merely "constructed by social evaluations."[41] Once the philosopher of turbulence and passion, Nussbaum refashions herself, in this new dispensation, as a modern Stoic, undisturbed by the retrograde enthusiasms that afflict less perfectly balanced minds.[42]

A spirit of sternly insistent progressivism presides over Nussbaum's work since 1990, in which the presiding spirits are Kant and the Stoics. Never notable for its range or variety, Nussbaum's account of emotions becomes even more restricted. Indeed, restriction becomes an integral part of her account of emotion itself, which she now describes not as valuable in itself but as part of a larger mental process dominated by rationality, serving in "a carefully demarcated cognitive role" (PJ xvi). Although *Poetic Justice* condemns the hyperutilitarian Gradgrind in *Hard Times*, Nussbaum's approach has its own Gradgrindian insistence. Literature, she says, is useful because it cultivates emotions, and emotions are useful because they foster a human community. The most useful literature is therefore realistic fiction, for which Nussbaum has a well-nigh Lukácsian admiration; and the most useful emotion is compassion, or "compassionate identification." Although Nussbaum remains, as in phase one, primarily concerned with the thoughts and feelings of the individual, that individual is no longer a panting reader whose mind is filled with the drama of the text, but a judge, a policy maker, a theorist, an administrator, all of whom, she says, could profit from a dose of compassion even as they remain, like a reader, outside the scene of action (*Sex and Social Justice* 171).[43] Ecstasy departs, and a disintoxicated and socially responsible spirit of gravity settles in. And whereas before, the reader looked up, as it were, to exemplary models, now the judge looks down in an attempt to gain necessary information before rendering judgment.

This spirit of restriction and utility is not just matched but, in a way that must be tracked with care to be appreciated, enabled by a spirit of expansion, even inflation, in which Nussbaum affiliates with the entirety of the human species, and urges everyone to do the same. Not everyone does appreciate it. In her essay in *For Love of Country*, she says that patriotism is bad—jingoistic, potentially violent, exclusive, and superficial—and a wide-minded and peaceable "cosmopolitanism" would be preferable.[44] So aggressively does Nussbaum make this unexceptionable case, however, that the respondents to her essay, including such luminaries as Kwame Anthony Appiah, Sissela Bok, Judith Butler, Amy Guttmann, Gertrude Himmelfarb, Hilary Putnam, Elaine Scarry, Charles Taylor, and Michael Walzer can find virtually nothing in it to agree with. Even Amartya Sen, although sympathetic to Nussbaum on several levels, can only defend her by suggesting that some of the worst consequences her attackers envision as following from her arguments might not, in fact, necessarily come to pass.

There does seem to be something about the way Nussbaum presents her argument that is almost designed to elicit its own negation. Her representations of the kinds of attachments that people have, the things they care about, what is primary and what secondary, what near and what far in human life, are so consistently counterintuitive as to seem deliberately contrarian. Labeling as "irrationality" the point of view that understands one's own feelings as natural, describing national boundaries as "arbitrary" and "morally insignificant," and national leadership structures as psychologically regressive, Nussbaum seems determined to make people feel bad about themselves.[45] And by offering in place of these old attachments only the most bleached and savorless of substitutes, she seems determined, too, to see that they stay that way. We must, she says, "join hands" across national boundaries and think of ourselves, like the Stoics, as citizens not of some mere country but of the human race; we must try to "make all human beings part of our community of dialogue and concern" (FLC 9). Species identification comes first, although she does allow that what Sen calls a "supplementary allegiance" to those near and dear may come later (114). A keen interest in national identity betrays immaturity, whereas cosmopolitanism, "by contrast, requires a nation of adults, who do not need a childlike dependence upon omnipotent parental figures" ("Kant and Stoic Cosmopolitanism" 11). Adults should be able to content themselves with "reason and the love of humanity, which may," she concedes with an unmistakable tone of condescension, "seem at times less colorful than other sources of belonging" (FLC 15).

The responses from what may be regarded as her target audience suggest that Nussbaum has, at least, succeeded in parting company with her own class. She is criticized from left, right, and center for ignoring the force, not to mention the occasional necessity and frequent benefits, of national identities and national sovereignty. If one were to construct a single comprehensive response, it might be the following: Nussbaum's brand of cosmopolitanism represents a violently self-deluded form of "generous imagining"; it underestimates and undervalues history, ethnicity, religion, family, or indeed any of the special and limited attachments that give us our actual identities; it ignores the most dominant contemporary form of one-world identity, economic globalism, whose version of solidarity is conspicuously empty of moral content; it is blind, too, to the fact that a world polity based on cosmopolitan principles could only be a tyranny; and it fails to consider such alternative concepts as "rooted cosmopolitanism" that give local attachments their due. Only an essay so bizarrely one-sided as Nussbaum's could have elicited from these cosmopolitan and independent-minded thinkers such a display of flag-waving.

As statements about how people ought to think about themselves, Nussbaum's arguments are peculiarly empty and anodyne. Their real interest is disclosed only when we consider dullness itself as one aspect of her attempt to give voice to reason, on behalf of the species. The most rigorously banal of Nussbaum's books, *Cultivating Humanity* (CH) (1997), is also the most intriguing in this respect. The premises of the book are all drawn from contemporary liberal-academic piety: that American higher education is Eurocentric; that students have not been taught to question their own assumptions; that a twofold failure of introspection and of knowledge about the world has made us morally arrogant, regarding other ways of life as deviant, lesser or confused versions of the true path—ours (*see* CH 40). The remedy she proposes is also noncontroversial: to learn about other customs and beliefs so that we will come to understand that our "natural" feelings are historical constructs, and might be changed. Surveying a number of recent developments in the study of religion, non-Western cultures, sexuality, and African-American studies at selected American universities, Nussbaum found that all these constituted gestures in the right direction, and so approved of them all.

The most compelling aspect of this book is its determined vacuity. Nussbaum's work was edgy and iconoclastic, with a fascinating enthusiasm for the pathological, when it praised middle-class heterosexual love in romance-novel terms, and has become oppressively normative as it has turned to homosexual rights and the culture wars. Her prose, once transgressive and "experimental," has lost all its pigmentation as its purpose has been reduced to reassurance and affirmation. Perhaps Michael Jordan, who once refused to endorse Jesse Helms's opponent with the comment that "Republicans buy Nikes, too," would understand Nussbaum's motivation. For *Cultivating Humanity* is clearly directed at a very large audience. It is an audience that, in its indiscriminate immensity, likes to be told that "a new and broader focus for knowledge . . . is necessary to adequate citizenship in a world now characterized by complicated interdependencies" (114); that black Americans need to be included "as inquirers and their history and traditions as part of the curriculum" (165); that "a central role of art is to challenge conventional wisdom and values" (99); that the goal of African-American studies is "truth and understanding for all students, as from their different starting points they approach the inclusive goal of world citizenship" (169); that our approach to education should be "liberal and democratic, informed by a conviction that all citizens are worthy of respect and that certain fundamental freedoms deserve our deepest allegiance" (102). This market is responsive to the need to "learn more about non-Western cultures" (115) and understands that "all students should gain some understanding of the major world religions" (145). They probably already believe that "a classroom is a place of inquiry that should be open to all who will do the work in a spirit of inquiry and mutual respect" (173). They will certainly be cheered by the thought that "Billy Tucker's philosophy class . . . focuses on the Socratic ability to question and to justify, using this as the underpinning of a concept of citizenship" (12). And they will be pleased to know that "Eric Chalmers' English class focuses on the imagination, pursuing the goal of world citizenship through practice in narrative understanding" (13). They may well have had flickering intuitions like those of "Connie Ellis, a forty-three-year-old waitress at Marion's Restaurant in Sycamore, Illinois," who, on the occasion of the Fourth of July, 1996, is reported to have said, "You can't narrow it down to just our country anymore—it's the whole planet" (52). With the exception of her harsh treatment of Brigham Young University, which fails to teach its students that the point of studying religion is to learn to be enlightened citizens of the world, the entire production reeks of the banality of goodness.

Dull though it may be, *Cultivating Humanity* is driven by a quite fantastic project, an effort to become *the subject of experience* for the American academy. To research this book, Nussbaum made extended visits to a core group of fifteen campuses, cultivated "informants" at these and other institutions, and deployed graduate students to interview students and faculty at other institutions and organize the massive files that resulted. She became, for a time, a kind of focal point at which the entire American academy came to countenance, the one mind in the roiling scene capable of informed and dispassionate judgment. Her emollient prose is nothing less than the rhetoric of the nation—even the world—itself, her arguments so fully informed, so saturated with data, that their necessary form is cliché. With *Cultivating Humanity*, cosmopolitanism has become not just a concept but a discursive mode, one that has absorbed into its colorless clarity all contending parties—except, of course, Mormons.

Stanley Fish has described "boutique multiculturalism" as a flabby liberal attempt to respect or celebrate the other that invariably collapses when it confronts some actual practice such as animal sacrifice that offends liberal sympathies.[46] Nussbaum's multiculturalism has its limits, but it is not flabby, for it is explicitly rather than implicitly normative and often bracingly illiberal in its methods. Nowhere is this "Mormon" illiberality more dazzlingly on display than in the already-famous *New Republic* 1999 review of the works of Judith Butler, "The Professor of Parody."[47] According to an argument that Nussbaum had clearly been contemplating for some time, Butler is a leading example of a force "more insidious than provincialism" that is overtaking the American academy and American feminism, a substitution of words for reality, "a verbal and symbolic politics that makes only the flimsiest of connections with the real situations of real women." A spirit of disdainful abstraction suffuses, Nussbaum charges, a conceptually thin, methodologically unsound, rhetorically obscure, elitist critique that is more than satisfied with coyly symbolic gestures of "resistance." On the personal level, Butler strikes Nussbaum as a willing object of uncritical adulation, evasive, bullying, ungenerous, preening, indifferent to Aristotle and Plato—in a word, "evil."[48]

Nussbaum is most affronted by the argument for which Butler is best known, that gender identities are not determined by biological sex but rather by "performance," and can, in principle, be performed any way we wish. In Butler's view, the very conventions that seem to limit our options open up a space of freedom in the form of parodic repetition, ironic and knowing gestures of assent that actually subvert the customs that structure them. The notion that we can "construct" an identity simply by, for example, cross-dressing seems to Nussbaum just as loony as the idea that such an "identity" might be politically "subversive." The gestures of display that, for Butler, loosen the bonds of nature and normativity seem to Nussbaum a feeble acquiescence in the status quo, self-indulgent parodies whose emancipation value in the real world—and reality, in the forms of "real politics," "real justice," and "the real situation of real women" is a constant reference in "The Professor of Parody"—is precisely zero. But the most egregiously self-defeating aspect of Butler's performativity, from Nussbaum's point of view, is its disdain for moral norms, which are treated by Butler only as opportunities for sly but triumphant evasion. Subversion is a good thing, Nussbaum argues, only if it is determined by a normative theory of human behavior that sets its direction and limits. Without a normative account of the human good, performative subversion can run amok. Justice, for example, is "performed," and could be performed differently, and Butler would have no argument against it. Without guardrails, we simply cannot say why subverting conventional gender roles is good and subverting conventional justice is bad. According to Nussbaum, Butler doesn't feel the lack because she is writing to an inbred coterie of like-minded initiates who agree on most things, who have things going pretty much their way, and are more than willing to work with the tools that a largely friendly culture provides.

A fine what-the-hell, rank-breaking, icon-busting quality sweeps through this polemic, every word of which carries conviction. Nussbaum clearly understands her review as a blow to the head of contemporary academic feminism, part of a hostile takeover bid.[49] Once conspicuous for its silence on the question of feminism, even as it advanced distinctly "feminized" qualities of caring and tenderness as high human achievements, Nussbaum's work at century's end was increasingly vocal about its feminism. *Sex and Social Justice* announced a "distinctive conception of feminism" grounded not, like Butler's work, in symbols but in "the real lives of women" (6); *Women and Human Development* pursued "a single clear line of feminist argument" (xiv).[50]

The very clarity of the dispute is, however, more than a bit misleading. Most of the arguments for which Nussbaum criticizes Butler are arguments Nussbaum has made herself. Butler's "hip quietism," her willingness to "[wait] to see what we get," is in some respects indistinguishable from Nussbaum's "moral luck" and "passivity," with the salient difference that Nussbaum is not hip. The special intensity of Nussbaum's attack may reflect her intuition that Butler's focus on the affective structure, the inner acts of dissent and resistance, of the individual subject repeats Nussbaum's own phase-one insistence on personal feelings; by rejecting Butler, Nussbaum may have been attempting to alienate that aspect of her own work.

But the more complex act of dissociation involves ideas Nussbaum continues to promote. She cites, as Butler's primary "contribution," the argument that identities are not given in nature but performed in culture. This is, if not precisely identical to, at least a fraternal twin of the idea of cultural distinctness that has dominated Nussbaum's thinking since around 1990. In *Sex and Social Justice*, Nussbaum devotes a long chapter to "Constructing Love, Desire, and Care" that mimics a number of Butler's arguments—that "society shapes a great deal, if not all, of what is found erotically desirable, and social forms are themselves eroticized" (253–75; 266); that "homosexuality" is a culturally constituted category; that genital organs do not necessarily determine gender identity; that gender is imputed from without as well as experienced from within; that even scientific accounts of sex are inflected by social values; and that "the role of society goes very deep, in shaping matters that our tradition has tended to define as . . . 'private' and 'natural'" (274).[51] Nussbaum seems to have taken in Butler's ideas but, like some snakes that swallow eggs, crush them, and spit out the empty shell, has rejected the person of Butler. It is almost as if the real animus behind Nussbaum's attack was the feeling that "the professor of parody" represented a ludicrously degraded, parodic version—of herself. Nussbaum might insist that the radical difference between her and

Butler is that she believes in good and evil, whereas Butler does not. But given all the positions they hold in common, that difference may not be as radical as, for example, the difference between good and evil.

Nussbaum's entertaining controversies may give the impression that she sees herself in an adversarial role, lobbing grenades over the fortress walls; but as her insistence on reason, humanity, world citizenship, reality, and a "determinate normative conception" of human being suggest, she in fact understands herself to be at the absolute center (WHD 6). The most symptomatic production of phase two is a singular artifact that began to appear with some regularity around 1990 and has been refined many times since then, appearing in *Sex and Social Justice*, and anchoring *Women and Human Development*.[52] The "List of Central Human Functional Capabilities" is an attempt to specify, in a spirit of "Aristotelian essentialism," the capacities that are truly human, whose loss, that is, makes us less than fully human.[53] The list includes such items as:

> Being able to live to the end of a human life of normal length . . . Being able to move freely from place to place; having one's bodily boundaries treated as sovereign . . . having opportunities for sexual satisfaction . . . Being able to use the senses, to imagine, think, and reason—and to do these things in a 'truly human' way . . . Being able to search for the ultimate meaning of life in one's own way. Being able to have pleasurable experiences, and to avoid non-necessary pain . . . [Being able to] experience longing, gratitude, and justified anger. Not having one's emotional development blighted by overwhelming fear and anxiety, or by traumatic events or abuse or neglect . . . being able to be treated as a dignified being whose worth is equal to that of others . . . In work, being able to work as a human being, exercising practical reason . . . Being able to laugh, to play, to enjoy recreational activities . . . having the right to seek employment on an equal basis with others. (WHD 79–80)

The list is intended as a guide to quality-of-life assessments and for legislation and public policy, which otherwise lack clear and publicly available standards of measurement, and represents Nussbaum's most radical attempt to claim the center by defining what a human being is.

The list has provoked much abuse, and not much else. Nussbaum, it has been asserted, has mistaken the ethos of the academic first world for a set of universal norms; by presuming that everybody wants the same things, she has blinded herself to cultural diversity; she has reduced the world's needs to a refrigerator list of to-dos; she has unwittingly suggested that Steven Hawking and Stevie Wonder are less than human; she has begged the question by using such phrases as "in a truly human way" or "to work as a human being" in her account of the human; she has introduced confusion with such phrases as "nonnecessary pain" (in an earlier version, "nonbeneficial" pain) and "justified anger"; she is a sentimental and reductive "family-of-man" liberal who believes that "the human" could exist apart from any culture or ideology; she has mistaken poorly informed arrogance for moral seriousness; and she has altogether ignored the problems associated with the fact that subjective interpretation and judgment must be involved in measuring particular cases against general principles. It is this list that Mary Beard describes as "a frightful muddle which verges on the ludicrous."

All these charges are to some degree justified. Nussbaum has addressed all of them at length, and yet they remain immediately plausible to all academics. Nevertheless, the list is Nussbaum's finest accomplishment in the task she has set herself, the use of philosophical argument to support specific projects of reform. It is the idea of such a list, rather than the list itself, that commands respect for its bold approach to a problem that lies well beyond disciplinary expertise, and the nauseated academic recoil from it is the surest sign of its particular kind of interest and merit. It does aspire to intervene on behalf of a conception of the good, and those who would quarrel with the particulars of the list might wish to propose a different list that reflects a better conception. Or, if they feel that the entire concept of a list of capabilities that could guide assessments and policy is wrongheaded, then they should be prepared to explain the difference between, on the one hand, the principles of "respect for otherness" and "cultural difference" and, on the other, hip quietism.

In *Sex and Social Justice* (SSJ), Nussbaum recounts the scene at an academic conference at which an anthropologist delivered a paper expressing regret that the introduction by the British of smallpox vaccine to India eradicated the cult of Sittala Devi, the goddess to whom people used to pray to avert smallpox. Clearly, the anthropologist concludes, "another example of Western neglect of difference." But just as clearly, Nussbaum replies from the floor, it is better to be healthy than ill, to live rather than to die. "The answer comes back; Western essentialist medicine conceives of things in terms of binary oppositions: life is opposed to death, health to disease. But if we cast away this binary way of thinking, we will begin to comprehend the otherness of Indian traditions." Provoked beyond endurance, Eric Hobsbawm then rises to deliver a blazing indictment of the traditionalism and relativism that prevail in the group, citing examples, including Nazism, of appeals to tradition that have been "politically engineered to support oppression and violence." He is nearly thrown out of the room by a host of enraged Foucauldian "mini-me"s ignorant of who, and what, he is (SSJ 35).

As this highly plausible anecdote suggests, there is a limit to the value of open theorizing, and some circumstances cry out for intervention. Although there is no bright line in space or time to tell us when that limit has been reached, we can say with confidence that needlessly dead bodies lie on one side and remarks by distinguished historians are on the other. The boundaries between disciplines, which preserve them from each other and from the moralizing world, are provisional rather than absolute. All disciplines, like all people, are subject to moral pressures. We live in a thick atmosphere of competing values, energies, and forces, a material atmosphere, as it were, in which choices must be made, actions taken, prescriptions ventured. Well-trained disciplinary professionals, even in the field of ethics, are often reluctant to confront this fact, especially when the issue involves the (animal-sacrificing, dowry-exacting, genital-mutilating) cultural other, because the responsibility it imposes is excessive and cannot always be met by writing more articles, attending more conferences, throwing out more Hobsbawms.

Thus a refusal of the rude closures of morality, which are sometimes theoretically impure or naive in their formulations, often takes the form of a retreat into disciplinarity, as into a cave.[54] Emerging from the cave— Plato's and others—Nussbaum has risked seeming to be muddled and frightful, the sheer magnitude of her task exposing her flaws but giving her work a warty Brobdingnagian grandeur. She has opened herself up not just to hostile arguments, but also to dismissive scorn from her peers. She has raised issues, including "the human," that simply cannot be addressed within the limits of a single discipline and seem, from a disciplinary perspective, unprofessional, even ridiculous. But one will find, in history, many people now revered who were once considered to be "on the verge" of the ludicrous. If intellectuals feel that risking scorn by raising large and intractable issues is a bad thing, then perhaps we should reassess what we are doing and why we are doing it.

There is a chance, after all, that some form of this list might fall into the right hands, and be used to do some good. If so, it will be possible to say of the present moment that Nussbaum—having gotten everything wrong, having set out on a path of monstrous arrogance, having deluded herself that she could exceed not just intellectual but national and even psychological boundaries, having identified herself directly and preposterously with reason, truth, reality, and humanity—is now, nearing the end of her marathon, on the brink of being useful.

Phase three should be worth waiting for.

CHAPTER 4

Criticism as Symptom: Slavoj Žižek and the End of Knowledge

1. As Other

With the publication in 1989 of *The Sublime Object of Ideology*, it was immediately apparent that the author, an unknown Slovenian scholar named Slavoj Žižek, had mastered all the skills required by academic discourse. An accomplished scholar who could boast of multilingual familiarity with an immense range of materials, a philosophical sophistication that few could match, a thorough mastery of the most difficult and cryptic texts, and a witty and engaging style, Žižek seemed to be possessed of every possible gift. Incorporating arguments and examples from literature, linguistics, psychoanalysis, film studies, philosophy, opera, theology, political theory, electronic technology, history, popular culture, and current events, he seemed to be attempting the impossible, a total theorization of the world. More metaphysical than the Germans, more pop culture than the Americans, more empirical than the British, and more theoretical than the French, Žižek combined all these traditions into a discourse of unprecedented heterogeneity. That his arguments, conducted with immense assurance and even bravado, ran precisely counter to the reigning tastes in all these traditions—he preferred Hegel to Kant and Lacan to Derrida; regarded philosophy, political economy, and psychoanalysis as entirely compatible; and held pop cultural artifacts to be the best possible examples of metaphysical concepts—only confirmed the impression that he had somehow escaped all of the normal constraints on thinking. Most impressive was that, even in what was apparently his first work, Žižek displayed no trace of apprenticeship, and gave little sign that he had ever been a petitioner at the gate of academia, earnestly demonstrating competence to his betters by making modest interventions in limited fields.

It was as if, developing in the darkness of the communist old world where everything was forbidden, he had never been taught that, out there in the free world, inquiry is also restricted by invisible codes and protocols, and there are limits to what an argument, a discourse, a discipline are permitted to address; and as if, his productivity having been dammed up by the conditions of academic life in Ljubljana, he burst forth fully formed at the first possible moment, his prodigious learning in place, his intellectual style set, and his commitments established.[1]

But within the general admiration excited by Žižek's early work could be detected signs of an obscure disquiet whose sources were deeper than the (not negligible) facts that few could pronounce his name or the name of his city, and that his very country could not be found in most atlases. So accessible in some respects, his work was mysterious and disconcerting in others. His background, the audience he imagined himself to be addressing, or even his overall intentions could be easily deduced. And some discerned in his phenomenal excess a barely concealed challenge, even a hostility, to Western scholarship and the political-social world in which it circulated.

Žižek is such an immediately appealing figure that he has always been in serious danger of being merely admired. But if we are really to understand Žižek's work, we must first confront his more alien attributes; we must engage his strangeness, which can be almost overpowering, before we can cull his contributions to knowledge. As a first step in understanding Žižek, then, we need something like an inventory of those aspects of his work that resist assimilation to the Western, especially the North American, context in which he has had such striking success. Only then will we be in a position to identify the core commitments that inform his work, the interlinked set of propositions that laces it together; only after having done that will we be able to determine what is and what might be most productive in his thought in a Western context.

Perhaps the most immediately apparent quality of Žižek's discourse is its breathtaking rapidity. He seems to bound over the tops of peaks others have laboriously scaled one at a time, seizing complex arguments in a masterly and synthetic manner that diagnoses others' hard-won conclusions as symptoms of a common failure to grasp the truth, a failure he immediately rectifies. His texts blast through the discursive version of the sound barrier, passing the point at which they might be considered simply accelerated versions of ordinary discourse and becoming something else altogether.

The standard format of argumentation is so deeply ingrained in academic culture that it generally goes unremarked. An argument begins with a hypothesis, a testable characterization of the data in a limited field. It proceeds by such means as adducing evidence, drawing inferences, proposing counterarguments, probing provisional conclusions in a spirit of skeptical inquiry, and eliminating contradictions, all of which lead toward a conclusion, a summative statement whose various elements have passed through the fires of rigorous and disinterested testing. This process functions as the form of fairness, an agreement to display the means by which a conclusion is achieved to ensure against the mere reiteration of prejudice or the interference of desire. Although this process cannot, of course, altogether eliminate flaws of observation, description, or reasoning, it does at least invite the scholarly conversation to continue, because conclusions arrived at in this way can either be challenged on the grounds of procedural flaws or can serve as the starting point for further investigation.

Žižek's work, by contrast, seems to be formed almost entirely of endgames in which the sense of conclusion, with its payoffs and rewards, is always present. A sharply diminished experience of orderly progress is compensated for by the continual feeling of arrival and by the constant surprises afforded by an exceptionally rich and quirky use of examples, which I will discuss in more detail later in this chapter. The effect is that of a stream of nonconsecutive units arranged in arbitrary sequences that solicit a sporadic and discontinuous attention. Žižek does not seem to believe that books should be *about* something; he reproduces his central themes compulsively regardless of the ostensible subject. He seems to write for the browser, for even the earnest reader who begins at page one has the constant impression of having opened to a page somewhere in the middle. This sense of an endless middle is achieved by reducing the conventional middle to almost zero. The typical Žižekian unit of discourse—a wittily titled passage of between five and fifteen pages—begins abruptly with the kind of confident assertion commonly associated with the conclusion; there is no phase of doubt, no pretense of unprejudiced inquiry, only a series of demonstrations, exemplifications, and restatements. Informed throughout by the spirit of conclusion, these units do not, in themselves, conclude, but simply gutter out at the end, like a sparkler; no sense of fairness attends the terminus and no invitation to further work by others is implied. The front loading of the argument reflects a distinctive understanding of the means and ends of thinking. The standard format supports and is supported by liberal democracy: its attempt to be presuppositionless corresponds to the assumption that the ultimate good is freedom and justice for all; the interval of doubt or uncertainty correlates roughly with free elections, when the place of power is momentarily (if only hypothetically) empty; and the submission of hypotheses to skeptical probing reflects at a distance the belief that truth should be independent of power and desire, that the best hypothesis should prevail. Structured as an invitation to challenges, this format silently presumes its own dominance, in the same way that liberal democracy presumes that the periodic upheavals it invites will, in the end, leave liberal democracy itself untouched and even strengthened. Emerging at the end of "actually-existing socialism," Žižek's work does not share the democratic provenance of the Western academy, and some of the distinctive features of his discourse might be seen as reflections or reflexes of their context.[2] What seems like a nearly frantic impatience in his work might, for example, suggest the volatile political and even military situation in Yugoslavia during the period in which he was coming of age; the declarative confidence with which he insists that the truth of things is *precisely the reverse* of received or conventional wisdom could be grasped both as a utopian leap out of Stalinism into an unmapped future and as a "totalitarian remainder," an emphatic habit of mind that was learned early, as the preferred, dialectical manner of refuting capitalist self-assurance.

Such theories are, of course, highly speculative, but Žižek's work invites such speculations. The fact to be explained is that Žižek does not grope toward certainty but begins there, and strives only for clarity of exposition. He writes not to open up a field of investigation, but to establish for the reader the truth he has already achieved. The introductory character of much of his work—*Sublime Object of Ideology* (SOI) is "an introduction to some of the fundamental concepts of Lacanian psychoanalysis" (SOI 7) and *Looking Awry* is subtitled *An Introduction to Jacques Lacan through Popular Culture*—actually signals a retrospective orientation of the kind seen in the pedagogical style that seeks not to provide a methodology that will teach a man to fish, but simply to provide the results of an unexplained methodology—the fish itself. This orientation is compounded by Žižek's proselytizing emphasis on the third or final phase of Lacan's teaching, the phase of achieved wisdom and ultimate radicality.[3] Even in those texts not explicitly labeled as introductions, the aim of explication, with its Owl-of-Minerva belatedness, emerges at moments when Žižek announces that something—a scene from a film, a joke, a cliché—constitutes the "very definition" of the Lacanian *objet petit a*, the Real, the gaze, the Borromean knot, enjoyment, the traumatic kernel, radical Evil, the Thing, subjective destitution, the *point de capiton*, the formulae of sexuation, as if definition had been his point all along.

The Žižekian difference is condensed in his exotic use of examples. For example:

> The comparison of German, French, and "Anglo-Saxon" toilets ("In a traditional German lavatory, the hole in which the shit disappears after we flush water is way in front, so that the shit is first laid out for us to sniff at and inspect . . . "), used as an illustration of "ideological perception" in which the truth is "out there"[4]

> Hans-Jürgen Syberberg's film of Wagner's *Parsifal*, in which the "wound" of Amfortas is "carried on a pillow beside him, as a nauseous partial object out of which, through an aperture resembling vaginal lips, trickles blood," a perfect example of the Lacanian *sinthome*, a signifier that, by existing outside the symbolic network, discloses the anamorphic "Real of enjoyment" (SOI 77)

> The "close-the-door button" in elevators, "a totally dysfunctional placebo which is placed there just to give individuals the impression that they are somehow participating, contributing to the speed of the elevator journey," an instance of the many forms of "fake participation" available to people in a "post-modern political process"[5]

> The skinheads who, when asked why they beat up foreigners, reply that they are concerned about cultural dilution and the loss of community; then, when pressed further, that their true worry is economic consequences among the working class caused by immigrant labor; then, meeting skepticism, that they simply enjoy beating people up; and finally, that they had been neglected as children and had not known a mother's love—an instance of several principles, including the way in which external or reflexive attributes, in this case the discourse of the social worker, can determine a subject's sense of identity.[6]

In *For They Know Not What They Do* (FTKN), Žižek describes the commonsense understanding of the metaphysics of meaning according to which the example is "just an external, passive resource which enables us to give plastic expression to our thought," a necessary prop, yet one that constantly threatens to become excessively seductive or distracting through its wealth of "external, particular content."[7] This understanding was refuted, Žižek says, by Hegel, who insisted that all identity is contingent on the conditions of its emergence, determined by "external" features that are simply posited retroactively as internal, like the skinheads' self-image as victims of neglect. The prime Hegelian example of the way examples work is the figure of Christ, the "most sublime example," Žižek says, of the principle that all of creation reflects the divine Idea (FTKN 42). Exemplifying exemplification, Christ stands at the very point at which principle and instance become indistinguishable in a kind of short circuit, and thus the point at which the metaphysics of meaning, with its dominant idea and passive instance, becomes unraveled in a disruptive "exchange of properties." Many of Žižek's most sublime examples are exemplified by Hegel's Christ, not illustrating so much as embodying the truth of the concept, in forms so compelling that they contend with the principle they should be illustrating.

A passage in the recent *Did Somebody Say Totalitarianism?*[8] illustrates the situation. Attempting to explain the "mistake" of the melancholic who in Freud interprets the present lack of a given object of desire as its loss, Žižek adduces, over the course of a rollicking ten-page section, a few helpful examples: Kant's notion of the "paralogism of the pure capacity to desire," a scene from Graham Greene's *The End of the Affair*, Hegel on the Crusades, Adorno on the conducting style of Wilhelm Fürtwangler, Giorgio Agamben's thoughts on melancholy, a relationship depicted in Edith Wharton's *The Age of Innocence*, Shostakovich's Eighth String Quartet, a joke about gypsies and the rain, a Lacanian refinement of a Freudian formulation, the popularity in the gay community of the film *Brief Encounter*, gay opposition to liberal policies, anamorphosis and the "sublime object" of ideology, the integral distortion of the "space of Ideality," the *objet petit a* as a "negative magnitude," the temporality of the Christian doctrine of the Incarnation, and the phenomenon of conversion (142–52). The effect is perfectly equivocal: the very abundance of the passage implies, more powerfully than any argument could, that the principle of "lack is not loss" constitutes a truth so fundamental that the entire world testifies to it; but, through an exchange of properties, the flood of examples also overwhelms the very principle of lack that unleashes them. So dazzling is the cataract of instances that the idea itself seems a mere pretext, a prop for its props, an occasion for its own undoing.

Examples are supposed to make things clear, but Žižek's cascading examples have a declarifying effect that extends well beyond the particular principle-instance dyad. If the conventional use of examples presupposes a metaphysics of meaning and, in the background, an orderly hegemonic social system, Žižek's examples, which reflect neither a metaphysics nor a physics of meaning, with neither idea nor material instance dominating, imply a far more uncertain and volatile arrangement of forces. In one respect, the bracing implication of his practice is that the world is full of thought, suffused with concept in ways we never suspected: the opportunities for theory expand as the domain of the meaningful is enlarged in a way that betokens a world of possibility. But in another respect, his examples suggest a closed universe, in which nothing is permitted to be random: constant theorizing is obligatory and simple perception requires the positing of connections between formal matrices and contingent particulars. A virtually totalitarian world in which everything is connected and significant looms up behind his texts, which seem to be produced by a mind that is radical to a suffocating degree.[9] In Žižek, pleasures and duties are, like examples and concepts, ambiguously intermixed, as he relentlessly extracts conceptual implications from the most random dreck of culture and discovers material or contingent impurities in every theoretical notion.

So unsettled is Žižek's work in this regard that the very idea of a discipline—an orderly inquiry producing falsifiable results in a limited field—is placed under considerable pressure. It is difficult to know exactly what he is, what field he occupies, because he is so heavily invested in a number of discourses, all of which seem to be immediately available to him. His work in film studies alone would qualify him as a leading film scholar and theorist. His references to popular culture evidence a prolonged and ecstatic immersion. And yet he is capable of an exceptionally astringent and sustained metaphysical rigor; by comparison with Žižek in full Hegelian gust, Richard Rorty, Robert Nozick, Michael Walzer, Charles Taylor, Stanley Cavell, Bernard Williams, Alasdair MacIntyre, and Thomas Nagel seem to be pop psychologists disseminating edifying ideas in the Great Books tradition.[10] Credentialed in philosophy and psychoanalysis, Žižek simply overrides any conflict of the faculties by practicing all at once. But despite multiple expertises, he seems to belong to no discipline whatsoever inasmuch as he manifestly takes holistic rather than sectoral knowledge as his aim.

Žižek's content is as aberrant as his form. He is often described as a Marxist, a commitment that could inform almost any kind of scholarly work. But the difference between his Marxism and that of Anglo-American academics can hardly be overstated. Especially in the English-speaking academy, the most salient Marxian contributions are the critique of political economy, the invention of ideology critique, the demystifying insistence on the concrete-historical at the expense of the philosophical-abstract, and the broadly oppositional political stance. Although often highly sophisticated in a theoretical sense, Anglo-American Marxism conceives of itself as a progressive, forward-looking discourse of material reality. Žižek's Marx, by contrast, is not the originator of a discourse, but a key figure in the Enlightenment tradition that began with Descartes, continued through Kant and Hegel, and culminated—no further theoretical advance is anticipated—in Lacan. Marx did not disprove in advance the individualist bias of psychoanalysis; he precipitated Freud, and thus anticipated Lacan, by "inventing the symptom," as Žižek puts it in *Sublime Object.*

Žižek's assessment of ordinary social reality is also nonstandard in a Marxist context, for he pins no hopes on the development of class consciousness, scientific consciousness, or indeed consciousness of any kind; in fact, he describes "reality," the sense people have of their world and how it works, bluntly as an ideological fantasy that we ratify and extend without knowing it. He is equally hard on utopian political visions, or any projection to a postdialectical state beyond class conflict: for Žižek, any such projection, as with any identification with the Cause, is inherently "Stalinist." Worse yet, from the point of view of orthodox academic Marxism, Žižek defines the dialectical method Marx derived from Hegel not as the steady advance on truth by way of confrontational testing but rather as a corrosive, anti-monist instrument of negation and desubstantialization.

Unlike most theoretical Marxists, including the Frankfurt School of Adorno and Horkheimer, Žižek does not dissociate Marx from actually existing socialism. Although in recent years such texts as *A Contribution to the Critique of Political Economy, The German Ideology,* and the *Grundrisse* have commanded the attention of those academics who continue to find Marx's writings theoretically productive, Žižek turns to the radically outdated *Manifesto,* which he finds uncannily prescient in recognizing the incipient postmodernism of capitalism's speculative economy, in which "all things solid melt into thin air."[11] The theoretical, and more than theoretical, error made by Marx resided, Žižek argues, not in the analysis of capitalism's madly destructive form of self-enhancement, which Žižek regards as an analytical triumph, but in the naive faith that the contradictions of capitalism could be overcome in a pure unleashed productivity not dependent on periodic wars and economic crises—in other words, in Communism. This dream of a spiral of productivity unchecked by contradictions was, Žižek insists, one of capitalism's *own* ideological fantasies. Thus, in a gesture that separates him from the vast majority of academic Marxists, Žižek argues that theoretical socialism was "a subspecies of capitalism."[12]

It might seem that Žižek's Marxism would be compatible with the emphasis on spectrality announced in Derrida's *Specters of Marx,* in which

Marx's texts are read deconstructively, against the materialist grain.[13] But Žižek is always critical of deconstruction, if respectful of Derrida, for its failure to recognize the positive, productive effects of such deconstructive antifetishes as difference, negation, spacing, iterability, and so forth. These factors do not simply interrupt or impede identity, Žižek insists, they constitute it. And this insight, he says, is Hegel's contribution to the tradition that includes Marxism. For most Marxists, Hegel is the philosopher who gave history its proper place in philosophy and grounded abstract reason in the real world. Hegel was, Marxists argue, fatally flawed in several respects—his panlogicism, his belief in the gradual self-realization of a World-Spirit, his understanding of the State as the worldly custodian of reason—but he did articulate the notion of totality that has served Marxism as the most comprehensive name for a condition beyond individualism, partial knowledge, class conflict, exploitation, and alienation.[14] For Žižek, Hegel should be revered by Marxists for precisely the opposite contribution—his discovery that alienation is the condition of all identity, a lesson imparted chiefly not by *The Philosophy of History* but by *The Phenomenology of Spirit* and *The Science of Logic*.[15] Žižek stresses the Hegelian argument that there is no subject without a gap separating the object from its notion, to which he adds the insistence that the subject is nothing but this gap in substance, this noncoincidence with itself.[16] Any closing of this gap, as when we think of the Nation as a true Home, or the Party as a direct agent of History, constitutes a virtually incestuous misprision, a version of Mother as Supreme Good. From Marx to the Frankfurt School and beyond, alienation was figured as the disaster wrought upon human beings by capitalism. For Žižek, it is the plain truth of the human condition. In this as in other respects, Žižek's Marxism seems not so much a variant of the Marxism still found in the American academy as the dialectical opposite of it.

Some differences might be attributed to the fact that Žižek was trained not in the liberal West but in Yugoslavia, where the reading of Marx was compulsory, not voluntary, and directly political, not theoretical, in its application.[17] In *Did Somebody Say Totalitarianism?*, Žižek demonstrates a thorough historical awareness of the obscene cruelty of the Stalinist and fascist regimes and suggests that the profoundly stupid cruelty of totalitarian regimes is more theoretically pertinent than theory itself in the dark illumination it casts on the institutions of the West, where the term "totalitarian" is often used, in a way that to Žižek suggests gross complacency, to describe the absolute other. The "close-the-door button" in elevators exemplifies the illusions of freedom and agency in contemporary democracy, illusions unavailable in nondemocratic societies, where the truth is confronted more directly in the form of a short circuit between authority and brutality. Žižek is virtually alone—joined only by a few, including his former wife Renata Salecl and other Slovenian scholars whose work he promotes and helps to publish[18]—in finding in Stalinism a direct index of the truth.

Stalinism becomes especially interesting, from the psychoanalytic point of view, in its insistence on the public display of loyalty. Coerced confessions, cynical professions of solidarity, and show trials—the most extreme examples of this display, in which an innocent person would concur with false accusations out of fidelity to the Cause[19]—all put consciousness or mind on the public stage, entirely separated from the private world of the subject. In so doing, they provide Žižek with material for one of his most ingenious projects, the redescription of the unconscious as a property of the world, a public outside rather than an inner fastness, a sanctuary known only to the introspective subject. Amfortas's hideous wound, carried on a pillow, could stand as a type of all Žižek's examples of the ways in which mental or abstract phenomena—the psychoanalytical symptom, the ideological formation, belief of all kinds, the capitalist system—are not inner phenomena, but "precisely the reverse," fully externalized material facts. Instructed by the Stalinist emphasis on "objective conditions," Žižek is uncannily attentive to the ways in which reflection is staged in the world. The Marxian commodity, for example, constitutes a "belief" in capitalism that relieves individuals, who think themselves free of all ideology, of the necessity of individual assent: the things themselves believe for them. Thus belief is like a "Tibetan prayer wheel," on which you write a prayer on a piece of paper, put the rolled paper into a wheel, and turn the wheel automatically, without thinking, so that you are "praying through the medium of the wheel. The beauty of it all," he concludes with a characteristic flourish, "is that in my psychological interiority I can think about whatever I want, I can yield to the most dirty and obscene fantasies, and it does not matter because—to use a good old Stalinist expression—whatever I am thinking, *objectively* I am praying" (SOI 34).

So, too, with the chorus of classical tragedy, and with canned laughter on television, which do our lamenting and our laughing for us; in all these forms, our thinking assumes the form of the un-thought, even the other-than-thought. Žižek is fond of an anecdote from Freud's *Psychopathology of Everyday Life* in which a woman's chance complaint about her fingernail enables Freud to unravel the entire complex crisis.[20] There is more and better thought, Žižek argues, in that woman's fingernail than in her mind. Even some "thoughts" are externalizations of other thoughts. Anti-Semitism, for example, represents a displacement onto "the Jew" of vague inchoate anxieties arising from social divisions, a displacement so effective that, to those in its grip, no evidence is capable of refuting it and all evidence appears to confirm it. If, in Hegel, "the Spirit is a bone"—a witticism Žižek repeats often—then in Žižek, the subject can be discovered only in alienated forms. Where orthodox Marxism opposes metaphysics to modes of production, and liberalism distinguishes between the private and public spheres, Žižek sees only an exchange of properties, a series of short circuits.

Žižek is unimpressed by the theoretical versions of common sense, and keeps discovering ways in which perception, judgment, and consciousness themselves are circumvented, deceived, or confused about their own natures. Ordinary rational thinking, he believes, is generally devoted to the production of orderly apologias for unreflected enjoyment, or *jouissance*, and so actually inhibits genuine insight, which is only obtained by "identification with the symptom" or "traversing the fantasy." One can get to the truth not by trying to think more clearly or to see the thing as it really is, but by embracing so fully the fantasies we inhabit that their fantasmatic nature becomes inescapable. Real cognitive insight, Žižek contends, is available in dreams, in which we confront not some little wish, as many Freudians would have it, but the traumas at the core of our being. Psychoanalysis, for him, is concerned with truth, not meaning, and the truth is often that there is no meaning, that structures of meaning are themselves fantasies. In the intellectual community, such views are, to put it gently, uncommon.

Early exposure to actually existing social force seems to have immunized Žižek to the charms of Foucault, whose account of pervasive, decentered power is, by comparison with the vividly present individuals who exercised power in its Stalinist or neo-Stalinist Yugoslav forms, bleached to the point of insipidity—dull as well as false. What Foucault's account lacks, in addition to a (stupid, brutal, often ridiculous) human face, is the dimension of obscene enjoyment that so manifestly characterizes Stalinist power. Žižek has a richly comic appreciation of the contorted circumstances in which people find themselves in totalitarian regimes; so oddly appreciative in so many ways are Žižek's invocations of "the good old days" when power was *mis à nu* so that people could actually see its unsublated workings, that, if it were not for the detailed, direct, and compassionate gaze at the functioning of high totalitarianism in *Did Somebody Say Totalitarianism?*, one might almost be persuaded that Žižek sustained a certain Stalinist nostalgia. He seems fully aware of the queasy charm exerted over Western audiences by his familiar references to Stalinism as a set of practices whose engaging artlessness one can understand. Such audiences generally imagine themselves to be in the business of "questioning received opinion" and "challenging prevailing assumptions," but the received admiration for Foucault and the prevailing horror in the contemplation of totalitarianism are not considered to be among the negotiable positions.

Ultimately, what totalitarianism discloses is the truth of Lacan, who functions in Žižek's thinking as a theoretical but actually existing Cause, if not precisely as a Stalin. The character of Žižek's adherence, even adhesion, to Lacan is unique in today's intellectual climate, where a withholding of full approval is regarded as an essential element of self-respect. For Žižek, the doxa of Lacan are not to be submitted to skeptical testing, but confirmed by any means necessary. Žižek conceives of his own project as the dot on Lacan's "i," or perhaps as the announcement that Lacan himself is the dot on the "i," the final link in the mighty chain of Western philosophical reflection, which includes Christianity, with its traumatic interruption of human life by the divine, its rejection of reason and its emphasis on believing in "the impossible"[21]; the philosophy of Descartes, with its identification of the subject as a pure point of subjectivity, a "vanishing gap baptized by Lacan 'subject of the signifier'"[22]; Kant's articulation of a domain, the moral law, that lay "beyond the pleasure principle"; Hegel's purification of Kantian thinking of all traces of the thing-in-itself and his emphasis on the self-alienation of the subject; Marx's transformation of the Hegelian dialectic into an analytical tool capable of conceptualizing such material forces as economics and history and his discovery that crises in the system actually reveal its innermost, symptomatic truth; and, finally and triumphantly, Lacan's psychoanalysis, which, especially as inflected by Althusser, fully realizes the universal dimension of all the above by constructing an account of the human subject grounded in Saussurean linguistics.[23] Žižek tries to render all this—"Lacanian 'dogmatics' (in the theological sense of the term)"—in the most attractive and crystallized pedagogy possible.[24] He plainly prefers the rigid, even antiacademic organization of the Lacanian community, with its angry doctrinal disputes and refusal of dialogue or mediation, to the Western academy's genteel cultivation of disinterested inquiry. His discourse is strewn with phrases such as, "Our Lacanian commitment compels us to conclude," that would simply never be found in standard academic discourse, where every effort is made to seem, and sometimes even to be, presuppositionless.

Žižek is perhaps most alien in that, unlike even other oppositional scholars or critics, he does not see himself as a member of the scholarly community. He notes that whereas most academic writers give a little glimpse, beneath an impassive professional style, of a "so-called lively personality," he is "the author of books whose excessively and compulsively 'witty' texture serves as the envelope of a fundamental *coldness* . . . . I always felt a deep sympathy for Monty Python, whose excessive humour also signals an underlying stance of profound disgust with life."[25] He has a keen interest in the formal dimensions of concepts, which can be expressed in formulae, graphs, and mathemes. The extended, muscular expositions of Hegelian logic that many readers page through are undoubtedly more important to the author than the more accessible parts that seem to express the "real" Žižek. And even those friendlier passages do not conform to the protocols of sociability that mark especially American social and academic discourse. They do not reveal a personality as such: their pace and density, their way of rocketing from one improbable example to another, one discourse or discipline to another, fill the air with astonishment and leaves the reader gasping. Žižek's arguments issue from an impersonal source that seeks not self-expression, much less dialogue, but a hammering form of persuasion. A bristling, dazzling surface with no tantalizing intimations of hidden depths or partially concealed subjectivity, Žižek's work gives the impression of a mind wholly saturated with the task of argument, a mind that actively refuses mediation and rejects intimacy.

Žižek presents, then, a deeper challenge to the norm than many realize, and forces us to determine what kind of relation his work has to the standard format, the ordinary canons of argument, and the society that sustains them. Is he a sublime theorist, a perfectly equipped academic mind capable of transcending the limitations that inhibit others, or an obscenity-obsessed Thing emerging from the black lagoon of Stalinism, dedicated to the overthrow of Western academic thought? We cannot simply "refuse the blackmail," as Žižek would put it, of making such a choice by regarding his work in another light altogether as a laying-bare of the mechanism, a naked disclosure of the actually existing premises that normally function as deep structure in academic discourse. For this option would require us to admit the inadmissible: that the phase of probing or testing in a standard argument is an engineered illusion, a charade performed for the benefit of the credulous en route to a predetermined conclusion; that what appears to be rational argumentation is actually a subtle doctrinal practice designed not to arrive at truth by "legitimate" means but simply to explicate a truth already possessed as a matter of faith; that disciplines achieve their specificity by making an unsupportable claim to have eliminated all that is not in their domain. If we took Žižek as a guide to the real character of conventional academic methods and practices, we would be forced to revise—actually, to discard—all our assumptions about academic work and indeed about rational thought as such. For if Žižek's practice were to be universalized, the result would be the destruction of the very idea of a field, a specialized professional discourse that arrives at a true account of a limited domain by progressive and rational means. It would mean the end of life as we know it.

Another option presents itself. We could simply set aside the question of the relation between Žižek and the scholarly community and consider his work as an extraordinarily developed reflection of the kind of milieu found in university towns—especially, perhaps, towns in which the university itself offers a stimulus to, but no real home for, free inquiry, towns such as Ljubljana in the good old days. It is possible to deduce from Žižek's remarkable work not only the movements of a formidable mind—to be frank, the most extraordinary scholarly mind of his generation—but also, as a kind of shadow, the pub-and-coffeehouse culture in which he might have come of age. Picture the scene at a bar after a raucous meeting of the Slovene Society for Theoretical Psychoanalysis in the heady atmosphere of new and widening freedoms, including imminent elections, in the late 1980s. Imagine a regular crowd of students, journalists, artists, filmmakers, poets, actors, all stifled in various ways by a political culture that tolerated but did not fully support them—thus producing a sort of democracy of unrealized talent—a noisy and disorderly group, the clink of glasses, an old jukebox, occasional small fights breaking out in corners of the room resolved with laughter and another round—and in the thick of it, a bearded young spellbinder, an academic Prince Hal (actually running for the presidency!) taking on all comers.[26] To some, such a scene constitutes an academic heaven, but it is more accurately considered as para-academic, for it exists not in the university but on its margins. Žižek's work, too, might be considered para-academic rather than sublime-academic, anti-academic, or essential-academic. Indeed, if Žižek were taken as a model for normal academic practice, the old notion that the purpose of a liberal education is to provide one with conversational artillery for the proverbial cocktail party would acquire a fantastic new validation.

2. And Otherness

The most disconcerting and the most entertaining feature of Žižek's thought is his habit of insisting that common knowledge—especially the common knowledge of self-aware, sophisticated thinkers—is completely mistaken, that it represents a misreading of material fact and an evasion of theoretical necessity that produces not a near miss but a precise reversal of the truth. The essential Žižekian claim is that our judgments, convictions, and even our very perceptions reflect a remarkably stubborn and ingenious will to self-delusion, which he can diagnose and correct. This claim, which might be considered the founding gesture of philosophy itself, has,

in Žižek's case, specific antecedents, including Hegel's dialectical negation and Marx's ideological camera obscura. But the most immediate and
pertinent source of Žižek's insistence on reversing common knowledge is
Lacan's reading of Saussure.

For Lacan, as for a great many other nonlinguists in the world of critical
or literary theory over the past thirty years, Saussure is virtually the only
theoretical linguist worth discussing. Lacan begins his pivotal 1957 seminar, "The agency of the letter in the unconscious or reason since Freud," by
announcing that he will "trust only those assumptions that have already
proven their value by virtue of the fact that language through them has
attained the status of an object of scientific investigation."[27] Those assumptions are contained in Saussure's *Course in General Linguistics*, a work that
has brought about nothing less than "a revolution in knowledge" (149).
Lacan makes no reference, even in subsequent publications, to any other
linguistic science, any further revolution; for him, it is Saussure alone
who provides the compelling scientific guarantee of the truth of language,
which in turn confirms the truth of Freud and leads directly to the truth
of man.

Given his profound respect for Saussure, Lacan's grasp of Saussurean
linguistics is strikingly partial, even distorted. When, for example, Lacan
appropriates Saussure's figure of "S over s," not only do signifier and signified change positions so that the signified is on the bottom, but, in a far
more significant innovation, the function of the bar between the signifier
and the signified is reversed. For Saussure, the bar joins the two, producing
one two-sided entity, like the front and back of a piece of paper[28]; for Lacan,
the bar divides them, so that the concept, the signified, "slides" perpetu-
ally beneath the phonemic signifier, which is incapable of grasping or adequately representing it. Lacan is in fact relatively indifferent to the signified,
and rarely mentions the composite of signifier and signified, the sign: the
thematics of his account are in general dominated by figures not of composition but of decomposition and disunity. Moreover, Lacan simply overrides
Saussure's account of language as a social product "deposited in the brain"
and replaces it with the claim that language constitutes human subjectivity
from the beginning. Such a claim had long been part of the humanistic tradition, but Lacan takes Saussure in an altogether different direction. Noting
that no aspect of the signifier—not the arbitrary relations among signifiers
that comprise the system of signs, nor the acoustic image required by the
signifier, nor the elements or "letters" of which the signifier is composed—
can be considered meaningful in itself, much less human, Lacan argues that
language constitutes a break or cut in human subjectivity.

Lacan's substitution of the material and mechanistic for the immaterial and ideal serves Žižek as a kind of template for his reversals, in which he argues for, to put it in the most general terms, the "agency of the letter" as a traumatic or senseless force operating within the human mind, an "object in subject" that blocks all liberal-humanistic pieties about moral, political, or cognitive freedom. For Žižek, language is a machine in the ghost of the Cartesian subject, a principle of automatism at the dead center of our fantasies of autonomy. And so we go, by a kind of metonymic sliding, from Saussure's account of language as a system of orderly social integration to Lacan's isolation of the signifier to Žižek's assertion that language is "a Stalinist phenomenon" (SOI 174). Many thinkers are crucial to Žižek's project, but it is ultimately on the distant and debatable authority of Lacan's "scientific" signifier-centered account of language that he bases his arguments that the unconscious is "ex-timate" rather than intimate, that naming is a retroactive and "arbitrary" act of constitution, and that the surest symptom of ideological thinking is the sober conviction that you have transcended ideology in a clean perception of reality.[29]

It is in the field of ideology—a field dominated by the signified—that the polemical force of Žižek's reversals of doxa is most strongly marked. Žižek clearly has nothing in common with those conservative thinkers who periodically declare an "end of ideology." Perhaps less clear, but even more extreme, is his radical divergence from those post-Marxist thinkers whose position on ideology is, like his, rooted in language. Marxists from Vološinov on have achieved sophisticated understandings of ideology by focusing on language as what Raymond Williams calls a material social practice, the means by which social evaluations are implanted in the individual. Agreeing with this understanding of language as far as it goes, Žižek proceeds to discount everything that occupies the attention of most such thinkers, beginning with the identifiably ideological features of a given language or discourse. He concentrates instead on the single brute fact of materiality—whose most elemental form is the "letter," the material support for the signified—as such. Ideology, for Žižek, has little to do with covert messages that whatever is is right, or that the ruling class is really doing an admirable job. The most general form of ideology in Žižek's sense is the deep-laid conviction that the subject is harmonious in itself and can be integrated without remainder into the social-symbolic order; the prototype for this faith is the belief that reality can translate directly and non-arbitrarily into a signifier.

Williams and his colleague on the British left, Stuart Hall, took language as the key to ideology in large part because they wanted to identify possibilities for self-determination and transformation beyond those envisioned by the vulgar Marxist economic determinism of the Second International. The reason that Hall retrieved Vološinov's claim that the sign is the arena of class struggle and that Williams described language as a dynamic, creative, and self-transforming practice was that both wanted to detach class struggle from violence and make it seem more responsive to directed effort, even to theoretical reflection, than it otherwise might.[30] Žižek refuses all such accommodations to intelligence and rejects all such earnestness as a rancid ideological fantasy. In his terms, we could only step out of this fantasy by making the gesture Williams criticized in Vološinov, "isolating the sign" from its social matrix, and doing so to lay appropriate emphasis on its arbitrary, rigidly deterministic, and mechanical character. Language is not, for Žižek, the meaning-saturated arena of class struggle, but its root cause: we fight each other partly as a way of evading the painful recognition that, as a consequence of being linguistic creatures, we are internally conflicted.

From some, we hear that others are trapped in ideology, but not us; from others, we hear that we're all in it, but that this is not necessarily a bad thing. Žižek tells us that we are all in it, and it is a very bad thing. We are all in it because ideology—contrary to the prevailing and traditional view that it blocks or redirects the free expression of individual or social desire—is a direct expression of unconscious desire. And it is a bad thing because such desire, whose kernel is "filthy enjoyment," leads away from the truth and toward dreams of wholeness or integration that produce, as necessary supports, such scapegoats as anti-Semitism's scheming, acquisitive, unpatriotic, wire-pulling Jew. We recognize, obscurely, that some primitive gratification is denied us, and so, all too naturally, we imagine that some external cause, some "Jew," has either stolen our enjoyment or has invaded our space and is trying to share it with us.[31] It is pointless to try to manage the force of ideology in our lives by vowing, for example, to respect Jewish otherness or to see Jews as they really are; we must instead traverse the fantasy, and "confront the Real of our desire" to persecute Jews. In contrast to prevailing leftist views, then, Žižek insists that the roots of ideology are psychoanalytic rather than social or historical.

It is difficult to find a political position that is widely shared among the intelligentsia of the first world that Žižek does not regard as an inversion of the truth. He does not, for example, feel that society would be improved by a higher level of patriotism, a greater commitment to order, or a more urgent call to civic duty. In fact, he relentlessly identifies the enjoyment specific to the sense of duty, the illicit gratification flourishing on the underside of adherence to the law.[32] Nor does he display any interest in recent liberal efforts to promote a cosmopolitan love of mankind in general that would be appropriate to an emergent global culture.[33] From his perspective, such wide-minded appeals to the family of man suggest an attempt to deny the reality of enjoyment by minimizing the force of irrational local identifications; if successful, they would only end in a "flat" or aseptic (as he puts it, "Habermasian") universe that produced amity by sacrificing spirit and vivacity. Nor, finally, has Žižek shown any interest in such conventional emancipatory projects as "giving voice to the voiceless," "liberating repressed drives," or "celebrating difference."

In short, he does not feel that we need more order, more enlightenment, or more freedom—each of which he recodes as a Cause, a Home, a subject-supposed-to-know, a Mother in whose bosom we can come to rest, a source of greater comfort and self-esteem.[34] What we do need, Žižek says, is more truth, which is to say, more Lacan. In particular, we need to have our noses kept to the grindstone of Lacan's insistence that the sign, the symbolic order, and therefore the human subject are cloven by an impassable bar; we need, that is, to keep reminding ourselves that "the other must not know all," that we must confront and refuse our desire to believe in the possibility of a superior, benevolently enfolding force—and, of course, refuse to collaborate or inform.

To say that Žižek's politics are psychoanalytic and linguistic is to say that they are founded not in the notion of a difference that must be contained, respected, or embraced, but in the concept of the universal. The centrality of universality in Žižek is commonly under appreciated because it was not fully theorized until quite recently, in *The Fragile Absolute* (FA) and *Contingency, Hegemony, Universality* (CHU). But it is clearly both his most fundamental premise and the one that determines his antagonism to other commonly held views on a range of issues. His commitment to universality gives him, for example, a far greater receptivity to Christianity than one commonly finds in the academy. Žižek notes that Christianity posits the universal within human life, and even makes the radical argument that Christ is most unmistakably divine at the moment of his utter humiliation, the nadir of his human existence. Christians learn what Žižek would teach everyone, that there is a point of view from which our immediate, ordinary sense of things is total nonsense, and also that the divine—one form of the "big Other," the symbolic order—is, in its subjective destitution, just like us; it does not "know all," and does not deserve our worship. Thus only from the perspective of the universal can we, according to Žižek, derive a proper understanding of the social, conceptual, and moral significance of mundanity. For the universal is always outside the order of social or political power and can often be traced in the shadowed features of those condemned to live in the background of history or society, unmarked by interesting differences and blurred in the mass of the "population" (CHU 313; *see* 90–135 *passim*).

Beginning, then, with Lacan's account of the signifier, Žižek arrives at last at the most far-reaching of his inversions of prevailing opinion, the assertion that we are all alike at the deep structural level of the unconscious, the level of the universal. Against those who argue that universality is a utopian dream, Žižek contends that it is present as a framework or terrain of intelligibility in every contingent circumstance: it does not loom like a spirit over our material lives, but rather inheres in them in an immediate and direct manner like, perhaps, form in an aesthetic work. Against those who contend that universality is an inherently oppressive concept, he insists that it is an indispensable political instrument, providing a concept of common humanity that enables us to delineate and protest specific injustices and acts of oppression. Without such a concept, people are left at the mercy of local arrangements, defenseless against the argument that their oppressors are simply participants in a given language game, that the injustices from which they suffer are to be seen "in their proper context" or that such matters are, after all, internal affairs. In this way, Žižek claims, a misguided politically correct racism writes off countless deaths by attributing them to ancient ethnic passions or traditional ways of life. The localization of conflict, conducted under the banner of difference, respects the otherness of the other at the cost of abandoning all responsibility.

Sometimes, Žižek insists, responsibility compels a refusal of mediation and respect. Intractable political problems are not solved by smothering hatred under a blanket of tolerance and respect, but by applying "*even more hatred*, but proper *political* hatred: hatred directed at the common political enemy" (FA 11). And it is only when we recognize the other as a person like ourselves that we can hate him in the most productive way. To surrender universality out of an empiricist embarrassment at invoking the nonverifiable or a multiculturalist suspicion of overarching principles of commonality is to neutralize oneself and empower evil.[35] Žižek is scornful on several levels of Western liberal pieties about the other, insisting that the sexual other, the ethnic other, the religious other are only other in our (corrupt) fantasies. Although psychoanalysis is often faulted for an indifference to particularity that appears apolitical and thus reactionary, it is, Žižek argues, the only theoretical perspective that, by positing formal structures of the human mind, can truly grasp universality, and therefore the only perspective capable of uniting the political and the ethical.[36]

3. And Others

I said at the beginning of this essay that Žižek has shown very little development in his thinking, that he seemed fully formed at the outset of his career. But over the past few years, he has begun to lay particular emphasis on the ethical act, a concept implicit in his earlier concern with Hegelian problems of identity and Lacanian approaches to ideology. The emergence of this concept has corresponded to a shift in the implied audience for his work, from the Slovenian and Lacanian milieus he occupied in the 1980s to the Western academy in which he has traveled so extensively over the past decade. As he has spent more and more time in lecture halls (in 2002, he calculated some 550 appearances over the last twenty-five years, mostly in the West, and his pace has if anything increased since then), his mood has turned sour. Some of his new friends in the free world seem to him as blinkered as Stalinists, squandering the liberties they enjoy by thinking their way back into deadlocks and dogmas, theorizing with no sense of philosophy and preaching with no sense of religion. In the confusion of the inauthentic clarity of the academy, the real nature of obligation and the real difficulty of ethical action have become obscured. And so while becoming, if anything, more frantically amusing than ever, he has also become, at the level of theory, a Savonarola.

The germ of Žižek's ethical argument is Lacan's dictum: Do not give way relative to [or cede] your desire.[37] From this sentence, which seems not just cryptic but provocatively antiethical, Žižek extracts two principles. The first might be rendered as: Do not give yourself over to desire; that is, do not become a slave to impulse driven by an unresisted need for gratification. The second paraphrase of Lacan's commandment would be: Do not accept any fantasy substitutes. The message here is more complex, for the injunction against ceding one's desire has the effect of representing desire as a duty, an imperative. Understood in this sense, Lacan's commandment seeks to block access to enjoyment and thwart the perversion noted earlier in which one derives obscene gratification from the identification with the punishing superego. Thus, in this second interpretation, we are instructed not to listen to our superego, or even to imagine that we have one; we should not, that is, try to overcome our barred nature by seeking illicit and fantasmatic gratifications, including the desires for ethnic purity or nationalist solidarity, in the belief that they can give us what we lack that we may stop desiring.

Desire, as Lacan says in the greatest of his seminars, *The Ethics of Psychoanalysis*, is to be conceived as a function of the signifier, whose movement, leading from point to point infinitely, constitutes both what we are and what we are not, our being and our nonbeing. With respect to what we are, Lacan provides a positive account of pathology in terms of one's own path, a particular destiny of one's own that resists the anaesthetizing oppression of moralizers, educators, and civic leaders. The exemplary figure for Lacan in this respect is Antigone, whose defiant refusal to cooperate with the civil authorities places her outside the securities of the polis and the guarantees of the symbolic order. And with respect to what we are not, Lacan argues that Antigone's self-destructive refusal to comply actually proceeds from her fidelity to the signifier, to language as the site of a cleavage in being.[38] Where traditional ethics would have you deny yourself by resisting the temptations proffered by desire, Lacanian ethics, modeled on the Saussurean signifying chain, would have you realize yourself by acting in conformity with your desire, keeping it—and thus your resistance to proffered goods and your connection to the truth of the death drive—alive.

These are the terms of Žižek's reading of Lacan on *Antigone* through the 1990s. But in more recent works, Žižek has begun to recognize another principle, more radical still, which is present but relatively unstressed in Lacan's seminar. Defying the king, Antigone not only removes herself from the civic and symbolic orders, but also gives birth to a new possibility of agency, altering the coordinates of social life. She does not force an adjustment of old laws to new realities, but reconfigures reality itself, transgressing the fantasy that structured it. She, too, is not expressed by her act so much as transformed and recreated. From this point, Žižek launches the general argument that a truly ethical act can *never* coincide with an existing norm, within which it must always appear impossible. For an act to be truly ethical, he says, it *must* transgress the norm, for only such a transgression can reveal the compensatory nature of norms themselves, and bring into the open the incomplete, yet-to-be-fashioned character of reality.[39]

So extreme is Žižek's recent thinking that it has taken him beyond Antigone herself. In *The Fragile Absolute*, he characterizes her sacrifice of all goods as "traditional," even as "masculine," rather than truly "modern." Her retention of the Cause or Thing—the burial of her brother in contradiction of Creon's order—is now seen as a point of regressive impurity. "In the modern ethical constellation," he says, one does not sacrifice everything but the Thing, "one *suspends this exception of the Thing*" by sacrificing it, too, so that one is left with absolutely nothing but duty itself. Thus the ethical act must, in the end, come to monstrous gestures of self-abuse, self-mutilation, self-destruction, "striking at oneself." Because division is our nature, such gestures are "constitutive of subjectivity itself" (FA 150).

One might think that in this case Žižek would be hard put to find examples, but he discovers a number of heroes who were willing to make a self-destructive leap into unreality in the name of duty. The Old Testament provides a chilling example in the person of Abraham, who was willing to sacrifice his own son. The New Testament furnishes another in the figure of God, who sacrificed his only-begotten son. Freud's response in *Moses and Monotheism* to anti-Semitism, targeting the founding figure of Moses by claiming he was not even Jewish, also qualifies as an act of properly ethical monstrosity, as does Medea's slaughter of her children. The signal instance in contemporary fiction of the modern ethical act is the wild attempt by Sethe in Toni Morrison's *Beloved* to exterminate what is most precious to her, as she tries to kill her two sons, and kills her infant daughter in order to save them from the dehumanization of bondage (FA 152–53). Stalinism also witnessed rare but inspiring examples of ethical impossibility, as in "the legendary event at Vorkuta Mine 29 in 1953," where modest demands made by prisoners were rebuffed with violence, resulting in a strike. The mine was surrounded by soldiers and tanks, and "when the troops finally entered the main gate, they saw the prisoners standing behind it in a solid phalanx, their arms linked, singing. After a brief hesitation, the heavy machine guns opened up—the miners remained massed and erect, defiantly continuing to sing, the dead held up by the living." At this point, the prisoners' defiance "seemed to suspend the very laws of nature," thereby illustrating "the Sublime at its purest." After "about a minute," however, "reality prevailed, and the corpses began to litter the ground" (*Did Somebody Say Totalitarianism?* 74–75).[40] In Žižek's examples, reality typically avenges itself on purity by producing a mass of corpses, a sequence dramatized by the Stalinist conclusion to Žižek's most recent example of ethical heroism, the "enacted utopia" of Lenin.[41] By comparison with these models, the Kantian categorical imperative (act in such a way that the maxim of your action might become a universal principle) represents a soft humanism, an evasion of the real difficulty.

So radical has Žižek become, in fact, that radicalism itself seems, from his perspective, flaccid and compliant. The radicalities of postmodernity, including the plurality of identities, transgressive idiosyncrasy, the multiplication of subject positions, the performance of identity—even the variant of radical democracy espoused by Ernesto Laclau and others—remain, for Žižek, firmly fixed within the framework of capitalism, with its structural demand for dynamism and revolution in the means of production, and therefore in the society at large. The noisy and aggressive elimination of every essentialist fixity includes a certain silent renunciation of any larger changes in the capitalist system. Our era, obsessed as it is with the politicization of science, sex, race, art, and so forth, has determined that capitalism itself is apolitical, beyond the reach of political debates. The hegemonic struggle today occurs within capitalism, and even radical critics seek merely to perform elective cosmetic surgery on the human face of capital. Postmodernists and others have succumbed to the blackmail that threatens people with loss of status if they disturb or even seriously challenge the system.

Everywhere Žižek casts his eye these days, he sees blackmailers and their willing victims. And once again the densely veiled form of "liberal blackmail" and thus of ideological closure today is the academic discourse on ethics, in which we find the persistent argument that any alternative to capitalism merely "paves the way for totalitarianism" (CHU 326).

The "return to ethics" in today's political philosophy shamefully exploits the horrors of Gulag or Holocaust as the ultimate bogey for blackmailing us into renouncing all serious radical engagement. In this way, conformist liberal scoundrels can find hypocritical satisfaction in their defense of the existing order: they know there is corruption, exploitation, and so on, but every attempt to change things is denounced as ethically dangerous and unacceptable, recalling the ghosts of Gulag or Holocaust . . . . (CHU 127)

The true path of duty, Žižek insists, is not around these ghosts, but directly through them. The capitalist framework is reaching its own inherent limitations, its capacity to contain its own mutations diminishing; we see rising unemployment, the erosion of national sovereignty under the amoral pressures of economic globalization, the much-heralded disappearance of the working class effected by means of third-world sweatshops, and the ghettoization of entire strata of society. Some breakout into a new reality is needed, and totalitarianism may, for a moment, be one of its names. In any event, we cannot refuse duty because of a mere monstrous appearance, because monstrosity is the condition of any true act.

The last straw in this desperate argument seems to have been the reaction of radical intellectuals to the North Atlantic Treaty Organization (NATO) bombing in Kosovo in 1999. Edward Said decried the "cowardly" risk-free bombing ("a fastidiousness . . . about the loss of American life that is positively revolting") and protested, in a judgment on which history has rendered its verdict, that the goal of removing Milosevic was "misguided and totally hopeless."[42] Noam Chomsky insisted, as did Said, that the United States was simply pursuing strategic objectives out of crass self-interest, and scoffed at the pious profession of "humanitarian" concerns for ethnic Albanians. We should, Chomsky argued, have followed the Hippocratic principle: "First, do no harm." Both he and Said argued that the United States should have pursued diplomatic channels, and Said urged a conference in which all those involved could discuss a settlement that respected the right to self-determination for all, implying that the Kosovar

Albanians might form a new nation. Chomsky urged as a check on nationalist or ethnic aggression a turn to the United Nations Charter.[43]

And Žižek? In an article circulated on the Web,[44] he agreed that strategic interests were at stake in the NATO bombing, and that the media presentation of the entire Balkan situation, with its blood-crazed aggressors and helpless victims who simply wished to live in apolitical peace, was racist. There were, he said, two stories about the Kosovo bombing—one casting NATO as the "armed hand of the new capitalist global order, defending the strategic interests of capital in the guise of a disgusting travesty"—the case made by Said and Chomsky—and another, made by the Clinton administration and its allies, in which the international community was seeking to enforce human rights standards on a brutal nationalist leader. The truth, Žižek said, was the opposite of each: that Milosevic was not the enemy of the New World Order, but its symptom, a deformed creature of the Western powers who had hypocritically cast him from the very beginning as an agent of stability in the region.

According to the standard wisdom in the West, the Serb people were essentially good but were manipulated by their evil leaders, and the roots of the conflict were ancient, even primordial. The truth, Žižek declared, was "precisely TURNED AROUND: not only are people not 'good,' since they let themselves be manipulated with obscene pleasure; there are also no 'old myths' which we need to study . . . just the PRESENT outburst of racist nationalism." The subtraction of these two myths from the analysis produces a clarity that can only be called glaring: "not yet ENOUGH bombs," he concluded, "and they are TOO LATE."[44]

Yes, bombs are bad; and yes, strategic-ideological interests determine their use in this case—and yes, we must bomb, even more, and ought to have bombed sooner. And no, we should not seek "self-determination for all," but must rather try to build

> TRANSNATIONAL political movements and institutions strong enough to seriously constrain the unlimited rule of the capital, and to render visible and politically relevant the fact that the local fundamentalist resistances against the New World Order, from Milosevic to le Pen and the extreme Right in Europe, are part of it.[44]

The Hippocratic Oath cannot guide us to the new order Žižek envisions in the exalted conclusion to his dispute with Ernesto Laclau and Judith Butler gathered in *Contingency, Hegemony, Universality* (2000), an order in which we would have "no taboos, no a priori norms ('human rights', 'democracy'), respect for which would prevent us also from 'resignifying' terror, the ruthless exercise of power, the spirit of sacrifice." We must be prepared to confront the worst, to break with ourselves, to bomb the other: "If this radical choice is decried by some bleeding-heart liberals as *Links-faschismus*," he proclaims, "so be it!" (326). If Žižek were in charge, life in the Balkans and elsewhere would not exactly be a cocktail party.

Noting Žižek's self-characterization as a "cold" thinker, the American editors of *The Žižek Reader* hasten to assure their audience that Žižek has not in fact departed from the compulsory amiability, the respect for reason, and the ethic of virtuous restraint that characterize the American academy. The Slovenian is just *joking*, they assure us, he is being *humorous* in his Slavic way; in fact, he has a "buoyantly ironic political programme" altogether congenial to unbombed Western readers.[45] But Žižek is not precisely one of us: not altogether other, he has never been a comfortable presence in the Western academy, and he is becoming less so as we continue to disappoint him with our pious force-phobia, our inability to imagine life without TIAA-CREF, our fastidious reluctance to make a *passage à l'acte*. So—once again—what is he? What relation does he have to the Western academic conversation? Can his current commitments be productively integrated into the ongoing discourse? Do we trust that bombs will, like the Lacanian letter, always reach their destinations? Can we imagine that the liberal ethos in which we flourish is a blackmail that must be refused or "precisely TURNED AROUND," and that ethical duty compels us to risk "resignifying" totalitarian terror, against others as well as ourselves? Can we endorse an ethics of total sacrifice, an ethics reserved only for a fanatical and even a suicidal few, a Leninist ethics of the vanguard? Or are these positions strictly impossible for us?

Žižek seems to have worked himself into an appalling position as the terminal consequence of a founding commitment to a catachrestical account of language. From an initial conviction that identity is the result of an arbitrary act of positing, Žižek has arrived at the conclusion that no ethical act can be strictly warranted by existing fact, and indeed that an ethical act must involve a shattering of the status quo. But others who have begun from the same starting point have nevertheless come to a principled account of action. Žižek might engage Derrida in particular on the terrain of ethics, taking up work Derrida has produced since the 1988 "Afterword: Towards an Ethic of Discussion."[46] Some have begun with a different account of language altogether and have still ended up with a vision of man as an altruistic "moral animal."[47] For others, the contingency of language leads in the opposite direction, away from ethics and its deadening imperatives. One would like to know exactly why Žižek thinks all of these options are theoretically wrong.

It would be especially productive if at this point Žižek could attempt, in an appropriate spirit of self-mutilation, to suspend his allegiance to Hegel, to surrender Lacanian dogmatics, and to entertain the question of Chomsky. Much of Lacan's mystique derives from the fact that he grounds his hypotheses about the mind in a science of language, giving them authority, scope, and profundity. But as we have seen, Lacan relied on Saussure for that science, and Saussure no longer enjoys unqualified respect among linguists, who in fact regard him not at all. Approaching language by way of syntax rather than signs, Chomsky reverses Saussure at every point. For Chomsky, language is a genetic endowment rather than a social construction, a capacity rather than a code; its form is therefore necessary rather than arbitrary, universal rather than local, and constant rather than historically mutable; the scope for individual innovation within the form is infinite rather than nonexistent. A study of the nature of language leads, for Chomsky, directly to an affirmation of solidarity, freedom, and creativity, whose value Žižek would certainly not dispute, even though Lacan never invokes them. Moreover, Chomsky plainly believes in the possibility of direct perception and truthful representation, free from ideological tincture. His political interventions consist largely of descriptions, or redescriptions, of events, which are intended, in an Orwellian spirit, to expose the corruption of the language represented by official statements, with the expectation that the simple, plain-English accuracy of his accounts will produce polemical and subversive effects.[48] Nothing in Chomsky follows from arbitrariness.

One of the more remarkable facts about the language-based theory revolution of the past generation is that not one of the theorists who launched their projects from the platform of language ever produced a serious reading of a thinker who, in addition to being the preeminent linguist of the era, also produced a number of major statements in political and linguistic philosophy, as well as an extraordinarily rich dossier of political dissidence. Lacan was simply one among many theorists who ignored Chomsky, but Lacan was more emphatic than any that his theories were grounded in a science of language.

Žižek could now make up for this missed encounter. There is, in addition to a number of salient differences, more than enough common ground to make for a productive debate, which might begin with a reading of Lacan's pronouncement, with which both Chomsky and Žižek agree, that "man's nature is woven by effects in which is to be found the structure of language."[49] Like Žižek, Chomsky proposes a universalist ethics and a radical politics based on a psychologistic account of language, and, again like Žižek, traces his intellectual lineage back to Descartes and Kant. Both share, moreover, a keen interest in F. W. J. Schelling, the subject of Žižek's *The Abyss of Freedom* and one among many philosophical sources Chomsky draws on in his attempts to establish a philosophical genealogy for his argument that freedom is a fundamental human endowment.[50] Chomsky is just as contrarian as Žižek, just as opposed to ideology, just as committed to the proposition of human uniqueness based on language, and just as insistent that transnational political and juridical structures are invaluable resources in the contemporary world. He is one of the very few contemporary thinkers who can match Žižek's capacity for political hatred. Moreover, Chomsky's linguistic thinking identifies a mechanistic structure, a structure that is in fact far more mechanistic than anything in Saussure, but which—since it constitutes only a capacity—seems more like a ghost than a machine.[51] And, finally, Chomsky has his own version of the Lacanian Real in the form of what Kant calls the irreducible yet never-realized human "inclination and duty to *think freely*," "the germ on which nature has lavished most care."[52]

With such interesting points of contact, the debate could center not just on the particulars of given events, but also on such fundamental questions as the grounds of human freedom, the nature of language, the site and force of the ethical imperative, the question of whether political or ethical arguments can be justified in the absence of some non-arbitrary normative account, whether what Chomsky calls creativity might include what Žižek calls the retroactive constitution of the thing, and the possibilities for deriving political principles from determinable facts of human nature. Nor can these questions be evaded by simply allotting syntax to Chomsky while giving Lacan the symbolic order, for the real question is which of these dimensions of language is truly fundamental and which is epiphenomenal. Which, in other words, determines man's nature?

Žižek's failure to read Chomsky, which repeats Lacan's similar failure, marks a rare and indefensible limitation in his willingness to engage with other thinkers. So acutely sensitive to the interchangeability of signifiers, Žižek has never attended to the grammatical system that makes such substitutions possible with no sacrifice of meaning. If Žižek could overcome his own distaste, both principled and visceral, for any theory grounded in nature, human nature, or instinct, and submit Lacanian dogmatics to the challenge presented by such texts as *Cartesian Linguistics*, *Reflections on Language*, and *Knowledge of Language*, the results would hold the highest interest.[53] Indeed, one might argue that Žižek owes us this encounter, and owes it precisely because Lacan refused it.

Then again, if we in the West could suspend both our amusement and our amazement, we might come to a more productive understanding of

Žižek, and—since he is a bone in *our* throat—of our own culture, academic and otherwise. If we could imagine Žižek as a *symptom* of the academic West, we might come to a sharper appreciation of the snags and inconsistencies in our own institutions and premises. The enthusiastic reception accorded to Žižek despite his bitter opposition to our most fundamental values and practices suggests that we are, as he would say, "enjoying our symptom," but also that, in our eager preoccupation with enjoyment itself, we have so far failed to understand what our symptom is a symptom of, and what it might, properly decoded, teach us about ourselves.

CHAPTER 5

Criticism as Obsession: Said and Conrad

1. Emulations

The death of a famous intellectual occasions self-examination by the survivors; and the death of Edward Said, of leukemia, in 2003 provoked among literary and cultural critics, and among many others who had been touched by his work, a prolonged ritual of introspection of a kind and intensity that exceeded even that seen a generation ago at the deaths, within a five-year span, of Roland Barthes, Jacques Lacan, Louis Althusser, Paul de Man, and Michel Foucault. For American intellectuals, their deaths had marked the end of a certain theoretical project or projects; the death of Said produced a different kind of response because his work had a different character. He was indifferent to the dilemmas of thought, and theory had little urgency for him except as the symptom of a massive institutional distraction from history. His emphasis was always on assertive, purposive, worldly action rather than on the dramas of the mind. All of his work was marked by an urgency that reflected a strong personal investment but also seemed to bear a larger meaning, an ethico-political import. His death was experienced by many as a personal grief and a blow to intellectual culture, but beyond that, as a loss for the world.

Accordingly, many of the memorials that poured forth expressed a sense of bereavement that was in a sense impersonal. Said embraced a wondrous combination of abilities and qualities—largeness of soul, deep political conviction, a commitment to both social justice and scholarly rigor, erudition, an immense *joie de vivre*, extraordinary intellectual curiosity, academic passion, an assured command of several languages and traditions, a firsthand experience of different cultures and cultural differences, and a great capacity for friendship—that many felt they would never see again. He also had qualities so rare in the academic world that it almost seems that their possession constitutes a disqualification for a career in scholarship: dramatic good looks, artistic talent, a bold and exacting sense of style which he half-humorously imposed on others as well as on himself, an aristocratic mien, a cosmopolitan ease with fame, and a fearless appetite for combat and controversy on a large stage. Most remarkably, this celebrated man was actually a member of a disadvantaged group and could speak of exile and dispossession from personal experience.

The last decade of his life was dominated not only by the routines and sufferings imposed by his illness, but also by the accumulation of awards, the giving of lectures and interviews, media appearances, and, unbelievably, by an accelerated rate of publication. And yet, even with the increasingly public nature of his life, countless people felt a powerful connection to him; a meeting, a conversation, a phone call from Edward Said tended to linger in the memory. He was the sort of person for whom people would gladly travel thousands of miles to attend a surprise birthday party. Acquaintance with him gave people a sense of being more fully in touch with the world than they would otherwise have been. A singular and original personality, he inspired among many not only awe but emulation; his considerable influence in the world of scholarship was spread by former students and admirers who took him as a model, even describing themselves candidly as "Saideans."

In certain respects, he was easy to emulate. So fully present in any given moment, he was utterly consistent in his abiding concerns and preoccupations. His entire career was informed by a set of linked premises:

- All acts, ideas, ideologies, and texts, are "situated" in that they emerge from determined historical contexts and specific experiences; knowledge always stands in some relation to power, which seeks to co-opt it, and often succeeds.
- A failure to recognize the worldliness, and therefore the impurity and heterogeneity, of action and understanding constitutes a blindness to reality.

- Among the symptoms of this blindness are the belief in a sacred origin and the quest for a perfect acontextual understanding; another is an overinvestment in biological principles of identity beginning with the family, with its clear roles, exclusionary principles of identity, and genealogical lines of authority.
- The most effective response to power's deforming influence on knowledge, and the best antidote to blindness, is the free exercise of the individual critical intelligence, as exemplified by scholarship, where respect for truth takes precedence over all other considerations.
- The essential mission of scholarship is the creation of secular communities based not on genealogy or race but on the voluntary and conscious creation of contexts, groupings, or institutions in which affinities are elective rather than predetermined.
- The most rigorous form of humanistic scholarship is philology, which is skeptical toward such quasi-filial entities as national traditions, and promotes instead the idea of a "world literature," a human heritage based on universal principles.
- "Exile" is the best metaphor to describe the philological, and therefore the scholarly, perspective.
- Hence, true scholarship is "oppositional," and entirely consistent with a sensitivity to the experience of loss and displacement suffered by those who are not in a position to become scholars, who cannot represent themselves or resist the representations of them generated by others, and who must simply suffer their losses without redress or compensation.

Said makes this argument not by mere assertion, but by compelling readings of exemplary figures. Early and late, he returns repeatedly to a few key figures, among them Giambattista Vico, Leo Spitzer, Michel Foucault, Erich Auerbach, Julian Benda, R. P. Blackmur, Ernest Renan, Georg Lukács, and T. W. Adorno. If one reason Said inspired emulation was that his central arguments were unchanging and accessible, another is that emulation in the form of admiration and ardent advocacy was an integral part of his sensibility. The first half of the argument traced above, for example, proceeds largely under the sign of Vico, on whom Said wrote as early as 1967, and to whom he referred frequently, most notably in the conclusion of *Beginnings*, and in a section of the key essay "On Repetition" in *The World, the Text, and the Critic* (WTC).[1] Enthusiastic and detailed references to Vico are difficult to find in the work of other critics, but Said revered Vico, praising in particular his autodidact's independence of mind and his commitment to a critique of linguistic representations. For Vico, history is a "gentile" human creation, an intentional, even creative and "poetic" artifact produced by human mind and will. Accordingly, the first step in investigation is always skeptical and philological. Said never discovered a better statement of his essential position.

Said was impressed at an early age by Vico's poetic or mythic account of the beginning of history, with feral giants striding the earth after the flood, gradually disciplining themselves into thinking creatures and eventually forming a rational society. He was impressed, too, by Vico's account of the cycles and laws of history that emerge from this beginning. "Men mean to gratify their bestial lust and abandon their offspring," Vico writes in the passage to which Said returns again and again; "the fathers mean to exercise without restraint their paternal power over their clients . . . the reigning orders of nobles mean to abuse their lordly freedom over the plebeians . . . . The monarchs mean to strengthen their own positions by debasing their subjects with all the vices of dissoluteness."[2] Said quotes and refers to this passage on more than one occasion, but his paraphrase indicates what he takes from it. "The sexual relations between men and women," he says,

> give rise to matrimony, the institution of matrimony gives rise to cities, the struggle of plebeians gives rise to laws; people in conflict with laws give rise to tyranny; and tyranny leads finally to capitulation to foreign powers. Out of this last debasement a new cycle will begin, arising out of man's absolute degeneration in the wilderness" (WTC, 112).

For Said, this allegorical master plot makes everything clear. Marriage, for example, is suddenly revealed as a means of interdicting an otherwise omnidirectional and unstoppable sexual desire so that the authority of the father will be recognized and preserved; but it also permits other kinds of relationships, based on choice rather than on biology—"affiliation" rather than filiation, cities rather than nomadic hordes—to take root. The principle of affiliation introduces eccentricity and contrariety into the closed system of biological repetition, and so gives rise to individual perspective, self-understanding, originality, and society. Thus Vico provides nothing less than an account of the basic structure of the observable world.

Other parts of Said's macro-argument are inspired and informed by Auerbach, with whom Said had an even more complex relationship. Said neglected no opportunity to praise the author of *Mimesis*—and translator of Vico—as an exemplary philologist. His first essay on Auerbach as philologist appeared in 1969; his last was an introduction to a new edition of *Mimesis* and appeared as a chapter in the posthumous *Humanism and Democratic Criticism*.[3] What strikes Said most forcefully about Auerbach is the productive role played in his work by loss and dispossession.

A German Jew exiled to Istanbul during World War II, Auerbach found himself having to recreate the Western tradition from the homeland of the mythic figure of the terrible Turk. From this alienated perspective, Auerbach could see the cultural tradition of Europe with fresh and critical eyes, as a specific thing with definite properties, a vast cultural structure of inclusions and exclusions. Said clearly saw himself in comparable terms, as a linguistically trained exile—from a country closer to Turkey than to Germany—with opportunities.

The practice of philology was, for Said, invested with a far greater drama, and was played for far higher stakes, than most scholars have recognized. He became the most insistent contemporary advocate for, if not a practitioner of, philology because he recognized, in this least exciting but most exacting of learned and culturally transmitted skills, not merely a deep concern for the preservation of the great cultural forms of the past in a way that would make them available for the present, but also the kind of relentless skepticism, the subjection of every textual appearance to rigorous scholarly examination, that dissolved all abstract notions of nature, nation, and home—in short, all notions of filiation.[4] Only when one is "out of place, exiled, alienated," Said wrote in the crucial essay on "Secular Criticism" that begins *The World, the Text, and the Critic*, can one truly see culture, the feeling of "being *at home in a place*," as the specific way in which power relations, exclusions, validations, and invalidations are affirmed (8). With his prodigious learning recontextualized by a new perspective, Auerbach could begin to conceptualize a world literature supporting a broadly humanistic agenda that transcended national boundaries and traditions. Said compared Auerbach with Matthew Arnold, whose dark genius lay in his unblinking, indeed wholly affirmative recognition of the implication of culture with the "quasi-theological exterior order of the State"; who brought to appreciative attention the host of quietly efficient ways in which culture identified, selected, and affirmed some things and cast out others; and who "covered critical writing with the mantle of cultural authority and reactionary political quietism." In contrast, Auerbach appealed to Said as an immensely impressive instance of the truism that in order to gain the world, one must lose home, leaving behind the assurance, confidence, and sense of solidity associated with being where you belong (WTC 28, 11; *see* 176–77). Said took from Auerbach not only a confirmation of the Vichian emphases on the human creation of history and the cultural importance of affiliative relationships, but also an understanding of the role played in the creation of such affiliations by modern scholarship.

Auerbach becomes all the more impressive when compared to another formidable intelligence whose grasp of the real mission of philology was imperfect. Ernest Renan's *Vie de Jesus* was one of the great monuments of the secularizing spirit of nineteenth-century scholarship, a challenge to revealed religion by the "New Philology." Renan could not have written this book, Said points out, without having first written a large work that attempted to demonstrate the "inferiority" of the Semitic languages of Arabic, Hebrew, and Aramaic, languages in which God was said to have spoken to man. This philological, or rather pseudo-philological task, had the secondary effect of helping to legitimate the colonial domination of the lands in which such inferior languages flourished. In this and other instances, philology participated in "Orientalism," that massive project of cultural self-conceptualization by which the West defined itself over and against the Middle East.[5] Renan's ideological allegiance to the West prevents him from grasping the crucial fact that the scholar is in essence what Auerbach became in fact, "out of place . . . standing consciously against the prevailing orthodoxy and very much for a professedly universal or humane set of values, which has provided significant local resistance to the hegemony of one culture" (WTC 15).

In one respect, Auerbach and Renan are comparable. Both exemplify what Said describes as a "three-part pattern" characteristic not just of philology but of criticism in general (WTC 20). Auerbach began as a German scholar in Germany; then—the second part—he found himself bereft of home and language but, miraculously, granted a new, more spacious perspective. The tradition he had taken for granted was lost, but also raised to the level of analytic attention, newly available for skeptical inquiry as a constructed entity informed not by natural necessity but by human purpose and interest. The hierarchies of stature, wealth, and power in the old, "natural" order could now be seen as products of contingent force: the home was after all but one place among many, and the real context was humanity at large. This sequence informed Said's famous essay "Traveling Theory" and served as a template for the way Said thought about criticism at its best.[6]

But there is a third part, where things seem to go wrong. What Auerbach actually created in his work was a powerful image not of a new global or broadly human culture, but rather of the cultural imperium of the West. Through an unwitting retreat into autochthony, Auerbach wound up testifying to the magnificence of the European tradition, which, according to Said, Auerbach associated with "vestiges of the kind of authority associated in the past with filiative order" (WTC 19). In case after case, Said discovers that the most gifted scholars find ways to proceed—actually, to regress—to this third stage of criticism where they rejoin their original cultural matrix, undoing what might have been a genuinely self-critical project. Scholars such as Auerbach who are "out of place" find ways to remain "very much *of* that place" (15). Their gains in critical freedom are only momentary because, in the third part of the pattern, criticism enacts a pathetic and merely imitative return to the principle of family authority. As evidence for this return Said cites "the curricular structures holding European literature departments," in which "the great texts, as well as the great teachers and the great theories, have an authority that compels respectful attention not so much by virtue of their content but because they are either old or they have power" (22). The great scholar may part his hair, wear a suit, and use utensils to eat, but in essence he is just a weakened version of the terrible father of the primal horde. Philology, and scholarship and culture in general, may be proxies for the war against the father, but they all fall, by an internal logic of their own, into parodic recreations of the patriarch.

Because Said applies this pattern to modern scholarly knowledge as such, the somewhat ambiguous implication is that this final retreat simply cannot be avoided. One is granted critical power only on the condition that one leaves home; but then, it seems, one betrays the condition by recreating, in a spirit of confused melancholy, home all over again. This is why criticism must, as Said says, be at all times "skeptical, secular, reflectively open to its own failings" (WTC 26). Criticism must always be open to its own failings because it is always failing; indeed, its achievements *are* its failings.

The third part of the pattern represents a distinctly pessimistic view of the fate of critical intelligence, a sharp disappointment arriving at the end of what had been an emancipatory narrative. Those who take Said as an inspiring figure would, in general, subscribe to the first two movements—home, and loss of home leading to a perspective at once alienated, spacious, and critical—but many would not identify the parodic recovery of home as the inevitable terminus. The more natural conclusion, for most activist scholars in the Saidean mold, would be to assert that the discovery of power's contingency and locality leads naturally to a commitment to resistance and insubordination. Most would, that is, conclude that, having liberated oneself from home, one should then complete the pattern by going on the offensive and promoting liberation in general. Especially in the last fifteen years of his career, Said himself lent powerful support to this understanding of the social and moral responsibilities of the critic. But he did so without ever renouncing, even in principle, the fatalistic pattern announced in *The World, the Text, and the Critic*.

What accounts for this fatalism? What mighty force could bring intelligence to its knees and force it to hand over its hard-won independence? The answer that emerges over the course of a number of essays written over many years is biology. It is impossible to read Said on issues of filiation and affiliation without noticing the striking prominence given to biological generation. Perhaps the only way really to account for Said's investment in Vico is to note that Vico describes the original filiative condition in the sexualized terms that Said would retain and elaborate in developing the rest of his macro-argument. Recall that Vico described the original condition as a state of bestial lust, which Said translates in "Secular Criticism" as "the procreative, generational urge authorizing filiative relationships," and "the chain of biological procreation" (20, 22). In the compensatory transpersonal affiliations that arise after marriage has succeeded in channeling this lust, the father's place "loses its unassailable eminence."

It is not clear whether Said saw himself as somehow escaping the traps into which others have fallen. But in the two essays on Jonathan Swift in *The World, the Text, and the Critic*, Said depicts a thinker who, in effect, refused to complete the pattern. Swift's mind, Said argues, was entirely occupied by the occasions of his writings: he had no overarching position to articulate, no consistent set of principles or allegiances, no power center to defend. He is "alert, forceful, undogmatic, ironic, unafraid of orthodoxies and dogmas, respectful of settled uncoercive community, anarchic in his sense of the range of alternatives to the status quo" (27). Swift exemplifies for Said the dictum, jarring in the context of the early 1980s when it was announced in "Traveling Theory," that "it is the critic's job to provide resistances to theory" (WTC, 242). In all these respects, Swift represents a kind of critical ultimacy, or as Said puts it, "critical consciousness in a raw form." One suspects that Said recognized something of himself in Swift, a suspicion supported by the highly torqued (and eminently Swiftian) comment that follows, in which Said notes that the essays collected in *The World, the Text, and the Critic* might imply, to some readers, "some radical uncertainty on my part as to what I do stand for, especially given the fact that I have been accused by colleagues of intemperate and even unseemly polemicism" (28). Purely oppositional, the true critic "stands for" nothing, in both senses.

According to Tim Brennan, one of the most accomplished of those touched by Said's genius for influence, philology gave Said not only an affiliative scheme focused on cultural traditions and the critical intelligence that discerned and articulated them, but also a set of exemplary careers on or against which he consciously modeled his own. "One could even say," Brennan writes, "that most of Said's essays, poised on either side of the watershed year of *Beginnings* in 1975, were efforts to look at these now-vanished masters by way of sketching a portrait of the intellectual he was (in those essays) forcing himself to become."[7] This account must, I think, be supplemented by a fuller understanding of Said's intimate and more-than-scholarly relation to those masters who guided him into the academic profession and indeed into citizenship in an alien society. We are invited to construct such an account by virtue of the fact that Said appropriated for the title of his own autobiography the same phrase he twice applied to Auerbach, *Out of Place*.[8] I will return to this fascinating document, noting for the time being only that it records, in almost unbelievably intimate autobiographical detail, virtually all of the elements Said would later list as attributes of the philological perspective, which are described not as theoretical postulates but as facts about his life.

In *Out of Place* (OP), as in countless other essays and interviews, Said describes himself as an exile, a man who, after leaving home, has to construct a compensatory sense of affiliative identity. The dominant figure in the home is Said's father, who is described as a Vichian patriarch, exercising power without restraint, an overmastering and relentlessly critical presence, a man from whose "powerful virility," expressed in whippings and canings that continued into adulthood, the boy "shrank in consternation" (OP, 160, 210). Eventually, the father sends the teenaged Edward to study in the United States, where he finds himself suddenly swimming in multiple affiliative streams—great writers, great critics, great universities, great cultural traditions. In such a circumstance, emulation emerged as the most efficient way of imagining one's way out of filiation and the family and into the new situation, a way of completing and negating the effects of exile by acquiring new skills. Emulation became the intellectual style of this deeply stylish if psychically mutilated man.

For many years, Said confesses in his memoir, he continued to feel himself an outsider with insider's credentials, forced to lead "numerous lives, being a non-Egyptian of uncertain, not to say suspicious, composite identity habitually out of place, and representing a person with no recognizable profile and no particular direction" (61). These phrases seem to represent not Said's own self-understanding, but the understanding that Said had of others' understanding of him; they also represent, however, a defiant assertion of what he later came to feel was an indispensable credential for a scholar: only a person who was out of place could imagine a *weltliteratur* that spoke to a broadly human rather than to a provincial national tradition. The universalist ideals associated with humanism enlisted, at this moment, his full commitment. But just as his career was getting under way, the 1967 Arab-Israeli War gave Said an entirely new perspective on himself. Having grown up in a family in which politics was seldom discussed and Arab or Palestinian identity never asserted,[9] Said suddenly discovered what sort of home, what kind of nation, he had actually lost. He spent much of the rest of his life advocating what he described in *The Question of Palestine* as "a broadly representative Palestinian position."[10] In so doing, he would reclaim the origin and complete the three-part pattern he would subsequently identify. To read *Out of Place* after reading Said's critical texts is to realize that the three-part pattern Said described was not merely an abstraction but rather a critical-theoretical version of a series of crises and difficulties that began, literally, at home.

2. Identifications

The phrase Said applied to himself was not original with him. He found it in the material he worked with in graduate school at Harvard, the let-ters of Joseph Conrad. "You and your ideals of sincerity and courage and truth," Conrad wrote to R. Cunninghame Graham in 1898, "are strangely out of place in this epoch of material preoccupations . . . you seem to be tragic with your courage, with your beliefs and your hopes. Every cause is tainted."[11] These letters served as the basis for Said's 1964 dissertation, which two years later was published as his first book. Near the end of his life, Said told Peter Mallios, who was interviewing him on the subject of Conrad, that in this exchange of letters, he himself identified with the out-of-place champion of lost causes, Graham.[12]

In the first instance, however, he discovered himself in Conrad, the most commanding of the figures who solicited his interest. It was Conrad whom Said described in a late essay as a "*cantus firmus*, a steady ground-bass to much that I have experienced . . . I don't know a better, more ency-clopedic description of the world from which I come than is provided by Conrad's novels."[13] There might seem to be little commonality between a Polish seaman-writer and an Arab-American academic born more than eighty years later, but there were, in Conrad's life, numerous points of pur-chase for Said, who eagerly sought them out. In a more direct sense than Said, Conrad was an exile from a conquered and erased land. Lord Jim's half-conscious leap from the ship, the *Patna*, is perhaps a closer analogue to Said's departure from Palestine than Conrad's decision to go to sea, which, however, was taken at just the age Said was when he went to Amer-ica. Both men wound up living in relatively privileged circumstances near the center of imperial power. Conrad described himself as "*homo duplex*"; as Said put it, "there were two Conrads,"[14] just as there were two Saids: the American academic and the Palestinian activist. They both became writ-ers, deploying an English that was haunted by abandoned languages and informed by alien cultural traditions.[15] If all Europe contributed to the making of Kurtz, the whole world seemed to contribute to the making of both Conrad and Said. Other similarities were temperamental rather than circumstantial. Both Conrad and Said had astonishing memories and the past was always with them. Conrad promoted music as "the art of arts"[16];

Said was an accomplished pianist and long-time music critic. And both were described by friends as "nervous," "high-strung," and "sensitive." As Mallios comments,

> once one starts looking, there are in fact extensive relations of continuity and correspondence . . . that run between Said and Conrad, all of which can become a bit uncanny and unnerving, as each additional considered increment contributes a new and vital thread that is essential to the web of continuities that seemed so self-sufficiently woven the moment before.[17]

But these points of contact only enabled a deeper relation with Conrad that served as Said's primary imaginative investment as scholar and perhaps in other roles as well.

Said first read Conrad ("Youth") as a fourteen-year-old in Cairo; then, in an experience whose impact was to last a lifetime, read more intensively as an undergraduate at Princeton. He wrote his dissertation at Harvard on Conrad in 1964; his first book and several of his earliest articles and reviews were on Conrad. These were followed by a long section in *Beginnings* on *Nostromo*; an essay on Conrad and the "presentation of narrative" in *The World, the Text, and the Critic*; an article on Conrad and the "two visions of empire" in *Culture and Imperialism*; an essay on "Conrad and Nietzsche" included in *Reflections on Exile*; the Mallios interview just mentioned; and a discussion of *Victory* in a book on "late style" that he was working on at his death. This list does not include a number of reviews, shorter essays, and briefer but often still consequential mentions of Conrad as illustrations of central Saidean concepts.

As the quotation from Brennan has already indicated, it is conventional to regard Said's career as beginning in 1975, with *Beginnings: Intention and Method*, a book that, Brennan says, "records that broad-ranging but also limited list of motifs that occupy Said for the better part of his career" (75). To begin at *Beginnings* makes good sense, for it is in this book that one encounters that mix of emphases—theory, "worldliness," the opposition of "secular" versus "religious" criticism, the great respect for the achievements of philology and humanistic scholarship generally, the emphasis on the generative or constructive capacity of representations—as well as the expansive range of reference and the sheer scholarly ambition that mark Said's entire career. But to treat *Beginnings* as a kind of ultrasound image of Said's later positions is, I think, to miss the distinctive element, the thing that truly distinguishes and differentiates Said from others who shared many of his larger commitments and goals. That thing, that striking and distinctive energy or force, can only be understood by backing up still further, beyond the fully articulated product of the forty-year-old scholar, to a more "innocent" point of genesis. That would be *Joseph Conrad and the Fiction of Autobiography* (JC). Considered by those few who have read it as something of an embarrassment—a dismayingly mediocre piece of apprentice work undertaken before Said truly became himself—this book has been quietly dropped from the Said canon. But it provides a richer and more illuminating perspective on Said's overall contribution than any other single document, and any understanding of Said as a thinker and as a person must begin with it.

For many who admired Said as an engaged and politically committed critic devoted to speaking truth to power, reading this book is a painful exercise, for it seems to represent a particularly unreflective instance of traditional humanism. As a graduate student, Said had noted that very few critics had made a systematic study of the eight published volumes of Conrad's letters; and with a graduate student's opportunism, he decided to mine these letters for clues to the fiction, focusing especially—another graduate student move—on the short fiction. The young scholar tracks the movement of motifs, themes, and concerns between the letters and the fiction, with particular emphasis on "facing the darkness," the dialectic between past and present, notions of truth and image, the growth of moral awareness, and the importance of forging a "vital association between a writer's work and his essential individuality" (JC, 28). The letters are treated as rough drafts of the crises and dramas represented in more finished and aestheticized form in the fiction, which depicts a "slowly unfolding discovery of his mind, his temperament, his character—a discovery, in short, that is Conrad's spiritual history as written by Conrad himself" (5).

Even in the context of literary criticism in the early and mid-1960s, *Joseph Conrad and the Fiction of Autobiography* is in many ways a reactionary work. It does not reflect the formal concerns of the New Criticism, but reaches back to an older man-and-his-works tradition. It betrays no sign of incipient sympathy with the movement that announced itself at the 1966 conference at Johns Hopkins University, attended by Barthes, de Man, Hippolyte, Lacan, and Derrida (although Said met Derrida during that year). Said's focus on the writer's inner struggles and spiritual quest seems untouched by the energies of either the present or the future of criticism. But in producing this regressive discourse, Said was discovering his own present and future, embarking on his own spiritual quest by way of a reading of Conrad, whom he constructed as a speculative image of himself, of who he was, and how he might comport himself and make his way in the world.

Perhaps the most striking feature of the book is its premise, that Conrad was primarily engaged not in the creation of aesthetic forms, but rather in a more urgent and uncertain process of self-discovery, self-recognition, self-healing, self-fabrication, and self-creation. Said seeks in Conrad's work transformations of experiences documented in raw form in the letters, in the conviction that making fiction is one way to make a self. The Conrad that emerges from this study is not a master craftsman or even an artist in the usual sense, but a struggling outcast beset by "the embarrassments and the difficulties of an overwhelmingly untidy existence as a French-speaking, self-exiled, extremely articulate Pole, who had been a sailor and was now, for reasons not quite clear to him, a writer of so-called adventure stories" (4). An immigrant in a land where nobody spoke his mother tongue, Conrad was displaced in several respects, his "selfhood . . . dissipating itself in a wide scattering of disparate impressions" with no central purpose (53). Born in a partitioned country,[18] Conrad was himself partitioned, his life broken into discrete phases, so that he was, in effect, "many different people, each one living a life unconnected with the others" (viii). And he had secrets. Said's Conrad was acutely conscious of his own inadequacy. He had recurrent fears about his own "laziness and incompetence," and above all a suffocating experience of shame (62). When Conrad wrote a story that was in any way autobiographical, Said notes, the story tended to probe "further and further into the shadows of Conrad's own sense of self-absorption, tended to reveal too many things about himself. And those, almost invariably, filled him with a deep feeling of shame" (97). A fear of being found out was apparently justified, for as Said argues, Conrad's "own personal history was a disgraceful paradigm of shameful things, from the desertion of the ideals of his Polish heritage to the seemingly capricious abandonment of his sea life. He had become . . . a creature of civilization, living in reliance upon the safety of his surroundings."[19]

This is, to say the very least, a highly idiosyncratic reading of Conrad. There is no evidence that would suggest that Conrad was unclear as to why he was writing; his letters and especially the autobiographical *A Personal Record* document that sense of an unwilled compulsion that one associates with born writers.[20] Nor have biographers uncovered any significant traces of a crippling sense of shame. One might plausibly attribute shame to Lord Jim, but Said is virtually alone in detecting an unalloyed shame in Conrad himself—hence his statement that "not enough has been written on [Conrad's] extraordinarily powerful sense of shame" (98). There is virtually nothing in Conrad that would indicate guilt about excessive self-absorption, about "abandoning" the sea (after twenty years), or about choosing to live on dry land out of the reach of violent storms.[21]

Here again, *Out of Place* provides the missing explanatory context. Perhaps the most shocking revelation in this extraordinarily detailed text is the disclosure that the young Said—a tall, strikingly handsome, athletic, intellectually precocious, artistically gifted son of privilege—grew up in an atmosphere of constant humiliation. His parents and teachers constantly accused him (at least in Said's account) of laziness, ineptitude, carelessness, insubordination, moral unworthiness, and a chronic failure to "do his best." His parents in particular rarely missed opportunities to single out particular character traits and even body parts for special criticism: back, hands, stomach, chest, and, above all, mouth. "My father would swiftly thrust his hand out," Said recalls, "put his thumb and second finger on either side of my mouth, press in, and hold the area with a number of energetic short jerks to the left and right, all the while producing a nasty, buzzing sound like 'mmmmmm,' quickly followed by 'that weak mouth of yours'" (OP, 66). "Look," a camp counselor told him, "I saw you take that hot dog"; and the young Said "stood transfixed in shame and wordless embarrassment" (137). Or: "I was reduced to a state of complete confusion, and a kind of babbling helplessness" (30). Or "Who was this ugly brute to beat me so humiliatingly? And why did I allow myself to be so powerless, so 'weak'—the word was beginning to acquire considerable resonance in my life—as to let him assault me with such impunity?" (42). Or "I felt myself to be seriously unwilling to let myself be looked at, so conscious was I of innumerable physical defects, all of which I was convinced reflected my inner deformations" (55). Or "I can recall staring at myself disgustedly in the mirror well past my twentieth birthday" (66). Or "I was immediately seized with such terror, guilt, shame, and vulnerability that I have never forgotten this scene" (72). Or "I felt like an ass and blushed uncontrollably. . . . Of course I was guilty. Of course he now knew it" (73). Or "I felt I was a failure, both physically and morally" (77). Or "To my great humiliation George beat me with ease every time we played" (196). Shame is not an occasional childhood experience, but the theme of his entire early life, on which were played a thousand variations. Not enough has been written on Said's extraordinarily powerful sense of shame.

For Said, Conrad's singular and monumental achievement consisted of making his shame productive, which he accomplished by turning away from his inner difficulties and getting down to work. Said is aggressively hostile to any attempt to explain Conrad by reference to "unconscious" energies, and repeatedly insists that nothing is to be gained by introducing a general theory of the unconscious as a way of understanding Conrad or his work.[27] Rather, he insists, Conrad worked in the world, confronting life as he found it, and the critic has no more need than Conrad to look for a "deeper" explanation. Nor does Conrad yield his secrets to a Marxian analysis: "the Marxist conclusion, class consciousness, does not suit the bias of this study," which is oriented entirely toward "the exigencies of Conrad's personal situation" (12).[23] The productive engagement was not between Conrad and his inner demons or drives, and not between Conrad and his class, but between Conrad and the world in which he found himself. As Said puts it,

> Conrad's individuality resides in a continuous exposure of his sense of himself to a sense of what is not himself: he set himself, lumpish and problematic, against the dynamic, fluid processes of life. Because of this, then, the great human appeal and distinction of Conrad's life is the dramatic spirit of partnership, however uneasy or indecorous, his life exemplifies, a partnership between himself and the external world. I am speaking of the full exposition of his soul to the vast panorama of existence it has discerned outside itself. He had the courage to risk a full confrontation with what, most of the time, seemed to him to be a threatening and unpleasant world. (9)

I quote this passage at such length because it gives an excellent sense of the immediacy, vividness, and sense of scale that, even in a small-bore, dissertation-ish piece of apprentice work, Said was capable of achieving. Particularly noteworthy is the freedom Said feels to interject his own reflections about life and existence into a work whose primary function, after all, is to demonstrate professional competence.

Conrad managed to win his battle and make his way, according to Said, by creating a "manufactured impression of himself as a composed individual" that camouflaged whatever intuitions Conrad may have had about his own unworthiness or ineptitude (JC, 58). His method was essentially to "[hide] himself within rhetoric," his famous indirection and obscurity representing not modernist virtuosity or technical experimentation but a way of testing himself against difficulties and of representing his own sense of disjointedness in the form appropriate to it. His style is a moral rather than an artistic achievement, "the concrete and particular result of his immense struggle with himself. . . . Pain and intense effort are the profound keynotes of Conrad's spiritual history" (4). This difficult story ends well, for the result, Said argues, is nothing less—and nothing more—than "the achievement of character" (13). *Joseph Conrad and the Fiction of Autobiography* is a not a work of literary criticism as much as it is a study of triumphant individualism.

For Saideans, this first book represents juvenilia; for Conradians, it is simply beside the point, for its arguments simply do not make any contact with established Conrad criticism. Conrad's reputation has been sustained by those readers who see in his work an exceptionally fertile field for analysis and interpretation. Said, by sharp contrast, explicitly rejects the entire concept of "depth" in Conrad, and in criticism generally. Rejected, too, is the picture of Conrad developed by Conrad criticism in the mid-1960s as a man of superior insight, vast experience, and artistic courage—a master mariner, master storyteller, and master craftsman whose best work represented not just a technical accomplishment of the highest order, but an undaunted confrontation with the irrational, the unknowable, and the unfathomable. Said's Conrad is bewildered, confused, uncertain, groping, harassed, insecure, driven. His work—on the evidence of Said's book— says next to nothing about race, sex, empire, hearts of darkness, or secret sharers. Instead, Said places squarely before his readers the spectacle of a lumpish and problematic, but hardworking and determined fellow who is trying to make his way in a threatening and unpleasant world.

If the Conrad of conventional criticism is hard to locate in this book, however, Said himself is not. It is remarkably easy to see in Said's Conrad a refracted image of Said himself, the man who overcame a deep and confused sense of inferiority, who abandoned his homeland by choice rather than necessity, who was "tortured by a finite number of intolerably fixed situations to which he seemed to return everlastingly" (as to a *cantus firmus*), who overcame pain through intense effort, who was "forced to surmount his laziness and incompetence and to produce something" (JC, 6, 62). Nor does Said discourage this comparison. He told one interviewer in the mid-1980s, "I felt, first coming across Conrad when I was a teenager, that in a certain sense I was reading, not so much my own story, but a story written out of bits of my life and put together in a haunting and fantastically obsessive way."[24] Conrad provides Said with an opportunity for self-exploration without the embarrassment, and even gives him the subject for his next book. All Conrad needed to achieve himself, Said writes, was to renounce any hope of regaining his home or language and find a "starting point," a "beginning or initiative . . . with enough connection to his own life to give method and consistency to what he wrote" (53). Said later told Mallios that *Beginnings* began, in a sense, with the famous passage in *Heart of Darkness*: "Going up that river was like traveling back to the earliest beginnings of the world . . . ."[25] Long after *Beginnings*, Said was still going up that river. As he described Conrad, the young scholar saw not only his past life but his future, the main principles, features, and emphases of his entire career, unfolding before him like a scroll in code:

At any rate, if he could do nothing else, he had to escape from the anonymity of common human destiny; that was the only way to confirm the reality of his individuality. There was for him no available movement of defiance, as there had been for his father, in which to play a part. He had to create the movement, his role in the movement, and the gesture of defiance all on his own. Such, as he understood it, was the cruel joke played on him by history when it offered him only a stunted, incomplete legacy of national identity, dissipated in an obscure and chaotic world. (JC, 38)

The motivation for this intensely felt passage is unclear in the context, but it leads directly to the final argument in the book, that Conrad ultimately found himself not by looking within but by looking outside, at history. The Great War, Said argues, presented Conrad with a large analogy for his inner turmoil. In the destruction of Europe, Conrad saw his own disorder magnified, as if the trouble in his soul "had suddenly taken Europe for its stage" (79). Expressed, as it were, geographically and historically, Conrad promptly shed his habitual obscurity, melancholia, and obsession with darkness; he began to write more lucidly, his plots became more consecutive, a new spirit of reconciliation and calm entered his work, and he became able at last to portray characters who "[transmute] suffering into stillness and peace" (197).

In a book that is consistently idiosyncratic, this argument is perhaps the most anomalous. The notion that Conrad's career arcs up towards resolution and calm contradicts not just Thomas Moser's influential 1957 thesis about Conrad's career—that it spiked sharply at the beginning, sustained itself for about a decade, and then tailed off dramatically[26]—but also the most common hierarchy of Conrad's texts, which places *Heart of Darkness*, *Lord Jim*, *Nostromo*, and *The Secret Agent*, all produced between 1899 and 1906, on top, and *Under Western Eyes, Chance, Victory, An Arrow of Gold*, and *The Rover* lower down. In Said's account, *The Shadow Line*, composed in 1915, represents a moment of ultimacy, a vision of a "deeply satisfying paradise" that brings the protagonist a sense of "ideal completeness, self-fulfillment, permanence," all achieved with "lyrical ease" (183). The final insight granted the protagonist is "that life is a blessing: any life, even the sick, hard one, is worth living" (194). The trajectory goes, then, from pain, struggle, and shame to achievement, calm, and reconciliation.

My argument, then, is that the chief interest of this book is not as a discussion of the "fiction of autobiography" in Conrad, but as a kind of fictional autobiography by Said, a testimony to a passionate, immediate, multilayered, and occasionally oppositional bond with a man in whom Said sees all the themes, energies, and obsessions that would come to define his mature critical positions and drive his own "spiritual quest." The entire book is an intimate and detailed portrait of Said himself—his commitments, drives, interests, fears, obsessions, and dreamy fantasies of a happy ending—filtered through the medium of Conrad. This portrait of the critic as a young man is not one Said could have produced if he had tried, partly because his self-understanding was manifestly a work in progress as he was writing this, but more directly because he was not, at the moment, thinking primarily or directly about himself. He was engaged rather in the kind of creative, absorptive work he said Conrad was engaged in; he was trying, as he said Conrad was, to imagine his way into a new identity in an adopted land by writing books and constructing a public career that would effectively overwrite the image he had of himself as pathetically and shamefully out of place.

3. Prolongations

The Conrad book is, then, the innocent origin, or perhaps the latency period, of Said's career, informed by preliminary versions of the certain recognitions, emphases, or energies that would later evolve into elements or characteristics of his fully matured critical positions. The most notable of these is a keen responsiveness to what might be described as turbulence, incoherence, or division in the field of identity. *Joseph Conrad* begins with the assertion that Conrad was in effect "different people, each living a life unconnected to the others," a description Said would shortly apply to himself (viii). Considering the remarkable consistency of his concerns and his fifty-year residency in the United States, this claim was mysterious to some of his friends, who had no difficulty seeing his life as a unity.[27] Not all émigrés have felt that their identities lay about them in pieces, but for Said, division seems to have been an essential part of his self-conception from the very beginning. Nor was it confined to that experience common to creative people of suspending one's ordinary concerns and surrendering oneself wholly to the exigencies of the task at hand. Said's doubleness took the form of an insistence that one part of himself was incommensurate with, and unaccountable to, the other. He begins *Out of Place* with an anguished meditation on the distinction between "Edward" and "Said," which he later transforms into the split between "my public, outer self, and the loose, irresponsible fantasy-ridden churning metamorphoses of my private, inner life" (OP, 137). He took heart from Chomsky's confident assertion of non-relation between his linguistics and his politics and ignored (like Chomsky) ample evidence that the connection is quite strong and clear.[28] What is asserted as a fact seems also to have been a wish to establish some principle of difference, to be his own doppelganger, to keep another "self" in reserve—hidden within rhetoric, as he says of Conrad.

Everything in Said's experience confirmed this doubleness. As a teenager, he confided to his mother that, "despite the almost comic lineup of failures and endless troubles" he found himself in at school and everywhere else, he sensed that he was "someone both gifted and unusual" (OP, 60). As an adult, he confesses, he sensed the opposite, that despite his extraordinary record of successes and honors, he was acutely vulnerable and exposed, so that "to this day I find it unbearably difficult to look at myself on television, or even read about myself" (55). As his fame grew, this sense of vulnerability actually seemed to increase, and manifested itself in what became a characteristic explosiveness, often out of scale with the provocation, in public exchanges. In the last decade of his life, Said developed a global reputation for combustibility, and although his admirers sometimes sought to explain his rages by pointing to the historical gravity of the issue at hand or the particular affront that had provoked him, his rages remained as events requiring explanation.

Said went much farther in the direction of rhetorical violence than most scholars, and he got there in a hurry. He blasted Ernest Gellner, who had reviewed *Culture and Imperialism* in *TLS*, as "an academic Rumplestiltskin, stamping his little feet when he doesn't get his way, appearing more unbalanced in attitudes that are now too extreme even for him to get away with."[29] At least Gellner was a mature scholar secure in his reputation and standing in the world; not all of his targets were so fortified. When Said was elected president of the Modern Language Association for 1999, an assistant professor, Jon Whitman, wrote to *PMLA* from Tel Aviv saying that he was resigning his membership in protest because Said's

> public assaults against individuals whose views reasonably differ from his own deeply violate fundamental values repeatedly professed by the Modern Language Association. At times such assaults have passed beyond the forms of disparagement that often characterize contemporary academic disputes. They have passed into acts of aggressive contempt and blatant dehumanization.[30]

Whitman supported this charge with a list of phrases deployed by Said in the course of debates: "solemn idiocies," "a semideranged world entirely his own," "patronizing and hypocritical self-congratulation," "tasteless and jejeune [but] not surprising," "wacky," "puerile," "a small frightened man," and "characteristic idiocy." "The more reflective the critique of his views," Whitman said, "the more enraged his reaction." Said, the world-famous president-elect of the Modern Language Association, replied by claiming that he was the victim of an assault with historical implications. On all the occasions cited by Whitman, he insisted, he had been attacked "at least as unreasonably as anything I either thought or said afterward"— and besides, "many of the people he claims I've dehumanized are friends." What's worse—far worse—is that Whitman's animus "resembles that of a partisan, recently nationalized Israeli, once again fighting a Palestinian. Whitman's letter is, I believe, an extension of the Zionist-Palestinian conflict masked as an argument against public misbehaving; it is drenched in the usual hypocrisy about norms of conduct. . . . Who has appointed Whitman referee anyway?" The only explanation for Whitman's behavior must be that he—once an "amiable, respectful, never contentious student" of Said's at Columbia—must be enacting some "oedipal rebellion." Which, however, could not erase the fact of "Israel's intransigent bellicosity."

A disturbing combination of bombast and self-pity defines Said's tone in such exchanges, and they are many. Said was incapable of hearing criticism, and simply unwilling even to engage in dialogue with anybody who demurred, however slightly, from his positions; and when people did not demur, but tried to meet him in the middle, he was, as Whitman notes, at his most aggressively defensive.[31] In perhaps his most widely noted performance, he characterized Robert Griffin—whose position was that "no resolution is possible without recognizing the principle of Palestinian self-determination," and "that Israel should negotiate a withdrawal from the occupied territories as soon as possible"—as "an ideological simulacrum whose only purpose is to attack, defame, harass Palestinians with the aim of stopping their irreversible progress toward self-determination." Said then invoked images of political prisoners languishing in Israeli jails and of Palestinian women beaten with clubs or shot with plastic bullets, their loved ones killed or maimed, with the implication that Griffin was somehow responsible for, or at least complicitous with, these abuses. Said concluded by insisting that because Griffin was speaking as a hypocrite and a knave, he should immediately clear out of "a discussion he has degraded" and begin to "atone for the crimes he defends."[32]

Although Swift (according to Said) invariably "[attacks] what he is impersonating," Said seems on this and other occasions to impersonate what he attacks, engaging in reductionism, name calling, and personal and ethnic slurs (WTC, 87). He seems determined to represent himself as the victim of an attempt to vilify or shame him, determined to find himself embroiled or locked in opposition, especially when debating people whose political positions are consistent with his own. The principle of absolute nonreconciliation is maintained and mirrored by what Griffin calls Said's "two conflicting epistemologies, a postmodernist one for his political enemies who are enmeshed in a web of historical determinations, and a classical one for himself, whose perspective is consonant with truth."[33] To Said, his opponents—and to reply or respond to Said was to oppose him—were all Orientalists, claiming to speak the truth but unwittingly serving imperial or colonial ends. Indeed, they cannot avoid this miserable fate, for there is no essential Orient that can be accurately represented (*see Orientalism* 322, 273).[34] And yet, Said can blast his enemies for failing to cite specifics, use Arabic sources, or uphold basic standards of scholarly rigor.

These "conflicting epistemologies" might be mapped onto the two mutually unaccountable parts of his personality—an official, public, philological self, and the loose, irresponsible, postmodern, constructivist self—that Said described in *Out of Place.* Such a mapping would enable us to see his outbursts as compulsive restagings of the antagonistic structure by which he felt himself to be internally defined, with the violence of his response representing an attempt to unify his identity in opposition to an external enemy. Or, we might say, his battles constitute reenactments of the humiliations of childhood, met this time not with acquiescent shame but with discursive belligerence. Such explanations would be merely speculative, of course, but some explanation is required that accounts for the sheer strangeness of Said's eruptions by tracing them to desperate personal urgencies, because the occasions themselves do not always have the fuel necessary to sustain such a blaze.

Take for example the attack near the end of *Orientalism* (O) on Bernard Lewis's explanation of Islamic concepts of revolution. The Arabic word for revolution, Lewis notes, is *thawra,* which means "to rise up (e.g., of a camel), to be stirred or excited, and hence, especially in Maghribi usage, to rebel." The term is associated with sedition, "as one of the dangers which should discourage a man from practicing the duty of resistance to bad government."[35] Said begins his response by accusing Lewis of Orientalist condescension in comparing revolution to a camel. Moreover, Said continues, Lewis is inaccurate, because many contemporary Arabs "have an active commitment" to revolution. Worst of all, Lewis's poor attempt at etymology is deformed by an essentializing misprision that repeats ancient slurs about Arab sexuality. Indeed, Said charges, Lewis's phrases hint

> much more broadly than is usual for him that the Arab is scarcely more than a neurotic sexual being. Each of the words or phrases he uses to describe revolution is tinged with sexuality: *stirred, excited, rising up.* But for the most part it is a "bad" sexuality he ascribes to the Arab. In the end, since Arabs are really not equipped for serious action, their sexual excitement is no more noble than a camel's rising up. . . . instead of copulation the Arab can only

achieve foreplay, masturbation, coitus interruptus. These, I think, are Lewis's implications, no matter how innocent his air of learning, or parlorlike his language. (O, 315–16)

What could possibly account for this bizarre outburst? Even if we accept the dubious premise that Lewis was making a comment about Arab sexuality, he was certainly not repeating the usual Orientalist depiction of the "lustful Turk" or Arab, who, as Said comments on many occasions, is said to enjoy an easier, less restricted, more various experience of sexuality than, for example, the repressed British or the active but conventional French.[36] A more proximate explanation is that Said is registering some deep-laid fear that he himself was "really not equipped for serious action," and given to fumbling uncertainty. Such fears are in fact detailed at depressing length in *Out of Place*, where he repeatedly describes himself as "timid," "sexually deprived," "woefully unsuccessful" with women, "sexually ill," and so forth. In perhaps the single most disturbing incident recorded in the entire book, his parents appear at his bedroom door, his father holding out his unstained pajamas: "Your mother and I have noticed . . . that you haven't had any wet dreams. That means you're abusing yourself" (70). Responding as it were on behalf of slandered Arabs, Said has confusedly substituted another, private scenario for the cliché he charges Lewis with retailing.

An even more revealingly misguided attack is leveled at William Edward Lane, author of the 1836 *An Account of the Manners and Customs of the Modern Egyptians*, an encyclopedic description of what Lane had observed and learned about Egypt during extended periods of residency. This was for many years the most authoritative and complete source on its subject, and remains in print today.[37] To Said, Lane is among the first and greatest Orientalists, which means that he has produced a congenial article for the consumption of a Western audience accustomed to empire as its birthright. Lane's very assiduousness in gathering information is, in Said's account, a small version of the appropriative imperial project. Lane's subjects demonstrate all the usual clichés, including "the sadomasochistic colossal tidbits: the self-mutilation of dervishes, the cruelty of judges, the blending of religion with licentiousness among Muslims, the excess of libidinous passions, and so on" (O, 162). Worst of all, Said charges, Lane is no real expert, because he never "joins" the society he studies. He did not, for example, take an Egyptian bride, a gift offered to him by an Egyptian friend who was concerned that, by not taking a wife, Lane was offending Egyptian sensibilities, and who had even gone to the trouble of locating a nearby widow. Even when the friend assures Lane that his new wife could be easily divorced when Lane returned to England, Lane refuses the gift. In Said's view, such a refusal to get with the program demonstrates Lane's "literal disengagement from the productive processes of Oriental society." Warming to his subject, Said charges that, by refusing to accept the proffered wife, Lane does more than absent himself from the pleasures of the Orient; he "literally abolishes himself as a human subject by refusing to marry into human society. Thus he preserves his authoritative identity as a mock participant and bolsters the objectivity of his narrative." To establish his credentials as an Orientalist, Lane felt he had "to avoid dating himself by entering the human life-cycle." If he had married, "his perspective would no longer have been antiseptically and asexually lexicographical." By "subduing his animal appetite," Lane interfered with "the ordinary narrative course of human life"—narrative rather than catalogue being the more authentic mode of representation—and so became "literally" inhuman, a monster of knowledge (163).

Nowhere does Said consider that perhaps Lane did not want to marry, or did not want a wife simply to be given to him. Nowhere does he mention, much less render an opinion on, the offer made by Lane's friend of a female slave as an acceptable substitute for a wife. Lane's own explanation—that he was planning to leave the country soon and did not think it appropriate to marry—simply does not impress Said. Everything about this passage strikes a jarringly discordant note of deep sexual anxiety and uncertainty, and betrays an astonishing lack of basic judgment masked by hypervirile declamation.

Perhaps the recurrent panic surrounding the subject of sexuality helps account for the immediate appeal of Conrad for the émigré-undergraduate that Said was when he first read him in depth. Conrad's works are dominated by intense male relationships; women, as Marlow comments in *Heart of Darkness*, are "out of it." The fraught, passionate attachments formed by men in Conrad's novels never rise to the level of the overtly homosexual, but they approach that level with some regularity, often seeming to do so without Conrad's awareness. Stories of life at sea or in the jungle are by and large stories of men together, and nothing more needs to be said than that; one must grant the artist his *donnée*. But on many occasions, Conrad's language, whether through suggestive indirection or oddly angled puns and homophones, registers a homoerotic affect, especially in *Nigger of the "Narcissus," "The Secret Sharer," Lord Jim,* and *Heart of Darkness.*[38] And, in this last text, Conrad approaches the issue directly in the portrait of the Russian youth who has discovered Kurtz at the Inner Station.

> They had come together unavoidably [Marlow says], like two ships becalmed near each other, and lay rubbing sides at last. "We talked of everything," [the Russian] said quite transported at the recollection. "I forgot there was such a thing as sleep. The night

did not seem to last an hour. Everything! Everything! . . . Of love too." "Ah, he talked to you of love!" I said much amused. "It isn't what you think," he cried almost passionately. "It was in general. He made me see things—things."[39]

Said mentions this incident in his Conrad book, but treats the Russian only as an "impassioned, eager, and innocent" young man in search of adventure, even a heroic soul willing to face "darkness" in search of "truth" (JC, 146). He does not speculate on what the amused Marlow may have been thinking that so alarmed the passionate young man. The banality of the treatment leaves one wondering why he introduced it at all; but in a larger sense, one wonders about the general neglect, in all Said's work on Conrad, of the highly charged relationships between men. It is a striking silence, given Said's career-long investment in Conrad, and one that might be best explained by referring to Said's well known argument about Jane Austen's *Mansfield Park*, in which he asserts that the reality of the slaveholding imperial economy is present in its very absence in the text, where it is not so much denied as assumed, and treated as a subject that, although important, is best passed over in silence.[40]

To many of Said's readers, the overpoweringly male orientation of his work is one of its most troubling features. At the beginning of a book-length introduction to Said, Valerie Kennedy notes that "Said's blindness to gender characterizes almost all of his work. . . . he has shown himself to be aware of his deficiencies in this respect. As he has said . . . there are no 'heroines' in *Orientalism*, and *After the Last Sky* also comments on its own failure to pay attention to Palestinian women."[41] The consequence of this blindness is best described by Conrad's narrator Marlow, who remarks in *Chance*—a book Said values much more highly than most Conradians—on the cost of violating the norm of heterosexual behavior: "Pairing off is the fate of mankind. And if two beings thrown together, mutually attracted, resist the necessity, fail in understanding and voluntarily stop short of the—the embrace . . . then they are committing a sin against life, the call of which is simple. . . . And the punishment of it is an invasion of complexity, a tormenting, forcibly tortuous involution of feelings."[42] Said understood this complexity perfectly.

The Saidean equivalent of "refusing the embrace" is the rejection of filial associations in favor of the gentile, voluntary creation of meaning—complexity as a consequence of the rejection of simplicity. We can see the rejection, and the consequences, in the compass of a single essay, "Conrad: The Presentation of Narrative," which was included in *The World, the Text, and the Critic*. Written during a sabbatical year spent in Lebanon in 1972, this essay took up the concept of presentation, a term that had, in the Conrad book, entirely positive connotations as the means by which one organizes oneself, makes a beginning, creates a world, enters history, performs oneself, achieves a character. The essay begins in this positive vein, pointing out that Conrad took great pains to establish worldly contexts for his tales—setting *Heart of Darkness*, for example, on board a ship in the Thames harbor—because he was acutely aware of the unreality of writing, and wanted to overcome this unreality by emphasizing the event of utterance, which is intended to convey "clarity, or realized intention" (WTC, 109). "Presentation" thus signifies worldliness, or at least does so until the very end, when Said suddenly realizes that in almost every case, what really underwrites this clarity or intention is "an inert substance like silver" in *Nostromo*, which is "felt mistakenly to be capable of embodying the visible, the timeless, the unmediated sensory possession of all reality" (109). So there is really no full presence or perfect clarity at all, and all of Conrad's repeated efforts to negate writing by representing specific circumstances of speech founder as narrator after narrator becomes "a talking insubstantiality" (110). By the end of the essay, presentation has been collapsed into representation and burdened with the adjective "mere."

To grasp the complicating pressures on Said's thinking at this time, we need to turn to the other text that was occupying his attention, *Beginnings* (B), which was begun around 1970, and that Brennan describes as "a booklength reflection on 'presentation,'" on the nondynastic, gentile production of meaning.[43] During that year in Lebanon, Said was studying Arabic literature and philology, and in this book, he introduced for the first time Arabic or Islamic materials. At the very beginning of his chapter 3, "The Novel as Beginning Intention," Said sketched a new context for literature that illuminated the specific role played by the novel in the Western tradition. In the Islamic tradition, he noted, the very desire to begin afresh by, for example, writing a novel, is "inimical to the Islamic world-view. The Prophet is he who has *completed* a world-view; thus the word *heresy* in Arabic is synonymous with the verb 'to innovate' or 'to begin'" (B, 81). In the Islamic tradition, there is no need to begin, because the world in its plenitude is already full, complete, and accessible to vision, belief, tradition. If for Europeans the prospect of beginning afresh and entering onto a free process of development and exploration is constantly celebrated, for Muslims, life is already fully explained by the Koran. In principle, there are no moral dilemmas because belief settles all questions. Such ideas may indicate a background for the rejection of psychoanalysis in *Joseph Conrad*; what is new here is the attribution of antipsychoanalytic notions to Arabic-Islamic tradition, which gives them cultural authority and also signals a nascent conflict in Said's allegiances. We can sense here the stirrings of an account to rival the strident individualism he had heretofore endorsed, an account more consistent with the Islamic worldview that, after the 1967 war, he had increasingly embraced not precisely as his own, but as one feature of the world into which he had been born, and therefore part of his identity.[44]

The introduction of the Prophet into critical discourse has complicated the argument considerably. The expanded context provided by Islam has made it possible to see that the gesture of claiming the authority necessary to begin—the gesture encapsulated in the term *presentation*—is not necessarily a sign of freedom; in another culture, individualism is anathema and beginning heretical. And not just in another culture. The history of the novel, Said argues, gives evidence of a conversion from the "classic" period of exuberant beginning to a later stage in which such assumptions were seen to be a sham because authority was now seen to reside in an inhuman process that enslaves people and defeats their aspirations. The primary example of this later stage, in which novelists take a darker, more involuted view of beginnings is *Nostromo*, a hypertextual discourse that represents not the material reality of South America but only "the author's dilemmas" in organizing his materials (B, 137).

The true nature of the tormenting dilemma faced by Conrad, and by Said, is condensed into the word Said chooses to designate the act of claiming of authority by the novelist-beginner—"molestation," a term whose ordinary meaning, never quite eclipsed by the meaning Said assigns it, suggests not successful self-creation but sexual victimization. "No novelist," Said asserts, "has ever been unaware that his authority . . . is a sham. Molestation, then, is a consciousness of one's duplicity, one's confinement to a fictive, scriptive realm" (B, 84). One can feel the strain as the once-buoyant concept of presentation is freighted with this new meaning. If, Said argues in one particularly tortured passage, earlier novels had proceeded from a desire to "create or author an alternate life and to show (by molestation) this alternative to be at bottom an illusion with reference to 'life,' the later version of this desire was a revulsion from the novelist's whole procreative enterprise and an intensification of his *scriptive* fate" (B, 137). From *Nostromo* on, Said contends, the business of beginning comes to be dominated by disgust for procreative and pseudo-procreative processes. Exiled from procreative reality and "the embrace," the writer, reduced to mimicry and insubstantial nothings, becomes a molester and the victim of molestation.

It is, in short, an argument about the value of novelistic beginnings that also registers religious objections to, and even a bodily disgust for, such beginnings. The result, at this inaugural moment in Said's career, the moment at which he truly becomes himself and presents himself to the world, is a conceptual impasse not just between Europe and Islam but also between "selves," with unresolved personal and political issues on one side and a determination to write oneself into a public career on the other. In the end, the image of the author—authors generally and Said in particular—that emerges in the folds and shadows of *Beginnings* is of a figure who invents himself compulsively, all the while realizing the sham, and shame, of his invention.[45]

4. Negations

The involution of Said's outlook can be measured by comparing his first discussion of Conrad's story "Amy Foster," in *Joseph Conrad*, with his last, in a 1998 essay called "Between Worlds," which was subsequently included in *Reflections on Exile* (RE). The story concerns a Polish man shipwrecked on English shores, who, although bereft of home and language, settles down in England, marries, and forms a family with an unresponsive and unintelligent woman. He never truly assimilates into the community and dies essentially alone, having been deserted emotionally by his wife.[46] The story is narrated by the village doctor, who meditates in Conradian fashion on Yanko Goorall and his mysterious life. In *Joseph Conrad*, Said argues that the story concerns the split between "pathetic action" and "the dramatic, interpreting imagination" (114). The story itself is not pathetic, however, both because of Yanko's "assertive individuality" and "genuinely buoyant nature," and because Conrad himself is "at once Yanko and [Dr.] Kennedy," action and imagination (149, 150, 114). Forty years later, the story appears to Said in a different light, as "the most desolate of [Conrad's] stories," a wrenching tale of exile, dislocation, and pure loss. In this reading, Conrad himself has shrunk, crowding into the figure of Yanko without the compensatory imaginative capacity of Dr. Kennedy: "It is difficult," Said comments in this later reading, "to read 'Amy Foster' without thinking that Conrad must have feared dying a similar death, inconsolable, alone, talking away in a language no one could understand" (RE, 555). The essential message concerns the "relentlessly anguished, raw, untreatable, always acute" experience of exile; and it is this aspect of Conrad that Said is referring to when he describes Conrad as a "*cantus firmus*, a steady groundbass to much that I have experienced."

The bond is close; and yet—"and this is the other part of it now," Said tells Mallios in 2003, "I have a feeling that Conrad and I would never, could never be friends" (290). Why not? Said lists several differences: he himself is idealistic, productive, politically engaged, committed, defiantly intransigent, unreconciled, resistant, and hopeful, whereas Conrad was "ironic and disengaged," severe, and uncompromising in his resignation. For

Conrad, lost causes were truly lost.[47] But another, equally pertinent, set of contrasts could also be drawn. Conrad was, as Said argued throughout *Joseph Conrad*, a perfect example of compensatory affiliation, a man who created a public career out of the ruins of loss and dislocation, identifying himself entirely with his new homeland. As a scholar living in the United States, Said had affiliated, too; but in laying claim first to an Arab and then to a Palestinian identity after 1967, he had, in effect, taken a 180-degree turn, completing the three-part pattern he would subsequently describe, and doing so with the same consequences he would trace in others.

Actually, he seemed to have turned in both directions at once. Both his filiative and affiliative commitments were undertaken in a spirit of total commitment, and the result was a political-critical position that was deeply mystifying because each position seemed not to complement but to negate the other. He was simultaneously committed and disengaged, partisan and independent; he was critical of all positions and parties, including the ones he represented.

Once again, the revealing tension in the argument is disclosed in the course of an engagement with Conrad, for the most condensed example of this self-interference is the discussion of Conrad in *Culture and Imperialism* (CI), "Two Visions in *Heart of Darkness*,"[48] a piece that represents not just a continuation of his early formative interest in Conrad but also the unmistakable signs of a parting of the ways. Said begins by running through an argument that had become routine for him about the way that "patriotism, chauvinism, ethnic, religious, and racial hatreds," especially when they assume the "primacy and complete centrality of the West," can lead to "mass destructiveness"; "the world," he points out, "simply cannot afford this many more times" (CI, 20). It is not clear why Said regards this as a necessary statement, but the real surprise is to follow: these attitudes, he says, find direct expression in *Heart of Darkness*. No longer, apparently, does Said regard this tale as a triumphant achievement by a man trying to repair the ruins of his life; now the text represents the imperial perspective, with Marlow's childhood recollection of staring at the "blank spaces" on the map representing the distilled expression of the Zionist attitude towards the land of Israel as a "place without a people."[49] Kurtz, Marlow, and Conrad himself all voice "world-conquering attitudes" whose effect is to make any alternative to empire literally unthinkable; the three of them can "only imagine the world carved up into one or another Western sphere of dominion" (24). Conrad simply could not see that what he represented as the "darkness" was in fact a separate "non-European world *resisting* imperialism so as one day to regain sovereignty and independence . . . . Conrad's tragic limitation is that . . . [he] could not grant the natives their freedom" (30). *Heart of Darkness* may be a great novel—Said doesn't say, and doesn't seem interested in the question—but it takes its place in a discourse that leads "inevitably to mass slaughter, and if not to literal mass slaughter then certainly to rhetorical slaughter" (25).

Thus the first vision. The second, "less objectionable" vision is not truly in the text, but is only generated by it (CI, 25). Conrad may have been unable to imagine any alternative to the cruelties of empire, Said argues, but because he retained a memory of his own exilic marginality, he managed to preserve an "ironic distance," and this distance produced "formal devices" that enabled his later readers to imagine something he could not, a free and proud postcolonial Africa, and a world free from Western domination (25). In other words, the second vision is not Conrad's at all, but a reflex of his experience that resulted in textual features that permitted others to have the vision even if Conrad could not.

This condescending and reductive treatment represents a low point in Said's critical career, a moment when his filiative impulse has led him to disavow his own *cantus firmus*, and to represent a man who began life as the orphaned son of a failed and broken Polish revolutionary as the voice—ironic, to be sure—of the imperial West, so that Said might better position himself on the side of the victims of empire.[50] But it was a low point from which Said would soon rebound. At just about the time this essay was written, between 1989 and 1991, a series of public and private events altered Said's outlook radically. In the wake of a notorious attack in *Commentary* magazine that depicted him as "The Professor of Terror,"[51] the atmosphere surrounding him grew more turbulent and unpredictable. At the same time, he was coming to a point of crisis concerning his long association with the Palestine National Council, which he left in 1991 after expressing disgust both with Arafat's refusal to acknowledge Israel's right to exist and his concessions at Oslo—in other words, both Arafat's intransigence and his weakness. He also criticized Arafat's failure even to attempt to grasp the dynamics of American culture, and the general air of corruption in the administration of the Palestine Liberation Organization.[52] When the first Gulf War broke out, Said found himself opposed to all sides, as a harsh critic of the American-led coalition, of Saddam Hussein, of Israel, of Kuwait's government, and of the Arab regimes that supported Saddam. A number of his writings during this brief war stressed the mendacity and backwardness of the authoritarian regimes that ruled most of the Arab world, regimes that disseminated unrealistic fantasies of Pan-Arabist nationalism, permitted the festering growth of reactionary Islam, implicitly or explicitly supported various forms of terrorism, and suppressed any genuine cultural and intellectual life. In the same year,

1991, he was diagnosed with leukemia; in part as a response to this crisis, he began *Out of Place* between bouts of chemotherapy, and began to think and write about "late style."

One can only speculate about the impact on Said of all of these public and private events, but one way of gathering them together into a unity is to say that they all represent failures of filiation, of biologically derived identity. After this point, affiliation and all its cognates and entailments—humanism, universalism, cultural traditions, the value of reason—come more assertively to the fore in his work. Despite his own insistence on non-reconciliation, intransigence, and resistance, Said began to soften with age and increasing consciousness of mortality. *Out of Place* represents not just an identity claim—indeed, a dismal testimony to the enduring power of home to inhibit the free development of the self—but also, paradoxically, a decisive, if loving, farewell to his family, the world he once inhabited, and the body itself.

There were exceptions to this general pattern, but the tendency is clear, and marked in the ways he recalled earlier moments of his career. Compare, for example, his various accounts of the message of *Orientalism*. The book itself concludes with the statement that the book constitutes a "reminder of the seductive degradation of knowledge, of any knowledge, anywhere, at any time" (O, 328). The 1994 edition contains a new "Afterword," which strikes a very different tone: "My aim [was] to challenge the notion that difference implies hostility" (350). In the first case, the emphasis falls on defiance and critique; in the second, on reconciliation. And then, in an essay written in the month before he died, he reflected on "*Orientalism* Twenty-Five Years Later"—a date he never reached—making it clear that, from that particular vantage point, the issue was not the degradation of knowledge at all, nor even the nonnecessity of hostility; rather, it was the positive contribution that can be made by "humanism,"

> a word I continue to use stubbornly despite the scornful dismissal of the term by sophisticated post-modern critics. By humanism I mean . . . [using] one's mind historically and rationally for the purposes of reflective understanding. Moreover humanism is sustained by a sense of community with other interpreters and other societies and periods: strictly speaking therefore, there is no such thing as an isolated humanist. . . . But what has really been lost is a sense of the density and interdependence of human life, which can neither be reduced to a formula nor brushed aside as irrelevant. . . . Humanism is centered upon the agency of human individuality and subjective intuition, rather than on received ideas and approved authority . . . humanism is the only and I would go

so far as saying the final resistance we have against the inhuman practices and injustices that disfigure human history.[53]

The same spirit of appreciation falls over Said's late revisitation of his arguments about *Heart of Darkness* in *Culture and Imperialism*. Speaking to Mallios in 2003, he recalls his account of the two visions of empire, but this time does not mention the mere "formal devices" that enable readers to glimpse a condition beyond empire that Conrad himself could not; on this occasion, he credits Conrad with "a kind of relentlessly open-ended, aggressively critical inquiry into the mechanisms and presuppositions and situatedness and abuses of imperialism."[54]

Said did not, to be sure, altogether lose his edge over the last decade of his life, but he became more evenhanded in his attacks, which were often leavened with intimations of a perspective beyond conflict, antagonism, and confrontation. At first a lonely (among Palestinians) supporter of a two-state solution for Palestine and Israel, he came, in the last few years of his life, to support an even less popular solution, a binational state predicated not just on coexistence but on shared responsibility for the creation of a common civic life. This solution has been criticized by many as unrealistic, utopian, and oblivious to realities on the ground; nor is it easy to square with his participation in the founding of the Palestinian National Initiative, whose platform does not mention a binational state.[55] It is possible, of course, that the binational solution represented nothing more than Said's own self-understanding, projected onto the map of the Middle East; it is possible, in other words, that Said had merely enacted the gesture he ascribed, unpersuasively, to Conrad, of solving his internal problems by projecting them analogically onto the world, displacing psychology with history and geography. Still, the idea of a binational state represents a generous imagining—utopian, perhaps, but proceeding from a large soul, and valuable as a marker against which more pragmatic solutions might be measured. If, for Said, Palestine-Israel was simply himself writ large—and when he describes Palestinians as decentered, displaced, in transit, and inescapably dual, the inference is hard to avoid—that was at least a more humane model than some others on offer then and now.

Over and above these specific returns, the issue of return itself had always been prominent in Said's thinking. In 1992, he wrote an essay called "Palestine, Then and Now," which was republished in *The Politics of Dispossession* as "Return to Palestine-Israel."[56] And throughout his career, the "right of return" claimed by both Israel and the Palestinians, as well as the return of occupied territories, had provided him with permanent incitements to discourse. But when, in his last, most purely affiliative book, *Humanism and Democratic Criticism*, he wrote of return, it was not a return home he was thinking of but the "return to philology."[57] He was thinking, too, of his adopted homeland that, because of its long tradition of hospitality to vast numbers of unsettled and dislocated peoples, was, he thought, the natural site for a cosmopolitan practice of humanism that reflected and celebrated the complexity and heterogeneity of the world. At the end, then, we can glimpse the lineaments of a fourth part of the pattern, a final renunciation of home and dynastic thinking, and a new investment in the values, institutions, and traditions of secular democracy, as sustained by a rigorous scholarly practice of truth.

In his interview, Mallios brings up the "Return to Palestine" essay, comparing it with Conrad's 1914 essay "Poland Revisited," in which Conrad records his experience of returning to a colonized homeland. "Really!" Said responds,

> Well, I must say I've read everything by Conrad, but this particular one I don't recall very well. It must have sunk in at some very deep level and stayed with me. Conrad is very interesting in this way. What is the phrase from *Heart of Darkness*: "the hint of half-remembered thoughts"? Because one of the characteristics of his style which I am deeply taken with is its reverberative quality: as if everything is an echo or quotation of something else. This echoic quality is why he haunts one—it's at least why he haunts me—and taking Conrad in at an early age, from the time I was in my late teens and twenties, must have inflected and informed my vision beyond my conscious recognition.[58]

In this lovely passage, a small island of reflective eloquence in the course of a very long, detailed, and illuminating interview, Said indicates not just the real (haunting) nature of his relationship to Conrad, but also the distinctive feature of his own work at its best, the capacity to apprehend and articulate the individuating features of texts, as if his sensibility were a tightly-stretched skin receiving the smallest vibrations and converting them to sound. Many have spoken of his extreme personal sensitivity, his undefended rawness—Christopher Hitchens described him as going through life "with one skin too few"[59]—and this quality, when contained and channeled, marked his best work.

Most of that work was in the field of intellectual history. He did not make his reputation as a hardheaded political analyst or actor. He lacked both steadiness and perspective, and his long association with Arafat remains for many an ineradicable stain on his memory that his eventual disengagement failed to remove. The dossier of his political statements contains many pronouncements that do not mellow with age and in fact continue to emit a poisonous glow. In his memorial tribute, Hitchens, a one-time ally and subsequent adversary, noted that Said's "moral energy wasn't always matched by equivalent political judgment."[60] Nor was Said a truly great literary critic, or even a great critic of Conrad. There are few passages in his published criticism of Conrad that match the nuanced delicacy of perception of his spoken words just quoted. In fact, he managed to be a great writer without writing great books. Perhaps the deepest reason he and Conrad "would never be friends" is that Conrad viewed every sentence as a moral and aesthetic challenge, and as Said once remarked of himself, he was "not an artist."[61] He was rapid, forceful, passionate, and often inattentive, unreflective, or careless. Writing as such cost him no particular effort, and for all his promotion of philology, he cared little for those critics who honed their sentences as if euphony and precision mattered. He contained multitudes, and on occasion contradicted himself—a different matter for a scholar or political commentator than for a poet. Early and late, he had—strange for a literary critic—a deep if rarely voiced and even perhaps rarely admitted distrust for verbal art, with its seductions and distractions. "Secular Criticism" concludes with an entirely gratuitous attack on the concept of criticism as an art. Far better, he says, in a statement that might be interpreted as a kind of proleptic defense against his own hypersensitive vulnerability to the unruly affect excited by works of art, to cultivate the "*critical* attitude" as the essence of the intellectual's vocation (WTC, 30).

In his best work, he himself was either foregrounded as subject or witness—as in the sporadically but beautifully evocative *After the Last Sky*, the powerful if sometimes tendentious exploration of *The Question of Palestine*, and *Out of Place*—or out of sight, as a scholar is hidden in the rhetoric of scholarship. His best book is very clearly *The World, The Text, and the Critic*, which has more of his strengths and fewer of his weaknesses than any other. With an impressive range and command of materials, intellectual seriousness, polemical force, sense of urgency, and passion, it stands as his *magnum opus* as a scholar and one of the most impressive academic books of its time. Its, and his, most compelling feature is difficult to describe: it is the sheer size of the thinking recorded in it, the magnitude, dimensions, and scale of it, the sense it sometimes gives of being the work of a Vichian giant engaged in a monumental labor of self-formation. More of the world's history, geography, violence, cultures, and energies coursed through Said than through most others, and all of it was directed toward articulation. He was large even in his limitations. He was, and was not, one of us.

Conclusion
Criticism in a State of Terror

A few short years ago, when "9-11," "WMD," "ground zero," "Guanta-namo," and "Abu Ghraib" meant nothing, or nothing in particular, criti-cism was in some respects operating in a far more congenial environment than today, several years later. When the world at large compels one to feel shock, astonishment, horror, outrage, and even shame—when passion is in every respect more immediately and profoundly appropriate than mea-sured reflection—criticism would seem to be disabled, rendered irrelevant by events. In a state of terror, which is perhaps the most comprehensive term to describe the political, cultural, and even the environmental con-ditions of the first years of the twenty-first century, criticism is not a first responder. Nor, indeed, does it respond directly at all. One could not easily reconstruct a record even of the most traumatic events of the past cen-tury by reading the criticism of that era, for criticism records not events but acts of attention, moments of informed and heightened focus that are performed, for the most part, by one person alone in a quiet room. So indirect or mediated is the relation of criticism to events in the world, in fact, that it seems that only some principle of deliberate avoidance or even inversion could explain the almost complete invisibility of those events within the domain of criticism. During the Second World War, New Criti-cism was the dominant critical mode in the United States; during the Cold War and the turbulent 1960s, an ahistorical formalism continued to be a

143

powerful force, supplemented by the archetypal criticism of Northrop Frye and eventually by rudimentary forms of structuralism; these gave way to deconstruction, Marxism, feminism, and high theory generally during the morning-in-America Reagan years; and in the era of technology, virtuality, and globalization, criticism has turned its attention to material culture and cultural particularities.

It is a remarkable record of countercyclical avoidance; and yet, as criticism enlists the deeper currents of individual being, it cannot fail to register its contexts, or to respond to a circumstance as extreme and ubiquitous as what I am calling terror. It is the character of criticism to record the shocks and jolts of history, but to do so in the form of a descriptive, analytical, or explanatory discourse on a discursive object. The premise of criticism is that the origin, nature, and significance of this object, or "text," are not immediately visible or apparent, and so require critical supplementation to be fully or adequately understood. The emphasis on the object entails a certain kind of focus or self-suppression such that the personal, historical, cultural, or ideological circumstances of the critic remain out of sight or at least carefully bracketed; all such circumstances are implicitly stipulated to be nonbinding or nondetermining on the critic, their influence restricted or contained. If these external factors, including the critic's beliefs about issues not directly pertinent to the text under examination, are perceived to be responsible for the criticism in ways the critic cannot account for or control, then the critic's implicit claim to critical probity is undercut, and the character of the criticism is compromised. This is true even of criticism where the gender, religion, ethnicity, or political convictions of the critic are foregrounded: the premise is still that *from my point of view*, the object really does look this way, have these features, and possess this kind of importance, not that I simply represent the object in this way because it suits my interests.

In the most general terms, "terror" names any aspect of the context of criticism that cannot be stabilized, neutralized, or suppressed so that the orderly production and reproduction of meaning can proceed. If external contextual forces are seen by the reader of criticism not as a background but as a preoccupation from which perception could not get free, if the critic himself or herself were seen as terrorized or terrified, then nothing that the critic said about the object would be persuasive. But the issue is delicate because if, on the other hand, the criticism were perceived to be completely oblivious to terror, it would be exposed to the suspicion that the critic is indifferent or insensitive, insulated somehow from the buffeting of the world, somehow inhuman. Effective criticism represents a nonresponsive response to its contexts, an apparently free, clean, or open encounter with the pertinent facts about the text in which the impact of the forces that sweep around the world is registered, but masked or mediated so these forces appear to inflect or provide a context for, but not to determine, the critical account of the object.

Modern criticism is born at the moment that the critic becomes aware of the threat of terror, of a context that threatens, but fails, to disturb the act of observation. The first critic for whom terror was a problem for criticism was Matthew Arnold, who announced in "The Function of Criticism at the Present Time" that the task of a critical, as opposed to a creative project was "to see the object as in itself it really is." Such a project, which he held to be absolutely distinct from "practical considerations" and polemics, could only flourish in certain political conditions. Critical disinterestedness could only be achieved if the world would let the critic be. Arnold concluded *Culture and Anarchy* with a memorable denunciation of the kind of social and political upheavals ("monster-processions in the streets and forcible irruptions into the parks") that intruded on the critic's attention, and an equally memorable affirmation of the superior wisdom of the state as the agent of order. In one sense, the appeal to objectivity and political reaction are rightly kept apart: criticism must not be determined by political conditions or political beliefs, because belief offered in the guise of critical observation represents a clear instance of bad faith. But in another sense, these two belong together, for criticism presupposes, in the most general sense, the effectiveness of the state in maintaining order. Criticism emerges and is valued only in a condition of social and environmental stability, and cannot function in an atmosphere of deep unpredictability or imminent violence. The very act of training one's attention on the object (the material text, the author, the tradition, the genre, the contexts, the form, the meaning, the milieu, the larger meaning), implies that one has succeeded in suppressing, excluding, or containing the various "terroristic" threats to such an act of sustained attention.

The act of distancing oneself from terror and the threat of terror—to register terror without being overcome by it—reveals, tests, and articulates character. Each of the critics discussed in this book has found a way to respond to terror by adapting it to previously established structures, deploying it as evidence of arguments to which they had already committed themselves, or enfolding it into ongoing concerns as a way of giving these concerns greater contemporary pertinence and urgency.

Perhaps the most impressive example among the four of an undeflected insistence on the priority of one's own critical project is the ongoing work of Martha Nussbaum. Since 9-11, she has written numerous articles, essays, and reviews; given countless papers, talks, and addresses of various kinds; and has published *Hiding from Humanity: Disgust, Shame, and the Law.*[1] This last project represents a further unfolding of her attempt, delineated in the discussion in Chapter 3, to anatomize, filter, rationalize, and generally identify and articulate the conceptual and political utility of the emotions, which she had at one time celebrated precisely for their violence and unpredictability. Rejecting the "no-emotion" approach to law, in which reason alone judges, Nussbaum argues that emotions often include within themselves distorted but genuine cognitive content, thoughts about objects as well as evaluative judgments, and should be respected for the reminder they give us of a common vulnerability, or as she often puts it, "disability." All emotions are not, however, equal. Unlike anger and fear, which register some present threat or vulnerability, shame and disgust are "especially likely to be normatively distorted, and [are] thus unreliable as guides to public practice" (13). Accordingly, the primary aim of the book is to marshal arguments that neutralize these two phobic emotions so that they are not made the basis of laws or policies that, Nussbaum points out, would have a disproportionately harmful effect on women and homosexuals. Tolerance and especially compassion, by which the sufferings of others are made real, must be enlisted against disgust and shame so that policies are crafted that enable people to realize to the fullest their fundamental human capabilities. A truly civilized nation, she argues, "must make a strenuous effort to counter the power of disgust, as a barrier to the full equality and mutual respect of all citizens" (117).[2]

One could characterize all of Nussbaum's work as a therapeutic and restorative immersion in the "lower" phenomena that have traditionally been ignored or even forcibly rejected by philosophy, Nussbaum's disciplinary home. Literature was the first of these outcasts to engage her attention, but over the years she has also turned, in the same recuperative spirit, to sensual pleasure, erotic rapture, sympathy, compassion, emotions generally, women, and suffering humanity in its most vulnerable or exposed forms. From the first, she has insisted that, far from being irrelevant to the lofty moral and political goals of philosophy, these rejected domains actually contain the key to the full realization of those goals. In her early work, she contended that literature, especially literature that represented instances of sympathy, affective identification, and passion, had stronger ethical credentials than philosophy, which overemphasized rationality and moral strictness. More recently, however, she has defined ethics as an orientation not toward an unregulated intimacy with other individuals but toward a compassion-based concern for humanity at large, with immediate or local affiliations acknowledged but subordinated to the universal, and private affect subsumed under the larger categories of justice and human flourishing. In recent years, Nussbaum has been reaching lower and lower for her subjects, but aiming ever higher with her arguments. The immense 750-page machinery of *Upheavals of Thought* (2001) tracks emotions from primitive object relations in Part One to "Ascents of Love" in the third and last part. And although *Hiding from Humanity* begins with "the fact that we are made of sticky and oozy substances that will all too soon decay," and with our impulse to "seek privacy for urination and defecation . . . sniff our armpits when nobody is looking, check in the mirror to make sure that no conspicuous snot is caught in our nose-hairs," the argument of the entirety is insistently lofty, moral, public, and abstract (14, 72). Beginning with ooze and armpits, the book rises massively toward "a passionate commitment to equal human dignity" (xv). It is civilizing work undertaken in a spirit of "strenuous effort," the construction of orderly, scrupulous, exacting argumentation in the service of universal peace and justice.

It is, however, in shorter pieces, talks, and essays written in recent years that one can best measure Nussbaum's fierce commitment to her own trajectory. In these, terror is often invoked, but folded firmly into Nussbaum's own concerns. In a number of these, she has begun with the fall of the towers of Troy and proceeded directly to the fall of "our own towers," an event that, however destructive, has provided extraordinary occasion for productive emotions. Terror, she says, has "this good thing about it: it makes us sit up and take notice." And what we notice, according to Nussbaum, is that an awakened responsiveness to the plight of the victims, informed by the right arguments, could lead to a more capacious, less belligerent view of the world, even to "a culture of critical compassion" informed by "a larger sense of the humanity of suffering, a patriotism constrained by respect for human dignity and by a vivid sense of the real losses and needs of others."[3] Announced with a moral and intellectual confidence developed over many years, this line of argument gathers together elements from every phase of Nussbaum's career. Everything points in one direction. Reviewing Said's *Out of Place*, she discovers that this deeply troubled and obsessive text precisely expresses her own earnestly reformist position. "It is," she writes, "exciting to see him affirm the idea that universal principles grounded in an understanding of common human capacities and problems have a radical potential as yet unrealized, spurring us to uphold justice and the bases of a flourishing life for all people."[4]

If, in what I called "phase two" of her career, Nussbaum worked in political philosophy dealing with questions of women and global justice, and in philosophical accounts of the role of emotion in ethical and political thought, an emergent phase three is even more spacious, and less exclusively invested in the human. In the 2002-03 Tanner Lectures on Human

Values, published in early 2006 as *Frontiers of Justice: Disability, National-ity, Species Membership*,[5] Nussbaum explored the limits of social contract theory in dealing with people with disabilities, ensuring justice and digni-fied life conditions for those beyond the nation state, and articulating the duties owed to non-human animals. In other words, Nussbaum has taken as her subject and in a sense her responsibility those who fall outside vari-ous circles of privilege, including that of humanity. In this work, the "capa-bilities approach" that had been developed to assess social policy especially in underdeveloped regions is applied to animals and their "flourishing," an extension that has drawn a sharp response from Peter Singer, whose 1975 *Animal Liberation* remains the key text in the contemporary discourse on animal rights.[6] It remains to be seen whether the discipline of philosophy will be able to accommodate such thinking, or whether some new kind of discourse, less specifically humanist in its orientation, will emerge from the books and articles that are surely to follow.

Elaine Scarry has discovered in terror violent affirmation of a different set of arguments. Rather than focusing on the reactions to the victims, she extracted from 9-11 different styles of "thinking in an emergency." On one hijacked plane, American Airlines Flight 77, the passengers stayed in their seats while the plane was flown into the Pentagon, with great loss of life; on United Airlines Flight 93, by contrast, the passengers apparently over-whelmed the hijackers and caused the plane to crash in a field in Pennsyl-vania. These differing responses, Scarry argued in a long essay published in *The Boston Review*, exemplified two conceptions of the relation between national defense and the citizenry: one model was "authoritarian, central-ized, top down; the other, operating in a civil frame, [was] distributed and egalitarian."[7] In the first instance, the citizens assumed the passive role that most citizens have long been accustomed to in matters of national defense, whereas in the second, they reclaimed their constitutional right to make decisions. Although "the Pentagon could not defend the Pentagon, let alone the rest of the country," the citizens on United Flight 93 deliber-ated, voted, and acted, averting an even greater tragedy.

From this parable, Scarry infers pragmatic as well as legal grounds (the Second Amendment) for lodging a certain kind of responsibility for national defense with the citizens rather than concentrating all "injur-ing power" in the executive branch. Since the advent of long-range mis-siles, the power of the congress to declare war has been steadily eroded under the pressure imposed by speed: both our descriptive and normative accounts of warfare, she points out, now turn on a phrase: the missiles will arrive, the intelligence must be processed, the president must decide on a response, and the decision must be communicated and acted on, all "in a matter of minutes." Scarry had long argued that fundamental rights and responsibilities could not be legitimately canceled or overridden by this rationale, and 9-11 proved her case wonderfully.[8]

The responses in *The Boston Review* ranged from profound gratitude that the republic contains such a brave and inspiring thinker to open contempt for Scarry's dangerous confusion about basic matters. Incredulous questions from the academics and military people enlisted to respond included: Can these two airplanes really be said to exemplify two different ways of thinking about defense? Can the citizen action on Flight 93 be considered a "success" given that everyone died? Does speed play no legitimate role in thinking about defense? Is a spontaneous group decision taken by people who feel that they are going to die in any event really a model for "a civil framework"? Would her arguments make the world, or any part of the world, safer—or far more violent? Paul W. Kahn offered his opinion that Scarry's concern with democratic self-defense "is an indulgence that may have tremendous costs to the rest of the world."[9] And Stephen M. Walt gave voice to a suspicion others indicated but did not state, that Scarry's entire essay was "an evocative metaphor masquerading as policy analysis." "Do we really want any group of Americans who believe they are in imminent danger," he asked, "to be empowered to use force to defend themselves, provided that they have 'deliberated' or 'voted' in some fashion? Of course not. Democracy is a wonderful thing, but lynch mobs can vote, too."[10]

In an impressively undisturbed response, Scarry invoked the concept that had informed much of *Dreaming by the Book*, "stretching." True, she conceded, "the concrete levers of self-defense and self-government may be beyond the reach of the citizenry right now, but are they 'out of reach' by a vast distance or instead by a gap so small it might be closed by a single day of concentrated stretching? The events of September 11—when the passengers on the Pennsylvania plane deliberated, voted, and acted in twenty-three minutes—suggest that the gap is small, that the governing levers are there and within reach." Then, the *pièce de résistance*: "Their being there, steadily within reach, is presumably what is meant by the words, 'gave proof through the night that the flag was still there.'"[11] It is doubtful that any of Scarry's respondents were persuaded that "America the Beautiful" represented better constitutional thinking than their own efforts. But Scarry was no more persuadable than they, and her refusal to concede any ground whatsoever demonstrates how tightly wrapped within their own metaphors Scarry's arguments were.[12] We see in her essay how a mass of difficult and even traumatic particulars can be "stretched" to fill the dimensions of Scarry's characteristic form of idealism, a conservative utopianism informed by Revolutionary-era rhetoric about the citizenry.

This utopianism comes into even sharper focus in another of Scarry's interventions during the era of terror, her 2004 essay "Resolving to Resist" published, once again, in *The Boston Review*. Unlike the hijacked airplanes of 9-11, this subject really requires and rewards her particular skill set; and in this essay, Scarry provides at once the most detailed account of what the Patriot Act actually licenses, and the most powerful arguments for rejecting it.[13] The argument represents Scarry at her absolute best. Freed from any need to spell out a particular course of positive action, she argues for a wholesale rejection of the Patriot Act, and a return to first principles of civil liberties. Although the constitutionalist argument about the Second Amendment and the "civil frame" of defense retains a persistent flakiness despite the great earnestness with which it is advanced, a similarly grounded argument applied to the Patriot Act is both powerfully evocative and practical. There is, to be sure, a characteristic metaphor lodged at the heart of this explicitly political argument, which emerges when Scarry notes that "the unifying work of the Patriot Act is even clearer if, rather than summarizing it as an increase in the power of the Justice Department and a corresponding decrease in the rights of persons, it is understood concretely as making the population *visible* and the Justice Department *invisible*." But the most distinctive feature of this remarkable text is its combination of assiduous research involving a huge mass of dully sinister particulars, and the high rhetoric of the Republic.

For Scarry, the Patriot Act—whose very form is encrypted, self-concealing, slinking in its obscurity, and relentless like an evil worm in the heart of Law—is best understood as an abuse of the concept of patriotism to license something that real patriots fought to proscribe: unlawful searches and seizures. The ban against such invasions of privacy was conceived against the background of the pre-Revolutionary Writs of Assistance issued by the British king, which enabled royal officers to search houses at will for smuggled goods. People died protesting this practice—and yet, our representatives, in a moment of patriotic confusion, have rushed to reinstate it, adding to "the unceasing injuries of the Bush-Rumsfeld-Ashcroft triumvirate." Today, Scarry writes, that moment of initial panic and confusion has passed, and the people, awakening to the fact that their rights have been hijacked, are rising up in protest. Resolutions urging the rejection of the Patriot Act have been passed in "first one community, then two, then eleven, then 27, then 238 . . . ." These resolutions

come from towns ranging from small villages with populations under a thousand—such as Wendell, Massachusetts (986),

Riverside, Washington (348), Gaston, Oregon (620), and tiny Crestone, Colorado (73)—to huge cities with populations of many hundreds of thousands—Philadelphia (1,517,550), Baltimore (651,000), Chicago (2,896,000), Detroit (951,000), Austin (656,500), San Francisco (777,000).

With its Lexington-and-Concord spirit and anthemic rhythm, this passage gathers towards the most powerful, or at least thrilling, formulation Scarry has yet achieved of citizenship as she conceives it:

> Whether the resistance to the Patriot Act gains more and more momentum or instead gets derailed, the town resolutions remind us that the power of enforcement lies not just with local police but with all those who reside in cities, towns, villages, isolated byways, and country lanes. Law—whether local, state, federal, or constitutional—is only real if, in the words of Patrick Henry, the rest of us will "put our hands to it, put our hearts to it, stand behind it" ("Resolving to Resist").

Perhaps the most striking feature of this text is the way it converts terror from an external to an internal threat, one that citizens might be able to control. For Scarry, the real terror is not the one perpetrated by suicidal fundamentalist fanatics from distant lands but the one created by an administration willing, indeed eager, to pervert fundamental American traditions and principles, including international law, in pursuit of its own authoritarian goals. If, on other occasions, her arguments seem to issue from a world of private meanings, metaphor, and evocation, her argument in this case asserts that the Patriot Act represents the Bush administration's fantasy of total control, and should be overturned by ordinary citizens (such as Patrick Henry) rising up in defense of traditional American values, principles, and rights as spelled out in plain English in the Constitution and Bill of Rights.

What Nussbaum finds in human capabilities and compassion, Scarry discovers in citizen's rights and constitutionalism.[14] What neither seems really able to account for is the fact that the immediate political object of their attacks—the Bush administration, which they both unhesitatingly portray as regressive, despotic, unlawful, violent, and incompetent—has at times enjoyed popular support. This is one of the hard facts that the recent work of Slavoj Žižek seeks to illuminate, and to reverse. Žižek has not discussed Scarry or Nussbaum, nor they him—in fact, none of these four has responded in any extended way to any of the others: missed opportunities all around![15]—but his ongoing critique is implicitly directed at both American fundamentalism and liberal earnestness. It is precisely these, rather than Islamic extremism, that he identifies as the true threat. The attacks on 9-11 did not scramble or disrupt reality, he argues; they clarified it, exposing the terror at the heart of liberal democracy. America did not get what was coming to it, but neither was it an innocent victim; it got—in the first instance—what it had, in countless novels and movies, imagined; and in a deeper sense, it got what it already was. Every feature attributed to the fanatical Other was, Žižek argues in *Welcome to the Desert of the Real* (WDR),[16] a feature, if not (like the Taliban) a creation, of America itself: the "clash of civilizations" is taking place within the United States, not between the United States and other countries. Everywhere, Žižek argues, there is confusion about the enemy.

The only true political enmity, from Žižek's perspective, is class antagonism; all other battles are displaced or "postpolitical" versions of this fundamental conflict. Capitalism, which hums along best in a climate of class envy but not class conflict, constantly seeks to moderate the more vehement collective passions and foster solidarity by calling attention to external enemies. Evidence of the success of the ruling-class effort to tamp down political divisions by drumming up patriotic unity can be found in the absence of genuine alternatives in the contemporary American scene, and by the universal failure to combat terror by passing through to what Žižek calls an Act—a reality-altering ethical breakthrough. Why have we failed to break through? According to Žižek, we make no progress as long as we deny our obscene libidinal investment in terror, an investment made not only by the bombers themselves, but also by the "rational strategists" behind them and even by the modern democracies that seem to oppose them. Fuddled by "false terms" such as human rights, freedom, liberty, democracy, we continue to think about lightness and dark, good and evil, when what is now needed is not more humanism but a new figure, a "freedom fighter with an inhuman face," a person capable of a "ruthless dedication to annihilation" undertaken *"out of our very love for humanity"* (WDR 82, 68). Every individual and group with a stake in the status quo is trying to defer the arrival of this new kind of hero. Rather than "waking up" to the "new reality" of the world after 9-11, we have taken the occasion to reaffirm our traditional ideological investments, with a vengeance. As Žižek expresses the new mood: "out with feelings of responsibility and guilt towards the impoverished Third World, *we* are the victims now!" (47). Heralded by some as a wake-up call, 9-11 was in fact a sedative.

The "debate" about torture provides Žižek with his best opportunity for exposing the democratic libidinal investment in terror. Against Jonathan Alter, who writes that we must "keep an open mind" about torture in the new, post-9-11 circumstances, and Alan Dershowitz, who says that if we cannot prevent torture we ought to try to regulate it by means of judicial review, Žižek insists that it is "absolutely crucial" that we do *not* keep an open mind or involve the justice system.[17] We should, in the event, "simply do it. Only in this way, by refusing to elevate a miserable necessity we had to do into a universal principle, do we retain the sense of guilt, the awareness of the inadmissibility of what we have done" (WDR 103). The clean conscience concerning torture sought by some liberals represents, for Žižek, an ultimate degradation, and it is a charge that sticks.

The total context of this charge, however, does not have the same convincing force. The sharpest contrast with the ethical collapse represented by liberalism is provided by Lenin, who, at least for a short time after 1917, kept alive the utopian spark of the revolution. Žižek has been promoting Lenin for many years, but Lenin's revolutionary *"passage á l'acte"* seems to Žižek even more pertinent as a model now, in the new era of postpolitical ideological conformity. As an academic, Žižek is not, of course, in a position to accomplish radical deeds himself, but he has recommended a few general guidelines in thinking about the optimal state of things, including "egalitarianism with a taste of terror" and "Islamic socialism,"[18] and he has made several specific recommendations. *Welcome to the Desert of the Real* culminates in a hastily conceived analysis of the conflict between Israel and the Palestine Liberation Organization as the trigger to the more general problem of Islamic fundamentalism. The key, he insists, is that Europe must assert itself as an autonomous political and economic force with its own priorities. This unified Europe should send troops into the Middle East and create by force two states, with the Jews leaving the West Bank in exchange for full recognition by the Palestinians. The West Bank and Gaza would be secured by international forces including "—why not?— NATO forces" (129). No more waffling: "Europe should simply take courage and *do* it" (144). This would indeed be a radical solution, but it would also require that "Europe" do what Žižek has criticized the United States for doing, bury its own internal conflicts, and indeed its own separate national identities, and set out on a military expedition that would involve "Europeans"—Swedes, Irish, Croatians, Germans, Poles—in relocation and "peacekeeping" missions, killing and being killed by both Israelis and Palestinians.

According to Žižek, modern democracy is, in the "Paulinian" sense, dead, inert. Liberals have, on principle, left the "place of power" empty—they are all Fidel Castros, faithful to castration—and have thereby aided and abetted the right, which has not hesitated to fill the place of power itself. Žižek's premise, in short, is that modern democracy permits no difference worthy of the name, no genuine dissent, no properly political form of conflict. In this desperate situation, it will take a figure as uncompromising, radical, and inhuman as Lenin, to break the knot, change the coordinates, and bring the world back to life. A Lenin, for example, or a de Gaulle—or a Gandhi—or a George W. Bush, who changed the coordinates of American political conservatism, the Middle East, American national self-understanding, the position of the United States in the world community, the moreal status of torture, all with a few swift strokes. Political events are not, as this depressingly obvious example attests, as predetermined by the machinations of modern capital as Žižek suggests. Nor do all difficult or dangerous situations require blood-drenched breakthroughs; nor do all forms of routine or convention cry out for their own "ethical" destruction. Not all forms of radicality are right or admirable, and some of them, beginning with those of Lenin and Mussolini, another Žižek hero (at least in his "early" years, before he succumbed to the temptation represented by Hitler), have within them an inner disposition to terror. It appears that 9-11, the astonishing event that signaled a shocking new distribution of force, has sedated not just the United States but also Žižek himself, drawing from him only increasingly peremptory and "theological" reassertions of his longstanding ideological investments, which have in fact come to seem less and less distinct from the terror they seek to combat.

The last word should go to the one who can no longer speak. On 9-11, only two years remained to Edward Said, and only a portion of his characteristic energy was available to him. The attacks themselves affected him both as a New Yorker and a prominent Arab-American activist. Much of his career had been devoted to arguing against stereotypes of Arabs as benighted, fanatical, or violent, and in favor of the view that Arab culture contained enough secular, democratic, modernizing elements to permit a genuine dialogue with the West. 9-11 hit these arguments like a bomb, but did not seem to strike Said himself with the same force. He responded within a few days with an article that registered the horror of the attacks, praised Rudolph Giuliani, and urged a critical delay before any military response, during which Americans could reflect on the deeper causes of anti-Americanism in the Arab world.

Perhaps one reason Said was so immediately able to marshal his resources at a time when he himself was very ill was that his imagination had been so thoroughly prepared for the incomprehensible event by his reading of Conrad. In this first response, published on September 16, Said virtually quoted from the meditations of the Christian financier Holroyd in *Nostromo*, who noted that "material interests," however sordid (a favorite Conradian word) their real motives, serve as their own justification because they inevitably create the peaceable conditions required for their own flourishing: "Political rhetoric in the US," Said wrote, has flung about words like "terrorism" and "freedom," "whereas, of course, such large abstractions have mostly hidden sordid material interests, the influence of the oil, defence and Zionist lobbies now consolidating their hold on the entire Middle East, and an age-old religious hostility to (and ignorance of) 'Islam' that takes new forms every day."[19] A few weeks later, Said deployed Conrad once again as a warning against the dangers of binary thinking:

> It was Conrad, more powerfully than any of his readers at the end of the nineteenth century could have imagined, who understood that the distinctions between civilized London and "the heart of darkness" quickly collapsed in extreme situations, and that the heights of European civilization could instantaneously fall into the most barbarous practices without preparation or transition. And it was Conrad also, in *The Secret Agent* (1907), who described terrorism's affinity for abstractions like "pure science" (and by extension for "Islam" or "the West"), as well as the terrorist's ultimate moral degradation.[20]

The attacks on 9-11 activated circuits in Said's imagination that had long structured his thinking about the world.

Especially considering Said's intimate relation to both the Arab world from which the 9-11 attackers emerged and the city they attacked, it is striking how little the event affected his intellectual commitments. Before 9-11, he had been thinking of "late style," and of the humanistic tradition he had long defended against the theoretical avant-garde; despite his ongoing activism and constant journalism, his major projects at the end of his life were concerned with academic rather than political issues: his posthumous book *Humanism and Democratic Criticism* (HDC),[21] for example, reaffirms in the most stunningly unfashionable terms the philological arguments that had informed his work from the beginning. This almost defiantly apolitical book focuses entirely on the individual, especially the free, critical, skeptical—the philological—individual, on whom the fate of democracy rests. The best long-term response to terror, Said suggests, is the general promotion of humanistic study, the implacable enemy of nativist or fundamentalist fantasies.

In some versions of humanism, no politics are permitted to intrude; for the theoretical critics who attacked humanism in the 1980s and 1990s, by contrast, humanism was simply the name given to a politics that did not or pretended not to know itself. In Said's version of humanism, there is a politics, but, paradoxically, it can only be realized by a passage through the individual. In fact, there are two such individuals on whom Said's humanism converges, the reader and the author. In reading, Said argues, one attempts to put oneself in the position of the author, attempting to think like the author, living the author's reality. The point of close reading is that it permits and even forces the reader to track the movements of the author's mind in the act of creation. The reader comes by this process to a sympathetic apprehension of the author's construction of an aesthetic work that, in its very nature, represents a protest against or a resistance to the given or actual. This counterconstruction might be called political, but the reading experience itself is not a political engagement; it is rather a "sympathetic dialogue," based on "erudition and sympathy," of two spirits who by this means are able to cross barriers of time and space and communicate with each other in a way that respects difference while cultivating commonality (HDC 92).

The most surprising note in the book is not the emphasis given to humanism, which an attentive reader of Said's would have noticed in many other works dating back to the very beginning of his career. No; it is the praise accorded the United States, the object of many of Said's bitterest attacks in the last decade of his life. A new note of appreciation for the complexity and dynamism of American society enters this last work almost, it seems, as if entailed by a commitment to humanism itself. Humanism, Said points out, "began in the Muslim madaris," and has often been associated with the Orient, as in Goethe's fascination with Islam and Persian poetry and, much later, Auerbach's exile in Istanbul (HDC 54). The most productive and authentic forms of humanism are not inward-turning or exclusive—Said regards T. S. Eliot as a sour perversion of the true humanist spirit—but cosmopolitan, skeptical, affirmative, and universalistic. Humanism today must be reactivated so that it may once again mediate the encounter between the West and the Orient. Myths of origin are not the answer: only in a country where "everyone is an outsider" can an authentic humanism truly flourish (48). That country is the United States. Again and again, Said specifically sites humanism in contemporary America, noting the "peculiar richness" of "this polyglot country in particular" as the natural locale for a criticism that could engage with the energy and unpredictability of "what is always present and arriving here in some form as the new and different" (48, 49, 24).

Despite the great differences between them, each of the four critics discussed in this book has responded to terror by affirming universal values and the human community. Two of them—Scarry and Said—have argued that the United States still represents a kind of portal to the universal, through constitutionalism in Scarry's case and through cultural dynamism and openness in Said's; Nussbaum and Žižek hold out for the universal in itself. At least as far as these four are concerned, terror has not suppressed criticism, nor has it deformed criticism's essential mission. What it has done is to generate a reinvigorated interest in the large issues of citizenship, justice, and human flourishing that normally remain deeply implicit in criticism; additionally, it has stimulated a commitment to a kind of thinking that transcends disciplinary categories and the relatively narrow range of issues that dominate academic discourse. By soliciting or calling out personal resources that have not been and cannot be defined by professional training or contexts, terror and the threat of terror have also challenged, refined, and expanded the characters of those critics who have answered that call. The responses of the four critics discussed in this book—and of many others who could be mentioned—have been so powerful, confident, and various that it appears, in fact, that these critics do not actually feel themselves to be living in a "state of terror"—an overarching condition in which the critical faculty is paralyzed—at all. Indeed, one of the most widely shared premises of political and critical engagement in the first years of the twenty-first century has been that "terror" is not merely a descriptive term for a condition in which criticism is irresponsible if not impossible, but is itself an object that must be seen clearly and whole, and, if necessary, redescribed or resituated. State-sponsored proclamations of terror have thus provoked in response individual acts of criticism that have invoked principles higher than the state. It is part of the character of criticism, and perhaps its most enduring justification, that it enables and structures intellectual and imaginative growth in those who can discover in themselves the capacity to respond to the turbulence of the world in a manner at once passionate, focused, independent, and disciplined.

Notes

Chapter 1

1. Charles L. Mackay, *Memoirs of Extraordinary Popular Delusions and the Madness of Crowds* (1841; repr. New York: Noonday Press, 1970). This book has been reissued several times. The entire book, which is far larger and even more wildly entertaining than the 1970 edition, is now online: http://www.litrix.com/madraven/madne001.htm.
2. Roland Barthes, "The Death of the Author," in *Image Music Text*, trans. Stephen Heath (New York: Hill and Wang, 1977), 142–8.
3. Michel Foucault, "What is an Author?" in *Language, Counter-Memory, Practice*, ed. Donald F. Bouchard, trans. Donald F. Bouchard and Sherry Simon (Ithaca, NY: Cornell University Press, 1981), 113–38. Both Barthes and Foucault were, from the very beginning of their careers, reacting to the existential humanism of Jean-Paul Sartre, Barthes by proposing a scientific study of semiotics and Foucault by insisting on all the ways in which human beings were determined by the discourses that described and defined them.
4. Michel Foucault, *The Order of Things: An Archaeology of the Human Sciences* (New York: Random House, 1973), 387.
5. Here I can only allude to the account of Foucault that emerges from James Miller, *The Passion of Michel Foucault* (New York: Simon and Schuster, 1993), an account affirmed, from a different point of view, in Geoffrey Galt Harpham, *Shadows of Ethics: Criticism and the Just Society* (Durham: Duke University Press, 1999), 67–98.
6. See especially Louis Althusser, *For Marx*, trans. Ben Brewster (New York: Vintage Books, 1970), in which ideology is described as a "system of representations" endowed with "a historical existence and role within a given society" (231).

7. Jean-François Lyotard, *The Inhuman: Reflections on Time*, trans. Geoffrey Bennington and Rachel Bowlby (Cambridge: Polity Press, 1991).

8. Jacques Derrida, *Of Grammatology*, trans. Gayatri Chakravorty Spivak (Baltimore: The Johns Hopkins University Press, 1978), 17.

9. Paul de Man, *The Resistance to Theory*, Theory and History of Literature, Vol. 33 (Minneapolis: University of Minnesota Press, 1986), 96; *Allegories of Reading: Figural Language in Rousseau, Nietzsche, Rilke, and Proust* (New Haven: Yale University Press, 1978), 153.

10. Paul de Man, *Allegories of Reading*, 206.

11. One conspicuous exception was Eve Kosofsky Sedgwick, who, noting that "a rich and conflictual salience of the vicarious" may be "embedded within gay definition," invited her reader to consider this as a possible or partial explanation for "the particular obliquities of my approach . . . . I can say generally that the vicarious investments most visible to me have had to do with my experiences as a woman; as a fat woman; as a nonprocreative adult; as someone who is, under several different discursive regimes, a sexual pervert; and, under some, a Jew." *Epistemology of the Closet* (Berkeley: University of California Press, 1990), 62–63.

12. Foucault, *Power/Knowledge: Selected Interviews and Other Writings 1972-77*, ed. Colin Gordon, trans. Colin Gordon et. al. (New York: Pantheon Books, 1980), 80. For "social": Karl Marx, *The Holy Family* http://www.marxists. org/archive/marx/works/1845/holy-family/ch06.htm; "scientific": Northrop Frye, *Anatomy of Criticism: Four Essays* (Princeton: Princeton University Press, 1957), 14–7; "secular" and "oppositional," Edward Said, *The World, the Text, and the Critic* (Cambridge, MA: Harvard University Press, 1983), "Secular Criticism," 1–30; "equivocal": Simon Jarvis, "An Undeleter for Criticism," *Diacritics* 32, no. 1 (Spring 2002), 3–18.

13. For an elaboration of this argument insofar as it applies to criticism as a genre, see Harpham, "Ethics and the Double Standard of Criticism," *Shadows of Ethics: Criticism and the Just Society*, 38–49.

14. See online at http://english.chass.ncsu.edu/freeverse/Archives/Spring_2003/Interview/interviews.htm.

15. Augustine, *Confessions*, trans. R. S. Pine-Coffin (Harmondsworth: Penguin, 1986), 11.1, 253; 13.20, 328; 12.18, 296.

16. Augustine, *On Christian Doctrine*. In *The Confessions. The City of God. On Christian Doctrine* (Chicago: Encyclopedia Britannica, 1952), 3.11: 17.

17. *Confessions* 13.22, 332.

18. Alexander Nehamas, *The Art of Living: Socratic Reflections from Plato to Foucault*, Sather Classical Lectures (Berkeley: University of California Press, 1998), 1.

19. David Hume, *A Treatise of Human Nature*, ed. David Fate Norton and Mary J. Norton (Oxford: Oxford University Press, 2000), Part 3. 3. 1: 368, "Of the Origin of the Natural Virtues and Vices": "Thus it appears that *sympathy* is a very powerful principle in human nature, that it has a great influence on our taste of beauty, and that it produces our sentiment of morals in all the artificial virtues."

20. Roland Barthes, "Writers, Intellectuals, Teachers," *Image Music Text*, trans. Stephen Heath (New York: Hill and Wang, 1977), 190–215. In the insistently binary terms of this essay, Barthes depicts method as a death-force—"No surer way to kill a piece of research and send it to join the great waste of abandoned projects than Method"—and pits it against a "space of dispersion of desire where Law is dismissed" (201). In the end, however, Barthes seeks not to eliminate Law but simply to "disorientate" it by subjecting it to what he calls *"floating"* (215).

21. Max Weber, "Science as a Vocation," in H.H. Gerth and C. Wright Mills, trans. and ed., *Max Weber: Essays in Sociology* (New York: Oxford University Press, 1946), 129-56, 137; originally published, 1919. Gerth and Mills translate the key word as "personality," and place it in quotation marks, but "character" is more exact.

22. Leonard Barkan, "Thomas M. Greene: Memorial Addresses," *Yale Alumni Magazine*, http://www.yalealumnimagazine.com/greene.html.

23. Roland Barthes, *Writing Degree Zero*, trans. Annette Lavers and Colin Smith, preface by Susan Sontag (1953; repr. New York: Hill and Wang, 1968), 10–11.

24. *Writing Degree Zero*, 10-11.

25. Samuel Johnson, *The Rambler* #68, November 10, 1750, online at: http://etext. lib.virginia.edu/etcbin/toccer-new2?id=Joh4All.sgm&images=images/ modeng&data=/texts/english/modeng/parsed&tag=public&part=14&divisi on=div2, #82.

26. Plutarch, *Plutarch's Lives*, vol. 2 of 2, trans.,and ed., Arthur Hugh Clough (New York: Modern Library, 2001), 139.

Chapter 2

1. Scarry's talk, "Beauty and the Scholar's Duty to Justice," as well as the talks by Bourdieu, Chomsky, and Fried, and a new introduction by Said, are printed in *Profession 2000*. Scarry's article is on pp. 21-31.

2. James Wood, "Eyes Wide Shut," *The New Republic* (28 February 2000), 27–32.

3. Peter Singer, "Unspeakable Acts," *The New York Review of Books* 33 (27 February 1986), 27–30.

4. As a further testament to Scarry's eminence, she received, in the spring of 2000, the Truman Capote Award for Literary Criticism in Memory of Newton Arvin, an award administered by the University of Iowa but determined by a distinguished panel of judges. Scarry shared the $50,000 award with Philip Fisher.

5. Elaine Scarry, *The Body in Pain: The Making and Unmaking of the World* (New York, Oxford: Oxford University Press, 1985).

6. Elaine Scarry, "The Made-Up and the Made-Real," *Field Work: Sites in Literary and Cultural Studies*, ed. Marjorie Garber, Paul B. Franklin, and Rebecca L. Walkowitz (New York and London: Routledge, 1996), 214–24. For a discussion of "consent," see Scarry, "War and the Social Contract: The

Right to Bear Arms," *Yale Journal of the Humanities* 2 (1990), 119–32; or a much longer version of this essay, "War and the Social Contract: Nuclear Policy, Distribution, and the Right to Bear Arms," *University of Pennsylvania Law Review* 139 (1991), 1257–316. See also Scarry, "The Declaration of War: Constitutional and Unconstitutional Violence," *Law's Violence*, ed. A. Sarat and T. Kearns (Ann Arbor: University of Michigan Press, 1992), 23–76.

7. Elaine Scarry, *Resisting Representation* (New York: Oxford University Press, 1994); and Elaine Scarry, ed., *Literature and the Body* (Baltimore: The Johns Hopkins University Press, 1988).

8. Elaine Scarry, "The Difficulty of Imagining Other People," *Human Rights in Political Transitions: Gettysburg to Bosnia*, ed. Carla Hesse and Robert Post (New York: Zone Books, 1999).

9. Count Joseph de Maistre, *Letters on the Spanish Inquisition*, trans. and ed. T. J. O'Flaherty (Delmar, NY: Scholars' Facsimiles and Reprints, 1977).

10. See Michael Levin, "The Case for Torture," *Newsweek* (7 June 1982), 13. For an excellent history of torture, see Edward Peters, *Torture* (Boston: Basil Blackwell, 1985). Singer's "Unspeakable Acts" reviews both Scarry and Peters, giving all the honor to Peters on the grounds of superior factual accuracy.

11. The terms "fact" and "interpretation" deliberately invoke Nietzsche, who seems to be the implied, if unconscious, target of Scarry's account. Some texts on pain with which Scarry's might be compared include David B. Morris, *The Culture of Pain* (Berkeley: University of California Press, 1991); David Bakan, *Disease, Pain, and Sacrifice: Toward a Psychology of Suffering* (Boston: Beacon Press, 1971); and Valerie Gray Hardcastle, *The Myth of Pain* (Cambridge, MA: The MIT Press, 1999).

12. Elaine Scarry, *On Beauty and Being Just* (Princeton: Princeton University Press, 1999).

13. Intellectual life in Cambridge these days seems to be a veritable Reign of Wonder, with Scarry being just one of a group of distinguished professors who cultivate an attitude of thunderstruck astonishment. These would include Philip Fisher (*On Wonder*), Stephen Greenblatt (*Marvelous Possessions*), and Stephen Jay Gould (*Wonderful Life*).

14. Friedrich Nietzsche, *Twilight of the Idols*, trans. R. J. Hollingdale (Harmondsworth: Penguin, 1969) #22: 80. In *The Critique of Judgment*, Kant argues that the sublime, like the beautiful, is an object of our liking, and that any judgment about the sublime, like any judgment about beauty, implicitly claims universal validity. For Kant, the feeling of the sublime results from an intuition awakening within us of the vastness of the imagination, which exceeds all possible objects, whereas the beautiful remains bound to objects. See Immanuel Kant, *The Critique of Judgment*, trans. Werner S. Pluhar (Indianapolis: Hackett Publishing Company, 1987), I. I. II. B. #29: 124–40.

15. See Joseph Valente, *James Joyce and the Problem of Justice: Negotiating Sexual and Colonial Difference* (Cambridge: Cambridge University Press, 1995), 1–4.

16. The strong emphasis on language in Scarry's thinking on war may be accounted for by the fact that her scant few examples of conflict are almost entirely drawn from the age of nationalism, which might also be described as the age of ideology, from the late eighteenth to the early twentieth century.

17. Friedrich Nietzsche, *Thus Spake Zarathustra: A Book for Everyone and No One*, trans. R. J. Hollingdale (Harmondsworth: Penguin, 1969), III.26: 230.

18. "Introduction" in Elaine Scarry, ed., *Literature and the Body* (Baltimore: The Johns Hopkins University Press, 1988), vii–xxvii.

19. Scarry has never adhered to Modern Language Association guidelines on nonsexist language; for her, good things are, in general, feminine things.

20. Elaine Scarry, *Dreaming by the Book* (New York: Farrar, Straus, Giroux, 1999).

21. Little autisms flicker up in Scarry, as when she begins her "Introduction" with a discussion of counting, which people do "with their bodies (tapping a finger; bobbing the head; bouncing the entire body slightly . . .)" (viii). A certain measure of Scarry's originality, which might be cast as a "refusal" to take for granted such routine concepts as beauty or imagination, could also be understood as an inability to grasp what others grasp effortlessly.

22. "The External Referent: History. Untransmissable History in Thackeray's *Henry Esmond*," *Resisting Representation* (New York: Oxford University Press, 1994), 101–42, 107–20.

23. *Resisting Representation,* 82.

24. For reasons that will become apparent later in the chapter, I have taken my definition of trauma from Larousse, which defines it as "*violence produite par un agent extérieur agissant mécaniquement.*"

25. Elaine Scarry, "The Fall of TWA 800," *New York Review of Books* XLV (9 April 1998) 6: 59–76.

26. In most respects a rigorously impersonal text, "TWA 800" does have several distinctively Scarryan moments, as when she notes of the EP3 Orion airplane that "the EP3's aspiration to be mistaken for a P3 is part of its larger project of electronic signal collection and self-fictionalization" (68).

27. For the official National Transportation Safety Board website on TWA 800, see http://www.ntsb.gov/events/twa800/default.htm. For arguments about missiles, which the National Transportation Safety Board has explicitly ruled out, see http://nw3.nai.net/~virtual/sot/twanews.htm. For a representative skeptical assessment of the technical argument in "TWA 800," see http://catless.ncl.ac.uk/Risks/19.66.html#subj6.

28. In correspondence with Scarry, James Hall, chairman of the National Transportation Safety Board, indicated that the inquiry would consider the possibility of radiation and predicted that the full results would be known within six months, or by the end of 1998. In fact, the investigation concluded on August 22, 2000, with no conclusion regarding electromagnetic radiation at all. See the exchanges between Hall and Scarry in *New York Review of Books,* 16 July 1998: 54–6; and *New York Review of Books* 13 August 1998: 61. These are also available in the electronic archives of the *New York Review* at http://www.nybooks.com/nyrev/.

29. Nor do subsequent articles published in *The New York Review* relieve the silence on this point. Although somewhat more specific in terms of the need for investigation and the form such investigation might take, they take no position on the main question of whether electromagnetic interference could ever be established beyond a reasonable doubt as the cause of any of these crashes. See "Swissair 111, TWA 800, and Electromagnetic Interference," *The New York Review of Books* XLVII 14 (21 September 2000), 92–100; and "The Fall of EgyptAir 990" *The New York Review of Books* XLVII (5 October 2000) 15: 49–53 (this article is the second part of "SwissAir 111, TWA 800, and Electromagnetic Interference"); also available online at www.nybooks.com.

30. In general, Scarry's descriptions of fictional characters stress their physical appearances, considered one detail—a nostril, an eyelid, a dress—at a time. For a contrast to this emphasis on the physical or visible, see Colin McGinn's subtle elaboration of the "Aesthetic Theory of Virtue," according to which virtue reflects certain aesthetic qualities. Although Scarry directly identifies beautiful surfaces with the concept of justice, McGinn insists that virtue lies within the mind, that the mental is primary and the material surface secondary. See McGinn, *Ethics, Evil, and Fiction* (Oxford: Clarendon Press, 1997), 92–104. The contrast between McGinn and Scarry is further underscored by McGinn's sensitivity to the ways in which evil is connected to pleasure, a prospect Scarry does not entertain (87–91).

31. As Scarry argues in *The Body in Pain*, consent defines the difference between conventional and nuclear war. In the former, both soldiers and civilians have some measure, however tiny, of consent to the act of war and its unpredictable consequences, whereas in the latter, they have none. Nuclear war is thus closer, in its "interior structure," to torture. See *The Body in Pain: The Making and Unmaking of the World*, 150–57.

32. Hampshire, *Justice is Conflict*, Princeton Monographs in Philosophy (Princeton: Princeton University Press, 2000). Hampshire makes an appearance in *On Beauty*, in a passage in which Scarry recounts a walk in the sand dunes with a "friend" to whom she describes her argument about beauty leading to justice. The friend—Hampshire, as she eventually reveals—refuses full endorsement, "'except, of course,' he added, turning suddenly serious, and holding out his 'two large hands, 'analogically,' by what they share: balance and the weighing of both sides'" (94). Reviewing this book in *The New York Review of Books*, Hampshire praises Scarry's evocation of the importance of beauty, which he brings into alignment with those of Kant and Schiller, but specifically repudiates any connection to justice. Hampshire, "The Eye of the Beholder," *The New York Review of Books* 46 (18 November 1999) 18:42–46.

33. It might even be suggested that Scarry herself provides, in unstressed form, all the thoughts necessary to refute her, as when she gives *The Body in Pain* the subtitle of *The Making and Unmaking of the World*. If her book actually followed the itinerary suggested by this subtitle, rather than the uplifting sequence of unmaking to making, the result would have been a completely different book.

34. Giorgio Vasari, *Lives of the Artists: A Selection*, trans. George Bull (Harmondsworth: Penguin, 1975), 261.
35. For a fuller repudiation of Scarry's arguments, with specific reference to the powerlessness of the aesthetic sensibilities of Hitler, Speer, and Goering to induce an acceptable sense of justice, see Todd Gitlin's review of *On Beauty and Being Just* in *The American Prospect* 11 (20 December 1999) 3; available online at http://www.prospect.org/archives/V11-3/gitlin.html. Gitlin is an excellent example of the Scarry reader who applauds the "importance" and "nobility" of the project, but rejects every one of its premises.

Chapter 3

1. Eddie Yeghiayan, compiler. Martha Craven Nussbaum: A Selected Bibliography. http://sun3.lib.uci.edu/~eyeghiay/Philosophy/Colloquia/nussbaum.html.
2. Martha Nussbaum, *Women and Human Development: The Capabilities Approach* (Cambridge, England, 2000).
3. Nussbaum's books have long acknowledgments sections. To take just one example, *Women and Human Development* thanks by name about 170 people, including not only scholars but also sex workers and the daughters of sex workers, and numerous unnamed others. It lists, too, more than thirty lectures and seminars based on the material of the book.
4. *Aristotle's* De Motu Animalium, 6.700b, ll. 19-25, cited in Martha Nussbaum, *Aristotle's* De Motu Animalium (Princeton: Princeton University Press, 1978), 38.
5. Martha Nussbaum, *Love's Knowledge: Essays on Philosophy and Literature* (New York and Oxford, 1990), 390.
6. Mary Beard, "The Danger of Making Lists," *Times Literary Supplement*, 17 March 2000, 6.
7. Jacques Derrida, *Writing and Difference*, trans. Alan Bass (Chicago: University of Chicago Press, 1978), 151, 152.
8. Jacques Derrida, *Of Grammatology*, trans. Gayatri Chakravorti Spivak (Baltimore and London: The Johns Hopkins University Press, 1978), 34. Derrida's influential reading of the double meaning of the *pharmakon* as both poison and remedy also refers to the *Phaedrus*. See "Plato's Pharmacy," in Jacques Derrida, *Dissemination*, trans. Barbara Johnson (Chicago: University of Chicago Press, 1981), 63–171.
9. Martha Nussbaum, *The Fragility of Goodness: Luck and Ethics in Greek Tragedy and Philosophy* (Cambridge: Cambridge University Press, 1986), 184-95.
10. Compared with the work of Donald Davidson, Charles Taylor, and Nelson Goodman, Nussbaum says, "the arguments of Derrida are relatively minor contributions." See Martha Nussbaum, "Human Functioning and Social Justice," *Political Theory* 20 (May 1992) 2:202–46. See also Martha Nussbaum, "Skepticism about Practical Reason in Literature and the Law," *Harvard Law Review* 107 (1994),714–44; here Derrida is associated with Robert

Bork, both of whom are cast as proponents of a "new subjectivism" who prize above all "freedom from disturbance" (734 ff.).

11. See Jacques Derrida, "Afterword: Toward an Ethic of Discussion," in *Limited Inc*, ed. Gerald Graff (Evanston, IL: Northwestern University Press, 1988), 111–60. For a discussion of this text, see Geoffrey Galt Harpham, *Shadows of Ethics: Criticism and the Just Society* (Durham, NC: Duke University Press, 1998), 38-49.

12. For Nussbaum on Adam Smith, see *Love's Knowledge: Essays on Philosophy and Literature* 338 ff.; Lionel Trilling, *The Liberal Imagination: Essays on Literature and Society* (1940) (New York: Charles Scribner's Sons, 1976), vii.

13. See Martha Nussbaum, *Cultivating Humanity: A Classical Defense of Reform in Liberal Education* (Cambridge, MA and London: Harvard University Press, 1997), 104–05.

14. See *Love's Knowledge: Essays on Philosophy and Literature,* and Martha Nussbaum, *Poetic Justice: The Literary Imagination and Public Life* (Boston: Beacon Press, 1995) on Leavis and Trilling; see Nussbaum, *The Therapy of Desire: Theory and Practice in Hellenistic Ethics,* 491, and *Love's Knowledge: Essays on Philosophy and Literature,* 230–44 on Wayne Booth. In *Cultivating Humanity: A Classical Defense of Reform in Liberal Education,* Nussbaum says that says her view of the universal community as a community of liberalism is modeled on Trilling (102).

15. Nussbaum, *Poetic Justice: The Literary Imagination and Public Life.* See F. R. Leavis, *The Great Tradition* (London: Chatto and Windus, 1948), 227 ff.

16. See especially "'Finely Aware and Richly Responsible:' Literature and the Moral Imagination," *Love's Knowledge: Essays on Philosophy and Literature* 148–67; and "Flawed Crystals: James's *The Golden Bowl* and Literature as Moral Philosophy," in *Love's Knowledge: Essays on Philosophy and Literature* 125–47. For a detailed assessment of Nussbaum's attempt to reconcile ethics and aesthetics, see Rüdiger Bender, "The Aesthetics of Ethical Reflection and the Ethical Significance of Aesthetic Experience: A Critique of Alasdair MacIntyre and Martha Nussbaum" at: http://www.ph-erfurt.de/~neumann/eese/artic98/bender/1_98.html.

17. In *Love's Knowledge*, Nussbaum documents three stages of her thinking in the mid- to late 1980s, which might be called "Up, Up, and Away." In the first, the ethics of Aristotle were conceived as an altogether adequate guide to the difficulties of life; in the second, emotion and erotic passion were elevated to a position of equivalence with morality; and in the glorious third, erotic love emerged triumphantly as superior to the moral view of life and even to philosophy, which is seen to be only a kind of propaedeutic to an ecstatic condition in which ethical judgment simply does not occur as we are led "beyond morality" (*Love's Knowledge, 350*). This last phase has not survived in Nussbaum's subsequent work, and it often has to struggle for dominance with phase two even in a single essay. Nussbaum is capable, for example, of declaring that "non-judgmental love . . . leads the lover at times beyond the ethical," and then, in the very next paragraph, of asserting

that "love and ethical concern . . . support and inform one another" (*Love's Knowledge,* 52, 53).

18. Nussbaum stands at the opposite extreme from the utilitarian philosopher Peter Singer, who has argued that ethical principles dictate that people should give 10 percent of their income, or anything more than they need to sustain themselves, to charitable causes. If Singer argues we should "give till it hurts," Nussbaum, responding to a more traditional utilitarian emphasis, urges us to maximize our pleasures. For a recent statement, see Peter Singer, *Writings on an Ethical Life* (New York: Ecco Press, 2000).

19. Martha Nussbaum, *The Therapy of Desire: Theory and Practice in Hellenistic Ethics* (Princeton: Princeton University Press, 1994), 312.

20. In another form of the ambivalence mentioned in note 17, Nussbaum sometimes contends that literature is a "supplement" to a rational-utilitarian perspective, and at other times argues the more extreme case that literature is simply superior to rationality as a way of understanding life. For the first, see *Poetic Justice: The Literary Imagination and Public Life*; for the second, see "Finely Aware," note 16. My sense of the mediocrity of *Poetic Justice* is based in part on the obviousness of its treatment of Dickens's *Hard Times,* which is the constant example of the novel as a genre. Very little that Nussbaum says about this most moralistic of Dickens's books advances on the literal reading of the text. *Hard Times* is commonly assigned to high school students precisely because of its moral obviousness, and it is hardly reassuring to see Nussbaum discover the morality that is instantly apparent to sixteen-year-old students, especially when moral assurance is the very sign of the Gradgrindian perspective she criticizes, and is little in evidence among the circus performers whom she treats as morally admirable victims.

21. See Luce Irigaray, *An Ethics of Sexual Difference*, trans. Carolyn Burke and Gillian C. Gill (Ithaca, NY, 1993), 44. Irigaray is commenting on Aristotle's *Physics* 4. 1–5. In *The Therapy of Desire: Theory and Practice in Hellenistic Ethics*, Nussbaum still speaks of the Socratic pupil, and even the Stoic philosopher, as "she."

22. Plato, *Phaedrus* and *The Seventh and Eighth Letters*, trans. Walter Hamilton (Harmondsworth, 1981), 64. It is important to Nussbaum that, in the "best" cases, the sex that occurred between teacher and pupil in Greece was "intercrural," between clenched thighs, rather than anal.

23. The word "misogynistic" is Nussbaum's, as quoted by Robert S. Boynton in "Who Needs Philosophy?" *New York Times Magazine*, 21 November 1999. See http://www10.nytimes.com/library/magazine/home/19991121mag-boynton.html. (Because this essay is more accessible online than in hard copy, I will not refer to page numbers, which are unmarked in the electronic version.)

24. Ibid.

25. In *Cultivating Humanity: A Classical Defense of Reform in Liberal Education*, Nussbaum retitles this project the "World Institute for Development Ethics Research" (xii).

26. Based on a series of lectures given in 1993, *Upheavals of Thought: The Intelligence of Emotions* (Cambridge, MA: Harvard University Press, 2001)

was described as forthcoming as early as 1994. The delay in the appearance of the book may have been caused by numerous factors, including, presumably, the rapidly changing status of emotions in Nussbaum's thinking during these years.

27. Martha Nussbaum, *Sex and Social Justice* (New York, Oxford, 1999), 79.
28. See Martha Nussbaum, "Non-Relative Virtues: An Aristotelian Approach," in Nussbaum and Amartya Sen, eds., *The Quality of Life* (Oxford: Clarendon Press, 1993), 242–69.
29. These phases overlap. "Non-Relative Virtues," written in 1986, may be considered the first product of phase two, but *The Therapy of Desire* (1994), with its focus on classical philosophy, can be considered the last major production of phase one. On the other hand, *Therapy's* emphasis on Stoic civic virtues and the regulation of emotions might qualify it as the first major production of phase two.
30. Nussbaum, "Non-Relative Virtues," 249.
31. Martha Nussbaum, "Platonic Love and Colorado Law: The Relevance of Ancient Greek Norms to Modern Controversies," in *Virginia Law Review* 80 (1994), 1515–651. A shortened version of this appears in *Sex and Social Justice* 299–331.
32. Daniel Mendelsohn, "The Stand: Expert Witnesses and Ancient Mysteries in a Colorado Courtoom," *Lingua Franca*, September/October 1996: 34–46; and Boynton, "Who Needs Philosophy?" See note 23.
33. Robert George, "'Shameless Acts' Revisited: Some Questions for Martha Nussbaum," *Academic Questions* (Winter 1995–96), 24–42 (the journal of the National Association of Scholars). The article is online at http://www.webcom.com/zurcher/philosophy/nussbaum.html#22a. The text details a list of charges against Nussbaum, including the case of the missing ampersand. George's deposition at the trial contains comments that seem to reflect a conservative position on sexuality, to say the least. See also his article "The Tyrant State," in which he argues from a Catholic perspective against the judgment in Roe v. Wade, which he says brings into question the legitimacy of "American democracy" itself; *First Things* 67 (November 1996), 39–42. George is the McCormick Professor of Jurisprudence in the Department of Politics at Princeton. In 1994, he was counsel of record to Mother Teresa of Calcutta in her amicus curiae brief to the Supreme Court to reconsider its ruling in Roe v. Wade.
34. Kenneth Dover, *Greek Homosexuality*, rev. ed. (Cambridge, MA: Harvard University Press, 1989).
35. "Platonic Love and Colorado Law: The Relevance of Ancient Greek Norms to Modern Controversies" (1628), contains Nussbaum's account of Dover's equivocations about his understanding of the key disputed term, *tolmêma*, which he had translated as "crime," but now, he tells Nussbaum in a letter, feels should be translated as "venture"—a translation that, as Nussbaum concedes, would decriminalize homosexuality at the cost of making nonsense of the crucial passage, which would refer to "a venture of the first order." Nussbaum's interesting review of Dover's peculiarly revealing memoirs, as

well as her own account of their collaboration against Finnis and George, is reprinted as "Sex, Truth, and Solitude," in *Sex and Social Justice* (New York: Oxford University Press, 1999), 332–40. The book as a whole is dedicated to Dover. Nussbaum argues that the younger male, often referred to in modern translations as a "boy," was actually most typically "the age of a modern college undergraduate" ("Platonic Love and Colorado Law: The Relevance of Ancient Greek Norms to Modern Controversies," 1551). But this would produce other unwanted consequences, from her point of view. The Hamilton edition of the *Phaedrus*, for example, describes homosexual seduction of a younger male as "monstrous wrongdoing"; if the "boy" were twenty years old, then the wrongdoing would refer entirely to the homosexuality, not to any possible exploitation associated with age, and that would make Plato positively homophobic. See note 22.

36. This was not, however, the issue in Colorado, which concerned the rights of homosexuals to claim minority status or protected status, or to make a claim of discrimination. Nussbaum has written a number of pieces arguing for equal rights for gays. These include, most prominently, "A Defense of Lesbian and Gay Rights," in *Sex and Social Justice* (New York, Oxford: Oxford University Press, 1999),184–210; and "The Study of Human Sexuality," in *Cultivating Humanity: A Classical Defense of Reform in Liberal Education* (Cambridge, MA, and London, England: Harvard University Press, 1997), 222–56.

37. The Kantian imperative to treat people as ends enables Nussbaum to introduce Enlightenment thinking in the course of a discussion of the way in which pornography "objectifies" women. See Martha Nussbaum, "Objectification," in *Sex and Social Justice* 213–24. Here, Nussbaum is concerned to disentangle those forms of objectification that degrade from those that merely excite, and thus form a valuable part of sex. For Nussbaum, the subject of sex brings out the Stoic best in Kant. See also Martha Nussbaum, "Kant and Stoic Cosmopolitanism," *The Journal of Political Philosophy* 5 (1997) 1:1–25.

38. References to John Rawls are distributed throughout *Sex and Social Justice* and *Women and Human Development: The Capabilities Approach*; for Jürgen Habermas, see Martha Nussbaum, "Feminists and Philosophy," *New York Review of Books*, 20 October 1994, 59–63.

39. Pure reason has come in for a number of critiques in recent years, having been accused of being implicitly oppressive, racist, and imperialist. See, respectively, Ashis Nandy, *The Intimate Enemy: Loss and Recovery of Self under Colonialism* (Delhi: Oxford University Press, 1983), 99; Franz Fanon, *Black Skin, White Masks* (London: Pluto Press, 1986), 110; and Veena Das, "Subaltern as Perspective," in Ranajit Guha, *Subaltern Studies 6: Writings on South Asian History and Society* (Delhi: Oxford University Press India, 1989), 310–24. For a series of pointed vignettes on the function of race in the discourse of reason, see Emmanuel Chukwudi Eze, ed., *Race and the Enlightenment: A Reader* (Cambridge, MA: Harvard University Press, 1997); and for a brief account of sex and reason in a long tradition of philosophical

discourse going back to the Greeks, see Genevieve Lloyd, *The Man of Reason: "Male" and "Female" in Western Philosophy* (Minneapolis, MN: University of Minnesota Press, 1984). For a discussion of contemporary accounts of rationality, see Geoffrey Galt Harpham, "Of Rats and Men; or, Reason in Our Time," *Shadows of Ethics: Criticism and the Just Society* (Durham, NC: Duke University Press, 1999), 99–119.

40. See "Human Functioning and Social Justice," note 10, which begins with a defense of "Aristotelian Essentialism," 239 ff.

41. "Kant and Stoic Cosmopolitanism," 20.

42. In *The Therapy of Desire: Theory and Practice in Hellenistic Ethics*, Nussbaum says she agrees with the Stoic effort to eliminate anger, but quarrels with their effort to eliminate other passions such as friendship, love, or grief (509).

43. Although conscripted by Nussbaum for liberal ends, compassion is one reflex of a conservative orientation that characteristically views suffering from the distance of privilege, as the onetime determination of George W. Bush to "build a vast army of compassion" suggests. Compassion, one might argue, is the form of social militancy favored by fortune's favorites. Treating it as "the basic social emotion," the affect that works toward justice, Nussbaum does not register the trickle-down aspect of compassion. See Martha Nussbaum, "Compassion: The Basic Social Emotion," *Social Philosophy and Policy* 13 (1996) 1: 27. Nussbaum's account of "poetic justice" has been criticized on other grounds by Alan Jacobs, who quarrels with Nussbaum's suggestion that Walt Whitman might be taken as a model judge. This, Jacobs argues, constitutes a grotesque misreading of Whitman, who would not have consented to have his faculties placed at the service of a legal bureaucracy. Whitman, Jacobs insists, wanted perfect freedom to "judge" according to his lights alone, and was indifferent to, if not scornful of, the civic-minded earnestness Nussbaum describes. See Alan Jacobs, "Martha Nussbaum, Poet's Defender," at http://www.leaderu.com/ftissues/ft9610/articles/reviewessay. html. Originally published in *First Things* 66 (October 1996), 37–41.

44. Martha Nussbaum, *For Love of Country: Debating the Limits of Patriotism*, ed. Joshua Cohen (Boston: Beacon Press, 1996). Nussbaum's essay is "Patriotism and Cosmopolitanism," 2–20.

45. In his response, Michael W. McConnell quotes Edmund Burke's *Tract Relative to the Popery Laws*: "To transfer humanity from its natural basis, our legitimate and home-bred connections, to lose all feeling for those who have grown up by our sides, in our eyes, the benefit of whose cares and labors we have partaken from our birth, and meretriciously to hunt abroad after foreign affections, is such a disarrangement of the whole system of our duties, that I do not know whether benevolence so displaced is not almost the same thing as destroyed, or what effect bigotry could have produced that is more fatal to society" (*For Love of Country: Debating the Limits of Patriotism*, 82).

46. See Stanley Fish, "Boutique Multiculturalism, or Why Liberals are Incapable of Thinking about Hate Speech," *Critical Inquiry* 23 (Winter 1997)

2:378–95. Reprinted in Stanley Fish, *The Trouble with Principle* (Cambridge, MA: Harvard University Press, 1999).

47. Martha Nussbaum, "The Professor of Parody," *New Republic*, 22 February 1999; online at http://www.thenewrepublic.com/archive/0299/022299/nussbaum022299.html.

48. Judith Butler and others who are more interested in symbolic than in real politics, Nussbaum says, "collaborate in evil." She repeats the term, with italicized emphasis, to Robert Boynton; see note 23.

49. A number of eminent feminist scholars rushed to defend Butler, but the spectacle of the empire writing back only strengthened Nussbaum's position. The clobbering counterclaims made by her attackers delineate the orthodoxy of contemporary academic feminism. Nussbaum is viciously confused, they argue, on many—indeed, on all—points. Specifically, they write, Butler is political, she is effective, she is subversive, she is antiauthoritarian—and anyway, she is a theorist, a thinker, and so doesn't have to be any of these things. In fact, her refusal to be directly political is a mark of her integrity and sophistication; her "provocative, open theories" compare favorably with Nussbaum's "closed moralizing." Indeed, Joan Scott warns, serious consequences would follow if Nussbaum were to be preferred to Butler: "when the gap between theory and politics is closed in the name of virtue, when Robespierre or the Ayatollahs or Ken Starr seek to impose their vision of the 'good' on the rest of society, reigns of terror follow." Perhaps the most darkly illuminating response comes from Gayatri Spivak, who describes Nussbaum's critique of Butler as a symptom of an appetite for cultural imperialism. "*How* does she know," Spivak asks, that Indian women would prefer to be fed, literate, enfranchised, and protected to being hungry, uneducated, exploited, beaten, and raped? Has she taken the rich tapestry of Indian life fully into account? "This may be her idea of what they should want," Spivak says, but her own research and experience have revealed that the "gender practice of the rural poor is quite often in the performative mode, carving out power within a more general scene of pleasure in subjection." Chastising Nussbaum for her inelegant moral confidence, her respondents do succeed in "putting into question," as theorists like to say, the difference between good and evil. Nussbaum's response was coldly nonciliatory. *New Republic* (19 April 1999); online at http://www.tnr.com/archive/0499/041999/nussbaum041999.html.

50. As early as 1994, Nussbaum was announcing an intention to reorient feminism, claiming that "the old norm of objectivity was in a sense more attractive for feminists than the [gender-specific] norms that feminists now defend." See Nussbaum, "Feminists and Philosophy," note 38; 63.

51. In an essay that makes many of these points, Butler actually bases her discussion on Nussbaum's hero Aristotle and refers to other thinkers Nussbaum cites as well. See Judith Butler, "Desire," in Frank Lentricchia and Thomas McLaughlin, eds., *Critical Terms for Literary Study*, 2nd ed. (Chicago and London, 1995), 369–86. In a recent review of a book by Edward Said, Nussbaum adopts another, friendlier form of appropriation, praising Said, in effect, for his insightful promotion of her ideas. In her account,

Said's notion of "exile" is equivalent to what she would call cosmopolitanism, his understanding of the role of universities is "basically Socratic" and identical to the one put forward in *Cultivating Humanity*, his critique of deconstruction as "effete" and "jargon-laden" is precisely her own, and his evolution as a thinker runs from an earlier Stoic tone "reminiscent of . . . Marcus Aurelius" to a later emphasis on "universal normative principles of justice . . . grounded in an understanding of common human capacities." Said, whose insistence on exile and dislocation as principles of identity has led him away from classically-grounded norms, might well have wondered if his reviewer had read him at all before praising him. See Nussbaum, "The End of Orthodoxy," *New York Times Book Review* (18 February 2001), 28.

52. Nussbaum lists nine other articles dealing with the capabilities approach, some of which contain versions of the list, in *Women and Human Development: The Capabilities Approach*, 34–35, n. 2.

53. The emphasis on capability rather than function is intended to guard against excessive prescriptive specificity. People may or may not choose to exercise these capabilities, which are intended as guides to policy, not to life. See Martha Nussbaum, "Women and Cultural Universals," in *Sex and Social Justice* 29–54; and "Human Functioning and Social Justice." Nussbaum's neo-Aristotelianism might be usefully compared with Noam Chomsky's neo-Cartesianism, which also defines human nature in terms of capacity, in his case a capacity for language. But although Chomsky has impeccable credentials on the libertarian left, his account of human nature is far more specific than Nussbaum's, for it is definitely allied with a particular set of political values, which it represents as simple, nonideological truth.

54. In *Getting It Right: Language, Literature, and Ethics* (Chicago: University of Chicago Press, 1992), I described the relation between ethics and morality in terms of openness—theoretical openness, the interval of reflection and uncommitted assessment in which all options remain possible—and closure, the moment of decision in which a specific course of action is chosen in accordance with a "transcendental" warrant (52–58). Critics of deconstruction have charged that it sought to prolong the gap of ethical openness infinitely, and thus refused, in a spirit of cognitive antisepsis, the responsibilities and risks that attend definite worldly action. It was the vulnerability of deconstruction to this accusation that led to its almost immediate collapse, in terms of academic fashion, in the wake of the discovery of Paul de Man's "wartime journalism."

Chapter 4

1. A citizen of Ljubljana, Slovenia, Žižek had, by the end of the 1980s, written a number of articles and two books in French (*Tout ce que vous avez toujours voulu savoir sur Lacan, sans oser le demander à Hitchcock* [Paris: Navarin, 1988], and *Le plus sublime des hystériques: Hegel passe* [Paris: Le point hors ligne, 1988]). *The Sublime Object of Ideology* (London: Verso, 1989), included material from the latter, and from texts published in Slo-

vene. Several of Žižek's early works in English were translations from his own French. Since about 1990, Žižek has written in English; occasionally, his works are translated by others into Slovene or Serbo-Croatian, and into many other languages. For a preliminary bibliography and a list of other Žižek resources on the web, see http://athena.louisville.edu/a-s/english/babo/snyder/Žižeklinks.html.

2. Slovenia introduced multiparty politics in the late 1980s and declared formal independence from the Serb-dominated Yugoslavia in June 1991.

3. The phases of Lacan were established primarily by Jacques-Alain Miller, Lacan's son-in-law, by whom Žižek was analyzed in Paris in the early 1980s. Miller worked tirelessly to order Lacan's somewhat chaotic teaching after his death and his work was crucial in establishing a Lacanian "school."

4. Žižek, *The Plague of Fantasies* (London: Verso, 1997), 4–5.

5. "Human Rights and Its Discontents," lecture at Bard College, November 16, 1999, transcript at http://www.bard.edu/hrp/Žižektranscript.htm.

6. See, for example, Žižek, "From Joyce-the-Symptom to the Symptom of Power," *Lacanian Ink* 11, available online at www.plexus.org/lacink/lacink11/Žižek/html.

7. Slavoj Žižek, *For They Know Not What They Do: Enjoyment as a Political Factor* (London: Verso, 1991), 40.

8. Slavoj Žižek, *Did Somebody Say Totalitarianism? Five Interventions in the (Mis)use of a Notion* (London: Verso, 2001).

9. My authority on radical thought is Artie Sternlicht, a character in E. L. Doctorow's *The Book of Daniel* who discourses on "the dynamics of radical thinking. With each cycle of radical thought, there is a state of genuine creative excitement during which the connections are made. The radical discovers connections between available data and the root responsibility. Finally he connects everything. At this point he begins to lose his following. It is not that he has incorrectly connected everything, it is that he has connected everything. Nothing is left outside his connections. At this point society becomes bored with the radical" (New York: Random House, 1971: 140).

10. The following example will suffice: "With regard to the tension (which provides the ultimate coordinates of the ethical space) between the Other *qua* the Thing, the abyssal Otherness which addresses us with the unconditional injunction, and the Other *qua* the Third, the agency which mediates my encounter with others (other 'normal' humans)—where this Third can be the figure of symbolic authority, but also the 'impersonal' set of rules that regulate my exchange with others—does not Antigone stand for the exclusive and uncompromising attachment to the Other *qua* Thing, eclipsing the Other *qua* Third, the agency of a symbolic mediation/reconciliation?" *Did Somebody Say Totalitarianism? Five Interventions in the (Mis)use of a Notion* 157–8. The concept is not in fact difficult, but Žižek's formulation is uncompromising.

11. Slavoj Žižek, *The Fragile Absolute or, Why is the Christian Legacy Worth Fighting For?* (London: Verso, 2000), 17. See also Karl Marx, *Manifesto of the*

Communist Party, in *The Marx-Engels Reader,* ed. Robert C. Tucker (New York: Norton, 1978), 476.

12. Perhaps the closest relative to Žižek's argument in the history of Marxist theory is Max Horkheimer's contention, in "The Authoritarian State" (1940), that Marx's utopian vision of a normative totality had been perversely realized in the capitalist spirit of administration in which the price for flourishing was integration. The point of transition between Marx and bourgeois society, Horkheimer said, was integral statism or state socialism. See Andrew Arato and Eike Gebhardt, eds., *The Essential Frankfurt School Reader* (New York: Continuum, 1982), 95–117.

13. Jacques Derrida, *Spectres of Marx: The State of the Debt, the Work of Mourning, and the New International,* trans. Peggy Kamuf (New York: Routledge, 1994).

14. See Martin Jay, *Marxism and Totality: The Adventures of a Concept from Lukács to Habermas* (Berkeley: University of California Press, 1984).

15. The section from the *Phenomenology* to which Žižek often seems to be referring is the section on the "world of self-alienated spirit." See *The Phenomenology of Spirit,* trans. A. V. Miller (Oxford: Oxford University Press, 1977), 317–8. The most pertinent section of *The Science of Logic* is Book Two, Chapter Two, "The Essentialities or Determinations of Reflection," a thirty-five page chapter that contains in unexpectedly pithy form most of Žižek's core beliefs on identity, beginning with the constitutive role of "internal repulsion." *Hegel's Science of Logic,* trans. A. V. Miller (Atlantic Highlands, NJ: Humanities Press International, 1993), 409–43.

16. See *For They Know Not What They Do: Enjoyment as a Political Factor,* 131 ff.

17. In a profile of Žižek, Robert Boynton describes how friends of the young Žižek, who had been unable to procure a university job because he was suspected of an insufficient fidelity to Marxism, secured for him a position with the Central Committee of the League of Slovene Communists, where one of his responsibilities was speech writing for members of the Committee. See Robert Boynton, "Enjoy Your Žižek! An Excitable Slovenian Philosopher Examines the Obscene Practices of Everyday Life—Including His Own," *Lingua Franca* 8 (October 1998), 7.

18. Žižek edits the *Wo es war* series for Verso, and the SIC series with Duke University Press, which have published a number of Slovenian scholars. The inner circle of the Slovene group consists of Žižek, Mladen Dolar, and Alenka Zupancic.

19. The discussion, at once particular and theoretical, in *Did Somebody Say Totalitarianism? Five Interventions in the (Mis)use of a Notion,* of the clashing ethical and political assumptions in the 1937 Bukharin trial is especially compelling. "We are not tormenting you [by prosecuting you]" the Central Committee insists to Bukharin, "you have been tormenting the Party over many years, and it is only thanks to the angelic patience of Comrade Stalin that we have not torn you politically to pieces for your vile, terroristic work . . . ." (109). Quoted from J. Arch Getty and Oleg V. Naumov, *The Road to*

Terror: Stalin and the Self-Destruction of the Bolsheviks (New Haven, CT: Yale University Press, 1999), 370.

20. See "Symptomatic and Chance Actions," in *Psychopathology of Everyday Life, The Basic Writings of Sigmund Freud*, ed. A. A. Brill, (New York: Modern Library, 1938), 128–40, especially 128–9.

21. Žižek's respectful attention to Christianity constitutes another anomaly in his *oeuvre*; but because his understanding of Christianity is totally secular, it does not represent a religious moment in contemporary philosophy. In fact, the scattered comments of Fredric Jameson on religion are more compatible with religious belief than anything in Žižek. Where Jameson sees in religion a species of utopian collectivity, Žižek argues that Christianity is "much too precious to be left to the fundamentalist freaks" and should be selectively appropriated for philosophical purposes (*The Fragile Absolute or, Why is the Christian Legacy Worth Fighting For?* 2). See Jameson, *The Political Unconscious: Narrative as a Socially Symbolic Act* (Ithaca, NY: Cornell University Press, 1981), 281–6. Žižek's most sustained exposition of Christianity, especially its account of how something emerges from nothing through the Word, is contained in his extended meditation on Schelling in Slavoj Žižek/F. W. J. von Schelling, *The Abyss of Freedom/Ages of the World* (Schelling's *Die Weltalter*, trans. Judith Norman [Ann Arbor, MI: University of Michigan Press, 1997]).

22. *For They Know Not What They Do: Enjoyment as a Political Factor*, 147. Žižek's "Cartesian" book is *The Ticklish Subject: The Absent Centre of Political Ontology* (London: Verso, 2000), whose introduction is called, "A Spectre is Haunting Western Academia . . ." and that begins with the words, ". . . the spectre of the Cartesian subject" (1).

23. Žižek's account of the tradition that finally produced Lacan is not uncontroversial. In *Contingency, Hegemony, Universality: Contemporary Dialogues on the Left* (authored by Judith Butler, Ernesto Laclau, and Žižek [London: Verso, 2000]) Žižek's friend Ernesto Laclau accuses Žižek of a gross misreading of the entire tradition and of Lacan's place in it. By emphasizing factors of "impossibility" at the expense of "necessity," Žižek has, Laclau argues, misrepresented virtually every thinker he discusses, including Lacan; he has, in short, "Lacanianized the tradition of modernity, most visibly in the case of Hegel, in a way which I see as hardly legitimate" (75).

24. *Looking Awry: An Introduction to Jacques Lacan through Popular Culture* (Cambridge, MA: The MIT Press, 1991), vii.

25. "Preface," *The Žižek Reader*, ed. Elizabeth Wright and Edmond Wright (New York: Blackwell, 1999), viii.

26. Žižek finished fifth in the 1990 elections, narrowly missing becoming one of the four-person rotating presidential team. He served as the Republic's Ambassador of Science in 1991. Žižek reportedly goes by the name of "Fidel" among his friends, a testament to his oratorical stamina. The scene evoked here is not entirely an invention. One of Žižek's first and best books, *For They Know Not What They Do*, consists of six seminars sponsored by the Slovene Society for Theoretical Analysis (of which he was founder and

president) given on consecutive Mondays in 1989–90. The book begins with a consideration of the sole mention by Freud (in a letter) of a Slovene, a man with "a thoroughly immoral Ego . . . obviously a good-for-nothing." "Our analytical art fails when faced with such people," Freud comments; but, Žižek contends, this derided Slovene nevertheless illustrates perfectly the Lacanian theory of the paradoxical linkage of enjoyment and the Law. See *For They Know Not What They Do: Enjoyment as a Political Factor*, 7–9.

27. In Jacques Lacan, "The agency of the letter in the unconscious or reason since Freud," 146–78 in *Ecrits: A Selection*, trans. Alan Sheridan (New York: W. W. Norton & Company, 1977), 148.

28. See Ferdinand de Saussure, *Course in General Linguistics*, trans. Wade Baskin (New York: The Philosophical Library, 1959), 113.

29. For a full-scale version of this argument, see Žižek, "The Spectre of Ideology" reprinted in *The Žižek Reader*, op. cit., 53–86. If the sense that we have stepped out of ideology is the surest sign that we remain in ideology, then, in a more general sense, one is truly caught in the web of power "only and precisely in so far as he does not fully identify with it but maintains a kind of distance towards it" (*The Fragile Absolute or, Why is the Christian Legacy Worth Fighting For?* 148). For this reason, we can resist social or ideological power most effectively not by repudiating it but by fully accepting its dictates, but doing so in an overly literal way that brings them to their point of their inherent contradiction. Christ is exemplary in this context. His insistence that he was merely here to fulfill the Jewish law bore witness to how his work effectively canceled the law: the fulfillment of the law *was* its negation. The same might be said of Žižek himself, who fulfills Lacan's law by superseding it (relegating most of it to stages one or two, exemplifying it in well-nigh hysterical terms, accommodating it to a long tradition of thinkers). As for his utter dedication to Lacan, is this not a way of traversing the fantasy and thus freeing himself of Lacan's influence? The most enslaved thinkers, Žižek might argue, are precisely those who maintain a critical distance from their heroes.

30. Stuart Hall, "The Problem of Ideology—Marxism without Guarantees," *Journal of Communication Inquiry* 10 (1986) 2: 28-42; and "The Rediscovery of 'Ideology': Return of the Repressed in Media Studies," in Michael Gurevitch, Tony Bennett, James Curran, and Janet Woollacott, eds., *Culture, Society, and the Media* (London: Methuen, 1982), 56–90. See also V. N. Vološinov, *Marxism and the Philosophy of Language*, trans. Ladislav Matejka and I. R. Titunik (New York: Seminar Press, 1973); and Raymond Williams, "Ideology," in *Marxism and Literature* (Oxford: Oxford University Press, 1977), 55–74.

31. This argument is the focus of one of Žižek's most theoretically ingenious interventions, "Enjoy Your Nation as Yourself!" in which he discusses the nationalist sense of the Nation and a distinctive national "way of life" as a "Thing" that is "in us more than ourselves" and inaccessible to others. The logic of nationalism is activated not by social homogeneity but by the tensions that arise when ethnic communities live closely together, produc-

ing an "inner antagonism" whose disquieting effects are neutralized by the fantasmatic Nation-Thing. The primary feature of nationalism is a mythic account of how other nations have "stolen our enjoyment," depriving us of that most excellent quality that would allow us to live fully. "Nationalism," Žižek says, "thus represents a privileged domain of the eruption of enjoyment into the social field." *Tarrying with the Negative: Kant, Hegel, and the Critique of Ideology* (Durham, NC: Duke University Press, 1993), 200–38.

32. The superego, Žižek says, is "an agency which bombards the subject with injunctions that are impossible to fulfill: it brooks no excuses . . . and observes, with mocking, malevolent neutrality the subject's helpless struggle to live up to its 'crazy' demands, secretly enjoying his failure" (*For They Know Not What They Do: Enjoyment as a Political Factor,* 232). Resistance to this sadistic force involves not a renewed dedication to duty but a complete and unsparing recognition of our true motives in following duty, motives that, like so much else, are illuminated by the rigors of Stalinism. Those who participated in executions, interrogations, torture, were not, Žižek insists, too cold, too lacking in human feeling. Rather, they were *not cold enough*, for they failed to recognize, and thus were in no position to resist, the enjoyment they experienced in inflicting pain according to their duty. Duty alone, he insists, is nothing but *pure* enjoyment.

33. Martha C. Nussbaum, *For Love of Country: Debating the Limits of Patriotism,* Joshua Cohen, ed. (Boston: Beacon Press, 1996), which consists of an essay by Martha Nussbaum ("Patriotism and Cosmopolitanism," 2–20), followed by responses from a number of prominent thinkers.

34. At this point, we can glimpse an unacknowledged point of contact between liberal versions of society that posit the possibility of complete freedom within the law and the totalitarian insistence on a complete identification with the Cause. Žižek is, however, alive to nuances within totalitarianism. In the remarkable tour de force *Did Somebody Say Totalitarianism?* he develops a number of intratotalitarian distinctions, with examples from actually existed forms of fascism and Stalinism, and occasional references to the Khmer Rouge. In the fascist or Nazi version of totalitarianism, the Leader is the Thing, whereas in Stalinism, it is History or the Party. The difference can be illustrated by the kinds of "subjective destitution" they created in their victims—the apathetic "Muslim" in the first instance, and the show-trial victim in the second—and by the behavior of the leader after a speech (the fascist leader will acknowledge applause by staring off into the distance, acknowledging that it is his greatness being recognized by the crowd, while the Communist leader will *himself* begin applauding, since it is not he the crowd is applauding, but the Cause). See especially "Hitler as Ironist," 61–88, and "When the Party Commits Suicide," 88–140.

35. By contrast with socialism and liberalism, both of which are based on the concept of human solidarity, fascism was based on the explicitly anti-universalist notion of a "people" gathered into a State. See Benito Mussolini, *The Doctrine of Fascism* (Firenze: Vallecchi Editore, 1936; orig. pub. 1931). Žižek might have had an interesting conversation with Mussolini, center-

ing on the (post-Hegelian, proto-Lacanian) convictions expressed in this article—that the State is of paramount importance, that duty is achieved by "the renunciation of self-interest, by death itself" (8), that conflict is eternal and class conflict is only one form of a deeper cleft, and that freedom-based liberal happiness is contemptible. Mussolini and Žižek agree on the fundamental premise of a crack in the ontological heart of human existence, but disagree on whether the Big Other can cure this wound.

36. In *Contingency, Hegemony, Universality: Contemporary Dialogues on the Left*, Butler begins her assault on Žižek by challenging the claim of psychoanalysis to articulate a notion of universality. The psychoanalytic version, she notes, would make the "incompleteness" of the subject—on which she, too, insists—based on "structurally static or foundational" factors rather than, as she would prefer, on "exclusions that are politically salient" (12). Her own understanding, based like his on Hegel, insists on the priority of the political, the particular, and the limited and contingent (not absolute) freedom of the individual. This book is fascinating reading for those capable of sustaining 330 pages worth of interest in watching three people, all both aggressive and defensive, hash out a limited number of inbred conceptual distinctions. Butler is a tenacious and uncompromising reader; Laclau attempts a more magisterial posture. Both of them try to moderate Žižek's runaway Lacanianism, with Butler complaining of insufficient historicity and Laclau brandishing the obscene spectacle of Bataille as an illustration of the consequences of excessive Lacanian enthusiasm. Žižek is himself, with a full complement of references to Wagner, *film noir*, Stephen Hawking, the film *Cat People*, Derrida, and so on. Of course, he defends Lacan in all cases, and plays his opponents off against each other. But the procedural requirement that each respond specifically to the others does force a useful and even entertaining pattern of deflections away from the narcissistic repetition to which all theoretical writing is prone. Žižek shows himself to be a remarkably effective close reader, a skill not always in evidence in his work.

37. Cf., Lacan: "from an analytical point of view, the only thing of which one can be guilty is of having given ground relative to one's desire." In *The Ethics of Psychoanalysis 1959–60*. Book VII of *The Seminar of Jacques Lacan*, ed. Jacques-Alain Miller, trans. by Dennis Porter (New York: W. W. Norton & Company, 1997), 319. Section XXIV of this work, "The paradoxes of ethics *or* Have you acted in conformity with your desire?" (pp. 311–25), is especially pertinent.

38. Lacan argues that Antigone's insistence on the rights of all humans, as distinct from animals, and on the relation she bears to her brother in particular, constitute an emphasis on language—the words *human* and especially the word *brother*—that sets her at odds with Creon, who is concerned with the civic and symbolic orders. Antigone follows an imperative that is determined by her position in a relational scheme, a linguistic system of differences without positive terms. Faithful to that system and to nothing else, she rejects enjoyment, which seeks gratification as an end, and embraces desire, which leads from point to point *ad infinitum*. See Lacan, *The Ethics of*

Psychoanalysis, 278–80. The stress on the connection between the symbolic order and the death of the subject marks this seminar as quintessential stage two Lacan.

39. See "The Ethical Act: Beyond the Reality Principle," *Did Somebody Say Totalitarianism? Five Interventions in the (Mis)use of a Notion* 165–73, and "The Breakout," *The Fragile Absolute or, Why is the Christian Legacy Worth Fighting For?* 143–60.

40. An example drawn from the annals of democracy might be the 1964 Civil Rights Act, which was harshly criticized by some, including the Republican candidate for president, Barry Goldwater, as unconstitutional. One of the Act's primary architects, Senator Everett Dirksen of Illinois, responded on the floor of the Senate to this charge, recalling other pieces of social legislation that had been criticized on the same grounds when they were first proposed. "Today they are accepted," Dirksen said, "because they were a forward thrust in the whole effort of mankind" ("Civil Rights Bill Passed, 73-27; Johnson Urges All to Comply; Dirksen Berates Goldwater," *New York Times* 20 June 1964, www.nytimes.com/learning/general/onthisday/big/0619.html).

41. Žižek has long been fascinated with Lenin as a man who, after a return to Hegel in 1914, undertook to transform Marxist theory into actuality. In so doing, Žižek argues, Lenin did not violate the essence of Marx, but rather took the responsibility, and ran the terrible risks (e.g., Stalin), of realizing that essence. Žižek favors the stern and specific letters of St. Paul over the sentimental Gospel image of Christ for the same reason, that Paul founds the Church by violently displacing the original teaching, and so brings the sublime message into the material world, even at the cost of its sublimity. The reactivation of the anti-democratic, openly terroristic legacy of Lenin is of course politically controversial, but in a theoretical sense, the most debatable aspect of the argument is surely Žižek's suggestion that an ethico-political model can be derived from the brief, wild, and violently negated utopian moment that followed the October Revolution of 1917. See "A Plea for Leninist Intolerance," *Critical Inquiry* 28 (Winter 2002), 542–66. This is a revised and abbreviated version of the talk Žižek gave at a conference on Lenin that he organized at Essen, Germany in February 2001, "Repeating Lenin"; see http://www.lacan.com/replenin.htm.

42. Edward Said, "Self-Determination for All," in *Al-Ahram* 8-14 April 1999, issue #424. Online at http://www.ahram.org.eg/weekly/1999/424/op2.htm.

43. Noam Chomsky, "The Current Bombings: Behind the Rhetoric," online at http://www.zmag.org/crisescurevts/current_bombings.htm. Chomsky is not always so pacific. In *A New Generation Draws the Line* (London: Verso, 2000), he compares the intervention in Kosovo with the "delicate respect" accorded to Indonesia as it eliminated resistance in East Timor. Even in retrospect, however, he insists that the bombing of Kosovo was unwarranted, and argues that there were more horrors in Kosovo under NATO than there had been under the Serbs (see 141). To hear Chomsky and Said speaking on Kosovo, on a panel sponsored and broadcast by Pacifica Radio, see "Noam Chomsky and Edward Said on Kosovo," 12 April 1999, at http://www.edwardsaid.org/.

44. Žižek, "Against the Double Blackmail," online at http://www.mii.
kurume-u.ac.jp/~leuers/Žižek-kosovo.htm.
45. Elizabeth Wright and Edmond Wright, Preface to *The Žižek Reader,* ed.
Elizabeth Wright and Edmond Wright (New York: Blackwell, 1999), 4.
46. Jacques Derrida, *Limited Inc,* ed. Gerald Graff (Evanston, IL: Northwestern University Press, 1988), 111-60.
47. See Robert Wright, *The Moral Animal: Why We Are the Way We Are: The
New Evolutionary Psychology* (New York: Pantheon Books, 1994).
48. For a recent account that praises Chomsky on these grounds even as it
criticizes the conceptual bases of his linguistics, see Rupert Read, "How I
Learned to Love (and Hate) Noam Chomsky," *Philosophical Writings* 15–16
(Autumn 2000–Spring 2001), 23–47.
49. Lacan, *Ecrits: A Selection*, trans. Alan Sheridan (New York: W. W. Norton &
Company, 1977), 284.
50. See note 21. Although Žižek stresses Schelling's discussion of God as different from himself and in danger of going insane before he created the universe, Chomsky quotes Schelling to the effect that "the highest dignity of
Philosophy consists precisely therein, that it stakes all on human freedom."
From F. W. J. Schelling, *Philosophical Inquiries into the Nature of Human
Freedom*, trans., and ed. James Gutmann (Chicago: Open Court Publishing
Co., 1936), quoted in Chomsky, "Language and Freedom," in James Peck,
ed., *The Chomsky Reader* (New York: Pantheon Books, 1987), 139–57.
51. In fact, if the Cartesian *res cogitans* is taken as "the ghost in the machine" of
the human body, and Lacan's signifier is a machine in the ghost, then Chomsky's language capacity might be described as the ghost in the machine in
the ghost in the machine. Still, Chomsky has been criticized for his replace-
ment of a properly human subject by a mechanistic grammar. For a scath-
ing critique of his "engineering" approach to language, see Roy Harris, *The
Language Machine* (London: Duckworth, 1987), 71–75.
52. Immanuel Kant, "An Answer to the Question: 'What is Enlightenment?'"
Hans Reiss, ed., *Kant's Political Writings*, trans. H. B. Nesbit (Cambridge:
Cambridge University Press, 1991), 54–60.
53. Chomsky, *Cartesian Linguistics: A Chapter in the History of Rationalist
Thought* (Lanham, MD: University Press of American, 1966); *Reflections on
Language* (New York: Random House, 1975); and *Knowledge of Language:
Its Nature, Origin, and Use* (New York: Praeger, 1986). Perhaps Žižek could
be urged to participate in other dialogues as well. A man who describes
himself as a "Pauline materialist" (Žižek, "Preface" to *The Žižek Reader* ix)
might wish to engage Daniel Boyarin, author of *Carnal Israel: Reading Sex
in Talmudic Culture* (Berkeley: University of California Press, 1993); and A
Radical Jew: Paul and the Politics of Identity* (Berkeley: University of California Press, 1994).

Chapter 5

1. Edward Said, "Vico: Autodidact and Humanist," *Centennial Review* 11, no. 3 (1967), 336–52; "Conclusion: Vico in His Work and in This," in *Beginnings: Intention and Method* (Baltimore: The Johns Hopkins University Press, 1975), 347–81; and *The World, The Text, and the Critic* (Cambridge, MA: Harvard University Press, 1983), 111–18.

2. *The New Science of Giambattista Vico*, trans. Thomas Goddard Bergin and Max Harold Fisch (Ithaca: Cornell University Press, 1968), 425; quoted in *The World, The Text, and the Critic*, 111.

3. See Erich Auerbach, "Philology and *Weltliteratur*," trans. with an introduction by Edward Said and Maire Said, *Centennial Review* 13, no. 1 (1969), 1–17.

4. As Auerbach says in "Philology and *Weltliteratur*," "our philological home is the earth: it can no longer be the nation." Quoted in *The World, The Text, and the Critic*, 7.

5. See *The World, The Text, and the Critic*, 222–24, 248–67, 268–89. In *The World, The Text, and the Critic*, Renan is compared implicitly with Raymond Schwab, and explicitly with Louis Massignon, Renan's twentieth-century successor in Orientalist tradition. Renan, according to Said, is in one phase of his work engaged in the project of "keeping Islam alive so that, in his philological writing, he might set about destroying it"; Massignon, "a mind altogether of another sort of magnitude," approaches Islam "to understand and feel compassion for it, then finally to exist in harmony with its anguish, its needs, its divine dilemmas" (*The World, The Text, and the Critic*, 281).

6. "First, there is a point of origin," Said says in "Traveling Theory," "a set of initial circumstances in which the idea came to birth or entered discourse. Second, there is a distance transversed, a passage . . . to another time and place where it will come into a new prominence. Third, there is a set of conditions . . . which then confronts the transplanted theory or idea . . . Fourth, the now full (or partly) accommodated (or incorporated) idea is to some extent transformed by its new uses, its new position in a new time and space" (226–7). "Traveling Theory," *The World, The Text, and the Critic*, 226–47.

7. Tim Brennan, "Places of Mind, Occupied Lands: Edward Said and Philology," in *Edward Said: A Critical Reader*, ed. Michael Sprinker (Oxford, UK: Blackwell, 1992), 74–95.

8. Edward Said, *Out of Place: A Memoir* (New York: Alfred A. Knopf, 1999).

9. See *Out of Place: A Memoir*, 117: "It seems inexplicable to me now that having dominated our lives for generations, the problem of Palestine and its tragic loss . . . should have been so relatively repressed, undiscussed, or even remarked on by my parents. . . . The repression of Palestine in our lives occurred as part of a larger depoliticization on the part of my parents."

10. Edward Said, *The Question of Palestine* (New York: Vintage, 1992; originally published, 1979), xi. See also *The Politics of Dispossession: The Struggle for Palestinian Self-Determination, 1969–1994* (New York: Pantheon Books, 1994).

11. Quoted in Edward Said, *Joseph Conrad and the Fiction of Autobiography* (Cambridge, MA: Harvard University Press, 1966), 32.

12. See Peter Mallios, "An Interview with Edward Said," in *Conrad in the Twenty-first Century: Contemporary Approaches and Perspectives*, ed. Carola Kaplan, Peter Mallios, and Andrea White (New York: Routledge, 2005), 283–303.

13. "Between Worlds," *Reflections on Exile and Other Essays* (Cambridge, MA: Harvard University Press, 2000), 554–69.

14. "Two Conrads" (*Joseph Conrad and the Fiction of Autobiography*, 57); "each one" (*Joseph Conrad and the Fiction of Autobiography*, viii). In fact, the more conventional view is that Conrad led three lives. See Frederick R. Karl, *Joseph Conrad: The Three Lives. A Biography* (New York: Farrar, Straus and Giroux, 1979). In his interview with Said, Mallios ventures the opinion that Said has "managed to reconcile this problem of 'duplexity' in a way that Conrad was never . . . ." " 'No, I haven't,' " Said interrupts, " 'I would say I haven't' " ("An Interview with Edward Said," 298). Rather than reconcile the problem, he aggravated it, insisting on the inherent irreconcilability between intellectual conviction and loyalty to tribe, sect, or country (see *Out of Place: A Memoir*, 217, 230, 280). In a 1999 interview, he seemed both to describe and to disavow himself, saying, "it seems to me there is a similarity between the practice and the function of the intellectual on the one hand, and politics on the other. What I find at this time is an urgent need for total separation between the two. Humbly, the most dangerous and worst scenario for intellectuals is to be involved in both the intellectual and political realms." Interview with Nouri Jarah in *Aljadid* 5 (1999), 28; online at http://www.aljadid.com/EdwardSaidDiscussesOrientalismArabIntellectualsReviving-Marxism.html.

15. Conrad learned English as an adult, but Said's relation to English is far more intimate. In the preface to *Out of Place*, Said describes Arabic as his "native language" and English the language of his education (xiii). But he also says, "I have never known what language I spoke first, Arabic or English, or which one was really mine beyond any doubt" (4).

16. "Preface" to *The Nigger of the "Narcissus,"* ed. Robert Kimbrough (New York: W. W. Norton, 1979), 145–48.

17. Peter Lancelot Mallios, "Contrapunctus: Edward Said and Joseph Conrad," in Andrzej Ciuk & Marcin Piechota, eds., *Conrad's Europe* (Opole: Wydawnicto Uniwersytetu Opolskiego, 2005), 177-94, 179-80.

18. After the last of three partitions in 1795, Poland was effectively divided among Russia, Prussia, and the Austro-Hungarian empire.

19. There are many other moments in which the power of shame is noted: "The powerful influence of shame is what, I think, makes this story ["The Return"] an epitome of Conrad's earliest group of short works" (*Joseph Conrad and the Fiction of Autobiography*, 105); and "[Leggatt's presence] on the ship endows X [Said's way of designating the unnamed captain-narrator] with an image of his secret self. But the image is both convert and strangely shameful" (*Joseph Conrad and the Fiction of Autobiography*, 157). He con-

tinued to emphasize shame in later readings of Conrad; see, for example, "Conrad: The Presentation of Narrative," written in 1972: "Much of the time obscurity, regardless even of extravagant outward splendour (as with Nostromo or Jim or the Black Mate), is a function of secret shame" (*The World, The Text, and the Critic*, 90–110).

20. Joseph Conrad, *The Mirror of the Sea* and *A Personal Record*, ed. Zdzislaw Najder (Oxford: Oxford University Press, 1988).

21. Guilt about leaving Poland is a separate issue, but is still not reducible to a sense of shame. Conrad was never in any doubt about the necessity of leaving Poland (whose leading intellectuals and artists had virtually all emigrated before and after him and which, geopolitically speaking, did not exist), but he was sensitive to accusations of betrayal. One criticism in particular struck home. Published in a Polish periodical in 1901, it attacked the general phenomenon of "The Emigration of Talent," with Conrad as the prime example, saying, "It is even hard to think about it without shame!" In response, Conrad explicitly rejected the suggestion that he should be ashamed of himself. Quoted in Zdzislav Najder, *Joseph Conrad: A Chronicle* (New Brunswick: Rutgers University Press, 1984), 256.

22. He insists, for example, that Conrad's achievement lies in his "admirably unerring command of *conscious* human psychology" (*Joseph Conrad and the Fiction of Autobiography*, 100). "Comprehension," Said writes in a more general vein, "is a phenomenon of consciousness, and it is in the openness of the conscious mind that critic and writer meet to engage in the act of knowing and being aware of an experience" (7).

23. For fuller critiques of Marxism, see *The World, The Text, and the Critic*, 27–29, and "Reflections on American 'Left' Literary Criticism," *The World, The Text, and the Critic*, 158–77.

24. In Imre Salusinszky, ed., *Criticism in Society* (New York: Methuen, 1987). 120–49.

25. Mallios, "An Interview with Edward Said," 296. The Conrad passage is quoted in *Beginnings: Intention and Method*, 232. The book began to take shape under the immediate pressure of a meditation on this passage, but also directly after the Arab-Israeli war, after Said's divorce from his first wife, and after the publication of Frank Kermode's *The Sense of an Ending*, to which it was intended as a reply.

26. Thomas Moser, *Joseph Conrad: Achievement and Decline* (Cambridge, MA: Harvard University Press, 1957). For an account of the rise, and perhaps fall, of this understanding of Conrad's career, see Ian Watt, "The Decline of the Decline: Notes on Conrad's Reputation," in *Essays on Conrad* (Cambridge, MA: Cambridge University Press, 2000), 170–85.

27. When Said wrote in general terms, he was quite capable of seeing "the actual *affiliations* that exist between the world of ideas and scholarship, on the one hand, and the world of brute politics, corporate and state power, and military force on the other." See "Opponents, Audiences, Constituencies, and Community," in *Reflections on Exile and Other Essays*, 118–47.

28. See Mallios "An Interview with Edward Said," 298. The most telling evidence of a denied unity in the work of Chomsky is the passage in *Reflections on Language* in which a discussion of technical linguistic issues abruptly turns into a philosophical and political discussion of the just society. See *Reflections on Language* (New York: Random House, 1975), 123–34.

29. Letter to the Editor, *Times Literary Supplement*, 4 June 1993: 17. Gellner is also taken to task for "sophomoric patter," "piffling trivia," "incompetence," and complicity "with imperial power."

30. Jon Whitman, Letter to the Editor, *PMLA* 114, no. 1 (1999), 106–7. Said's response is on p. 107. See also Rael Jean Isaac, "Edward Said v. Edward Alexander," online at http://216.247.220.66/archives/rogues/isaac8-4-99.htm.

31. See, for example, the exchange with Daniel and Jonathan Boyarin in *Critical Inquiry* 15, no. 3 (1989), 626–46. The Boyarins title their piece "Toward a Dialogue with Edward Said"; they speak as "Jewish nationalists" who attack anti-Arab racism in Israel and Israeli "repression of the Palestinians," and urge the recognition of "Palestinian national rights" (633). To Said, such positions suggest nothing more than the Boyarins' "embarrassment at Israeli practices," which include shooting children, "torture, murder, and mass oppression," all occurring "even as the Boyarins speak" (635–6).

32. Robert Griffin, "Ideology and Misrepresentation: A Response to Edward Said, *Critical Inquiry* 15, no. 3 (1989), 611–25; Edward Said, "Response," *Critical Inquiry* 15, no. 3 (1989), 634–46. I am not claiming here to adjudicate the many particular issues in this exchange concerning the history and policies of Israel, nor am I suggesting that scholarly peaceability and decorum are the only appropriate modes of what is, after all, a political discussion. I am only pointing out how insistently Said refuses any suggestion that there may be common ground between him and his critics.

33. Griffin, "Ideology and Misrepresentation," 624–25.

34. Edward Said, *Orientalism* (1979, repr. New York: Vintage, 1994), 322, 273.

35. Bernard Lewis, "Islamic Concepts of Revolution," in *Revolution in the Middle East, and Other Case Studies; proceedings of a seminar*, ed. P. J. Vatikiotis (London: George Allen & Unwin, 1972), 38–39. Quoted in *Orientalism*, 314-15.

36. One of the recurrent themes of *Orientalism* is the sexual projections of Europeans onto the Orient, where, according to Said, they sought "a different type of sexuality, perhaps more libertine and less guilt-ridden" than anything on offer in Europe. See *Orientalism*, 190.

37. William Edward Lane, *An Account of the Manners and Customs of the Modern Egyptians* (Cairo: American University in Cairo Press, 2003).

38. See Geoffrey Galt Harpham, *One of Us: The Mastery of Joseph Conrad* (Chicago: University of Chicago Press, 1996), 115–80.

39. Joseph Conrad, *Heart of Darkness*, 3rd ed., Robert Kimbrough (New York: W. W. Norton, 1988), 55.

40. Edward Said, *Culture and Imperialism* (New York: Alfred A. Knopf, 1993), 80–97, esp. 89.

41. Valerie Kennedy, *Edward Said: A Critical Introduction* (Cambridge, England: Polity Press, 2000), 6. At times, Kennedy points out, "Said's own description of the Orient as seen by the West seems to reproduce unwittingly the sexual stereotyping which he criticizes" (42). Kennedy also notes that "there are, ironically, times when Said as a reader seems to fall into a position of complicity with certain imperialist literary tropes or metaphors" (102). Among these is the assertion of imperial "pleasure" in his reading of Kipling's *Kim*, in "The Pleasures of Imperialism," *Culture and Imperialism*, 132–61. "Said seems to be seduced," Kennedy says, "by the practically all-male, celibate world of the novel. He celebrates the 'two wonderfully attractive men at its center' " (104). Although writing one of a series of books devoted to confirming the reputations of the already-eminent, Kennedy is almost relentlessly critical of Said on this and other subjects. Exceptions to the general rule of silence on the subject of sexuality are Said's two excited accounts of Tahia Carioca, an Egyptian belly dancer who impressed Said so greatly when he saw her at the age of fourteen that he sought her out and interviewed her in Cairo decades later. For an account of the former incident, see *Out of Place: A Memoir*, 193; for the latter, see *Reflections on Exile and Other Essays*, 346–55.
42. Joseph Conrad, *Chance* (New York: Signet, 1992), 338.
43. Tim Brennan, "Places of Mind, Occupied Lands: Edward Said and Philology," 83.
44. Said was raised Anglican, the son of a Lebanese mother and a Palestinian father, predominantly in Cairo. He spoke Arabic and English with equal fluency. His father had American citizenship, to which Edward was entitled on the condition that he live for five years in the United States before turning twenty-one; this was one reason he was sent to boarding school to finish high school. He was capable of assuming any aspect of these identities at a given time. Ebrahim Moosa gives this account of a conversation: "'So what religion do you follow, Edward?' I asked unabashedly. 'I am secular,' he replied. I remember retorting that he was dodging my question. Then he said something that startled me: 'I am Muslim,' he said teasingly. For a moment I thought he was playing me, and perhaps he did, for he knew that Islam was an important aspect of my identity. 'You mean Islam culturally, right?' I queried. 'I am Arab and I am Muslim. I am also American, Brahim,' Edward replied." Ebrahim Moosa, a post at www.quran.ca (August 19, 2005), a Web site devoted to the exchange of ideas centered on "Islamic education and discussion": http://www.quran.ca/modules. php?name=News&file=article&sid=152.
45. Shame appears in the discussion of *Nostromo* in *Beginnings* whenever Said discusses Nostromo's later fate, when, following his famous "rebirth," he becomes a rich man living off the silver he had buried: "Now he begins to feel a secret shame that intensifies his moral disgrace . . ." (*Beginnings: Intention and Method*, 134).
46. In Said's account in *Joseph Conrad and the Fiction of Autobiography*, this "desertion" becomes something else a few sentences later, when Said

provides what seems a gratuitous commentary: "A rather large degree of misfortune in the supposedly natural relation between man and woman . . . depends on the fact that a woman must always be sought and is always found wanting, even debasing" (114).

47. For Said's view of lost causes, see "On Lost Causes," *Reflections on Exile and Other Essays*, 527–53.

48. *Culture and Imperialism*, 19–31.

49. This connection is drawn explicitly in "Zionism from the Standpoint of its Victims," in *The Edward Said Reader*, ed. Moustafa Bayoumi and Andrew Rubin (New York: Vintage Books, 2000), 114–68; originally published in *The Question of Palestine* (New York: Time Books, 1979).

50. On occasion, this self-positioning was explicit. "I feel," he says late in the "Two Visions" essay, "outnumbered and outorganized by a prevailing Western consensus that has come to regard the Third World as an atrocious nuisance, a culturally and politically inferior place" (*Culture and Imperialism*, 28).

51. Edward Alexander, "The Professor of Terror," *Commentary* 88, no. 2 (1989), 49–50. Alexander's article does not mention Conrad's *The Secret Agent*, but Said would surely have registered the reference to the bomb-making "Professor." Said told Mallios that *The Secret Agent* is "a novel that has never really captivated my interest" ("An Interview with Edward Said," 294).

52. For a full account, see Njubar Hovsepian, "Connections with Palestine," in Michael Sprinker, ed., *Edward Said: A Critical Reader*, 5–18.

53. Edward Said, "*Orientalism* 25 Years Later," written as an introduction to a new edition of *Orientalism* and first published as "Window on the World" in *The Guardian* August 2, 2003; posted on MITFTAH, a Palestinian Web site, August 7, 2003: http://www.miftah.org/Display.cfm?DocId=2314&CategoryId=5.

54. Peter Mallios, "An Interview with Edward Said," 289. In the two pages preceding this comment, Said praises *Heart of Darkness* as "the most uncompromised, unafraid confrontation with the irrational and the unknown . . . that has ever been done" (288).

55. Said helped to found the Palestinian National Initiative, whose spokesman is Dr. Mustafa Barghouthi. See Edward Said, "Dignity, Solidarity and the Penal Colony," online at http://www.miftah.org/Display.cfm?DocId=2463&CategoryId=5, posted on September 27, 2003, two days after Said's death. For the Initiative's self-description, see http://www.almubadara.org/eng/initiative.htm.

56. Edward Said, "Return to Palestine-Israel," in *The Politics of Dispossession: The Struggle for Palestinian Self-Determination, 1969-1994 (New York: Pantheon Books, 1994)*, 175–99.

57. Chapter 3 of Edward Said, *Humanism and Democratic Criticism* (New York: Columbia University Press, 2004), 57–84.

58. Peter Mallios, "An Interview with Edward Said," 295.

59. Christopher Hitchens, "Edward Said," *The Observer*, September 28, 2003; online at http://slate.msn.com/id/2088944/.

60. Ibid.
61. This comment was made to Tim Brennan in conversation; quoted in Brennan, "Places of Mind, Occupied Lands," 85.

Conclusion

1. Martha C. Nussbaum, *Hiding from Humanity: Disgust, Shame, and the Law* (Princeton: Princeton University Press, 2004).
2. Nussbaum speaks of the emotions with considerable authority, but her understanding of them is by no means uncontested. Her account might, for example, be set alongside Philip Fisher's recent book *The Vehement Passions*. Fisher is less interested than Nussbaum in the softer emotions such as compassion, which he sees as weakened modern versions of more "vehement" archaic passions such as fear and anger. Whereas Nussbaum emphasizes the capacity of compassion to enlarge the sensibility and make imaginatively real a world outside one's limited arena of immediate experience, Fisher focuses on the way in which passions reinforce the isolating sense of "my world," a domain of personal experiences occurring in time, as opposed to "the world," the shared domain of rational, testable, common experience. "'The world,'" he argues, has been a hard-won accomplishment essential for notions of duty, justice, and reason; but the violent and inward-turning passions have never been altogether extinguished. See Philip Fisher, *The Vehement Passions* (Princeton: Princeton University Press, 2002).
3. See "The Role of Compassion after 9-11," online at http://wwwlb.aub.edu. lb/~webbultn/v5n1/20.html. See also "Compassion and Terror," online at http://www.columbia.edu/cu/lweb/news/libraries/2002/2002-04-02.kristeller.html.
4. Martha C. Nussbaum, "The End of Orthodoxy," *The New York Times Book Review*, February 18, 2001, online at http://www.nytimes.com/books/01/02/18/reviews/010218.18nussbat.html.
5. Martha Nussbaum, *Frontiers of Justice: Disability, Nationality, Species Membership* (Cambridge, MA: Belknap Press, 2006).
6. Peter Singer, "A Response to Martha Nussbaum," a reply to Nussbaum's November 13, 2002, Tanner Lecture, online at http://www.utilitarian. net/singer/by/20021113.htm. Singer insists that the "preference utilitarian" approach is more realistic and effective than the capabilities approach, which confuses facts with values. See Peter Singer, *Animal Liberation* (New York: Ecco, 2001; originally published, 1975).
7. Elaine Scarry, "Citizenship in Emergency," *The Boston Review*, October/ November 2002; online at: http://bostonreview.net/BR27.5/scarry.html.
8. For the earlier form of this argument, see Elaine Scarry, "War and the Social Contract: Nuclear Policy, Distribution, and the Right to Bear Arms," *University of Pennsylvania Law Review* 139 (May 1991), 1257–1316.
9. Paul W. Kahn, response to Elaine Scarry, *The Boston Review*, October/ November 2002; online at http://bostonreview.net/BR27.5/kahn.html.
10. Stephen M. Walt, response to Elaine Scarry, *The Boston Review*, October/ November 2002, online at http://bostonreview.net/BR27.5/walt.html.

11. "Elaine Scarry Replies," *The Boston Review*, October/November 2002; online at http://www.bostonreview.net/BR27.5/reply.html.

12. When Scarry does make a specific recommendation, which she does with considerable reluctance—in this case, in the response to her critics rather than in the essay itself—the results are deflating. "A country going to war," she writes, "ought to have to present its case in *both* democratic *and* international arenas. A negative vote in either arena should be sufficient to stop the war; formal authorization in both arenas should be required to go to war" ("Elaine Scarry Replies"). How many people would agree?

13. Elaine Scarry, "Resolving to Resist," *The Boston Review*, February/March 2004; online at: http://www.bostonreview.net/BR29.1/scarry.html.

14. It would be very good to have an extended exchange between Scarry and Nussbaum on this difference. There is at present just one instance of a near-conversation, in Scarry's reply to Nussbaum's "Patriotism and Cosmopolitanism," in which Scarry represents Nussbaum as a starry-eyed idealist and herself as a gritty realist. Most of the essay seems to have been written for some other occasion, but there is an intriguing sentence at the beginning that indicates the grounds for a serious debate, in which Scarry argues that "such attempts [as Nussbaum's] to replace nationalism by internationalism often turn out to entail a rejection of constitutionalism in favor of unanchored good will that can be summarized under the heading of generous imaginings." Elaine Scarry, "The Difficulty of Imagining Other People," in Martha Nussbaum, *For Love of Country: Debating the Limits of Patriotism*, Joshua Cohen, ed. (Boston: Beacon Press, 1996), 98–110.

15. Žižek does come very close to a direct criticism of Said in his comments on those who excuse Palestinian terror by pointing to the sufferings of the Palestinians (see *Welcome to the Desert of the Real: Five Essays on September 11 and Related Dates*, 128). Said may also be the implied object of a footnote decrying "the Leftist narcissism for the lost Cause" (53).

16. Slavoj Žižek, *Welcome to the Desert of the Real: Five Essays on September 11 and Related Dates* (London: Verso, 2002).

17. For the fullest representation of this debate, including articles by Dershowitz and many others, see Sanford Levinson, ed., *Torture: A Collection* (New York: Oxford University Press, 2004).

18. "egalitarianism . . .": quoted in Rebecca Mead, "The Marx Brother," *The New Yorker*, 5 May 2003; online at: http://www.rebeccamead.com/2003/2003_05_05_art_marx.htm; "Islamic socialism," WDR, 133-34.

19. Edward Said, "Islam and the West are Inadequate Banners," *Sunday Observer,* 16 September 2001; available online at: http://observer.guardian.co.uk/islam/story/0,1442,576703,00.html.

20. Edward W. Said, "The Clash of Ignorance," *The Nation,* October 22, 2001; available online at: http://www.thenation.com/doc/20011022/said. Said was never able to contemplate the possibility that contemporary Islam itself might be terror-prone. He argues in this essay that the bombings were carried out by "a tiny band of crazed fanatics."

21. Edward Said, *Humanism and Democratic Criticism* (Princeton: Princeton University Press, 2004).

Index